Running the
Border Gauntlet

Running the Border Gauntlet

The Mexican Migrant Controversy

LAURENCE ARMAND FRENCH

 PRAEGER

AN IMPRINT OF ABC-CLIO, LLC
Santa Barbara, California • Denver, Colorado • Oxford, England

Library of Congress Cataloging-in-Publication Data
French, Laurence, 1941–
   Running the border gauntlet : the Mexican migrant controversy / Laurence
Armand French.
      p. cm.
   Includes bibliographical references and index.
   ISBN 978-0-313-38212-3 (print : alk. paper)—ISBN 978-0-313-38213-0 (e-book)
1. Mexicans—United States.   2. United States—Emigration and immigration.
3. Mexico—Emigration and immigration.   4. United States—Relations—
Mexico.   5. Mexico—Relations—United States.   I. Title.
   E184.M5F74   2010
   973'.046872—dc22   2010001611

ISBN: 978-0-313-38212-3
EISBN: 978-0-313-38213-0

14   13   12   11   10   1   2   3   4   5

This book is also available on the World Wide Web as an eBook.
Visit www.abc-clio.com for details.

Praeger
An Imprint of ABC-CLIO, LLC

ABC-CLIO, LLC
130 Cremona Drive, P.O. Box 1911
Santa Barbara, California 93116-1911

This book is printed on acid-free paper ∞

Manufactured in the United States of America

Dedicated to the memory of Rumaldo de la Cruz Torres, cavalry captain in the Zapatista Forces during the Mexican Revolution

Contents

Map insert follows page 68

Preface

The United States and Mexico share a long and complex history, one that is not often portrayed in a favorable light in the popular press or media. Here we attempt to provide a more balanced perspective on U.S./Mexico relations, providing a clearer picture of this symbiotic relationship that extends to the early 19th century. This relationship also helps articulate the nature and extent of American imperialism fostered under the guise of divine providence (white supremacy) and Manifest Destiny (primacy over inferior humans, notably American Indians and Mestizos), including events leading to the U.S. Civil War. White supremacy was seen as the birthright of white, Anglo-Saxon Protestant (WASP) colonial separatists, setting the stage for class and caste divisions in the new American republic as well as providing the justification for U.S. imperialistic gains and influence—first in the Americas and later in the Pacific Islands.

The 13 original colonies were unlike other British colonies that eventually gained their independence in that the United States was the only one to emulate the same imperialistic behaviors that it claimed to abhor and used as a justification for its revolt against England. Moreover, the United States was the only former colony in the Americas to aggressively interfere in the sovereignty of other nations in the hemisphere (Monroe Doctrine), those who also successfully gained their independence from their European colonizers (France, Spain, Portugal . . .).

Furthermore, it is clear that the freedoms articulated in the Bill of Rights in the U.S. Constitution were not for all persons residing in the new republic but for a select privileged group of adult white males. Ironically, the most conservative justices currently serving on the U.S. Supreme Court (Chief

Justice John Roberts; Associate Justices Antonia Scalia, Clarence Thomas and Samuel Alito, Jr.), those adhering to a strict interpretation of the original dictates of the Constitution, would not have held these rights if they lived in that era in which the Constitution was framed. All are Roman Catholics, along with Associate Justice Anthony Kennedy, while Thomas is African American and Alito and Scalia are of non-WASP ethnic origins. Even then the U.S. Supreme Court was usurped or unduly influenced by the other branches of government when imperialistic interests were concerned, the most notable event being President Andrew Jackson's dismissal of Chief Justice John Marshall's ruling regarding Indian sovereignty. President Jackson then had the U.S. Army forcefully remove the Five Civilized Tribes (Cherokee, Creek, Chickasaw, Choctaw, and Seminole) from their traditional homelands to Indian Territory (later the state of Oklahoma) west of the Mississippi River so that white Protestant males could acquire the tribes' prime farmlands and villages. These actions early in the history of the United States provided insights into future misadventures and conflicts generated in the name of Manifest Destiny. Indeed, a close parallel can be found between the U.S. dealings with Indian tribes and its dealings with Mexico. Both groups were considered to be inferior to white Anglo-Saxon Protestants and therefore exploitable. These groups were exempt from the protections of the U.S. Constitution much like "foreign combatants" are in the current war on terrorism.

The stage for the exploitation of "outsiders," those not of the landed gentry and the correct Protestant persuasion, was set during the colonial era and reestablished as national policy early in the new republic beginning with President George Washington. The major European colonial powers in the New World subscribed to the dictates of European international laws, established in the 16th century, where it was established that the indigenous peoples in conquered lands were entitled to sovereignty and property rights. Apparently these rights were expanded to all tribes, even those who did not convert to Christianity (Catholicism or Protestantism). Under these rules, conflict with aboriginal groups was justified only when tribes refused Europeans the right to trade and to preach Christianity. Moreover, before the U.S. Monroe Doctrine, the colonial powers adhered to the "doctrine of discovery" which gave exclusive rights of trade negotiations with the European power that first laid claims to the territory. These were essentially the rules by which Christian capitalism operated during the colonial era worldwide. In the Americas two competing Christian ideologies were established—the British and Dutch Protestant colonial enterprises and the French, Portuguese, and Spanish Catholicism.

The emerging United States altered these operational rules, greatly restricting the status of indigenous groups residing within the boundaries of the new republic. President Washington set the stage for federal paternalism and exploitation of American Indians by assigning them less-than-human status, equating them with wolves and other predatory animals in a letter to

Congress on September 7, 1783. In referring to American Indians as simple-minded savages and expressing fear of continued bloodshed among Indians and white settlers, President Washington set the stage for the long-held policy of "trickery by treaty" in dealing with what the country labeled its inferior inhabitants—first American Indians and later Mexicans and mixed Mexican Indians (Mestizos). From the start, the United States held imperialistic designs like those of its European counterparts. The War of 1812 was an attempt to expand the United States north into Canada while, at the same time, illegal incursions were being made into Spanish Florida. Indeed, the new republic operated from a less tolerant rule book under the guise of divine providence spewing a history of segregation and discrimination against not only people of color (American Indians, Asians, Mexicans . . .) but also non-English white ethnic groups notably of Catholic and Jewish heritage. This sense of white supremacy and entitlement over the land and resources of the New World equaled or superseded the elitism of its European counterparts, making the United States one of the last white societies to abolish slavery in the Americas—an issue that clearly factored in the Mexican-American War of 1846–48.

Divine entitlement and intolerance began with the landing of the Pilgrims and their extreme form of Calvinistic predestination. Conservative Calvinistic Protestants sought out their own domain in the New World, away from societal intolerance of their sense of predestined moral superiority. America soon became the breeding ground for numerous insular religious groups and cults including the Mormons (Latter Day Saints). This sense of moral and racial/ethnic superiority paved the way for trickery and deceit among those seeking their riches at the expense of others. Here, the "means justified the ends" edict came to prevail in American capitalism, often resulting in preferential judicial considerations when laws were violated. "Cease and desist" orders were the rule for business misconduct in the United States with few exceptions until the late 20th century when corporate entities were finally being adjudicated for criminal liability. Some could argue that the sense of privileged entitlement within America businesses and politics, a secular outgrowth of Puritan Calvinism, is a major culprit in the worldwide economic meltdown of the early 21st century.

With this focus, the book examines the interwoven roles of the United States and Mexican geopolitics, history, and culture up until the present. Part 1 looks at the historical antecedents of U.S./Mexico geopolitics with the first chapter looking at the religious factor and the strains of racism relevant to U.S. expansionism. Chapter 2 challenges the myths and realities of the annexation of Texas and the justifications for starting the war with Mexico during the 1830s and 1840s. This section addresses the slavery issue in the emerging Texas republic and how this was a prelude to the U.S. Civil War. This era was one of political turmoil in both emerging republics, setting the stage for future international, often contentious, relations between these neighbors. The third chapter addresses the nature of border conflicts and their impact on migration trends and policies between the United States and Mexico. Included here is the not-so-glorious portrayal of the Texas Rangers and the rule of President Díaz, the United States' favorite border despot, and how these events eventually led to Mexico's own revolution at the turn of the 20th century. Again, we find that U.S. involvement and intrigue play a significant role in Mexico's destiny, leading to General Villa's 1916 raid on military facilities in Columbus, New Mexico—the first attack on the United States since the War of 1812.

The second part of the book addresses the Mexican migration issue from 1917 until the present along with the ensuing social and economic factors. Chapter 4 looks at the early U.S. immigration laws, initially directed toward Asians, and how these laws came to impact upon Mexican laborers. Addressed here is the Bracero Program, initiated during the Second World War to address agricultural labor shortages, especially how this international agreement set the stage for continued migration, both licit and illicit, of laborers to the United States. This section also addresses U.S. attempts to expulse these workers once they were deemed no longer necessary to the American economy. It was at this time that Mexican Americans, in a reaction to segregation and violence directed toward them, came to find their collective ethnic voice establishing organizations so to better play a role in the larger U.S. society. These organizations included the League of Latin American Citizens (LULAC) and the American GI Forum (AGIF). In chapter 5, intra-Hispanic conflict over the portrayal of Mexican Americans is addressed, including the rise of "bronze power" and recognition of Mestizos—Hispanics of mixed Spanish and American Indian heritage. This section depicts the role of Mexican Americans and their counterparts in Mexico during the upheavals of the turbulent 1960s—including the pro-democracy massacre in Mexico City. Also addressed is the conflict associated with the New Mexico land grant controversy. Equally significant is the emergence of the borderland as a semiautonomous socioeconomic entity straddling the international border along with its maquiladoras—international assembly factories employing mainly young Mexican women. Related to this issue is the role of the North American Free Trade Agreement (NAFTA) in transforming Mexico to capitalism. Chapter 6 takes this discussion further, looking at the social and human justice issues associated with recent U.S. immigration laws and attempts at keeping Mexican migrants at bay at the border. The rise of anti-Mexican vigilante and other hate groups during the late 20th and early 21st centuries has emerged as a contemporary expression of white supremacy, leading to the creation of physical barriers and the increased militarization of the U.S. side of the international border. Moreover, the increased militarization on both sides of the border has seen a dramatic rise in drug-related violence, making sections of the borderland a battlefield with increasing civilian casualties, including the unsolved rape and murder of dozens of maquilador workers. This chapter also looks at how the United States' war on drugs and war on terrorism have contributed to this violence.

The epilogue illustrates the efforts of educational cooperation between rural school districts in Puerto Palomas, Mexico, and New Mexico during the last 20 years and how this endeavor has now been destroyed by the violence associated with Mexican drug cartels attempting to deliver their goods to their American customers. Hope for better U.S./Mexico relations is hitched to the current Obama administration.

PART I

Historical Antecedents of U.S./Mexico Geopolitics

CHAPTER 1

Introduction: Religion, Race, and Imperialism

Since the terrorist attacks on the United States on September 11, 2001, and the ensuing war on terrorism, a heated debate has focused on border security. Although new measures appear to address all undocumented aliens, it is, nonetheless, evident that they continue their historic and controversial focus on nonwhite undocumented aliens who cross the U.S. southern border. This is clearly demonstrated by virtue of the intensification of money and manpower dedicated to the 2,000-mile U.S./Mexico border since 2001, in contrast to the policing of the longer (4,000-mile) U.S./Canada border; despite the fact that more apprehended Muslim terrorists entered the United States from Canada than from Mexico.[1] Even before the 9/11 terrorist attacks on U.S. soil, Mexican migrants were associated with increased job losses, welfare costs, and criminal activity. Mexican migrants served as the poster children of the negative stereotype of the undocumented migrant. Clearly, this negative image extends back to the early days of the U.S. republic with the annexation of Texas and the subsequent war with Mexico. From this contentious beginning, Mexicans in the United States, legal or undocumented, have been viewed alternately as a cheap labor source or as a threat to society. Part of the image problem is that Mexico has long been portrayed in the United States as yet another inferior third world nation, an image common to the U.S. perception of Latin America. In marked contrast, the United States presents itself as a tolerant, nonviolent, constitutional democracy where judicial fairness, due process, and the pursuit of liberty are afforded everyone. Moreover, it presents itself as fostering a socioeconomic environment where anyone can succeed. Indeed, it is the latter construct that attracts immigrants to the United States, often from impoverished countries.

But for Mexican migrants, this trek is a return to their own land, a situation that can be contrasted with Palestinian refugees attempting to return to their traditional home in what is now Israel, or Native Americans attempting to get some of their traditional lands back in North America. Hence, a review of U.S./Mexican history is required to lift the fog of persisting myths in order to offer a clearer picture of the complexities surrounding the current Mexican migrant controversy.

Clearly, race, religion, and socioeconomic differences play significant roles here. Nonwhite immigrants have traditionally had a very difficult time entering the United States. This racial/ethnic factor is illustrated by the obvious discrimination against black Haitians in contrast to phenotypically Caucasian Cubans attempting to seek asylum in the United States. Given that the manifest reason for this policy—that of the United States' strong anti-Communism stance—plays a significant role here, the latent function of racism still comes out strong as a major dynamic of exclusion relevant to Haitians seeking asylum. Moreover, extreme negative stereotyping is assigned to Mexicans, especially those of mixed Indian/Spanish origin—the Mestizos also known derogatively as *wet backs* and *greasers*. At the international level, former Latin colonies of Catholic imperialism (French, Spanish, Portuguese), notably those in the Caribbean and Central and South America, carry the stigma of being third world nations. And while some negative stereotyping has been assigned to French Canadians over the years, this pales in comparison to that shown toward Hispanics in general and Mexicans in particular. Today, Latinos are becoming the fastest growing ethnic group in the United States and are estimated to comprise 25 percent of the total population by 2020. And with this growth comes increased political power. This is already evident with the election of Antonio Villaraigosa as mayor of Los Angeles, the second largest municipality in the country. He now joins Bill Richardson, the governor of New Mexico, as a high-profile Mexican American in a leadership position.

In June 2005, it was estimated that there were some 10 million illegal immigrants in the United States—the vast majority of Mexican descent. Clearly, the current trend indicates that Mexican Hispanics are overtaking the traditional East Coast Latino power brokers—the Puerto Ricans and Cubans. The United States now joins Canada in having a significant and distinctive minority population. In Canada it is the French Canadians while in the United States it soon will be Mexican Americans. In both countries the minority group is viewed as an inferior subculture, less refined than its Anglo counterpart.

In marked contrast to French Canadians, Anglo Canadians are generally seen as being basically indistinguishable from white residents of the United States. Given these factors, any viable analysis of the current controversy needs to look at the historical antecedents of U.S. geopolitics to see how these events transpired. To better understand the interethnic controversy today we need to explore to what extent U.S. Anglo ethnocentrism was influenced by the combination of three critical factors: religious tolerance/intolerance, racial prejudice, and blatant imperialism—all justified by Manifest Destiny in the form of Christian capitalist democracy. This theme continues to be played out in the world today, most recently during the administration of George W. Bush and his attempt to impose his legacy of regime change on predominately Muslim societies.

THE RELIGION FACTOR

Contrary to popular belief, the United States republic was an active participant in the European colonial wars of the 18th, 19th, and 20th centuries. And these were, for a good part, religious wars pitting Protestant imperialism (British Empire) against Catholic imperialism (Roman Empire). Granted intra-group conflicts also existed such as the United States versus Great Britain, and France versus Spain, et cetera, but in the final analysis English-speaking Protestant societies like the United States favored Great Britain over Latin Catholic societies even when the latter was an ally. This phenomenon explains, in part, the negative stereotypes generated toward Spain and its colonies throughout the world, and the continued distaste for the French—a fact clearly illustrated by the anti-French sentiment relevant to the U.S. preemptive war on Iraq.

Protestantism and Capitalism

Max Weber, the noted 19th-century social philosopher, probably best articulated the relationship between Protestantism and capitalism. According to Weber, in his work *The Protestant Ethic and the Spirit of Capitalism*, this change of worldview was associated with the introduction of new Christian perspectives on predestination, notably Calvinism, Pietism, Methodism, and the Baptist Sects. Briefly stated, Catholicism, especially the doctrine practiced during the Middle Ages, posited that humans were predisposed with original sin and that life was a trial of good versus evil challenges, with a preponderance of one over the other, along with the appropriate sacraments, determining one's place in the hereafter. With the Reformation, especially the work of Calvin and his brand of Protestantism—Calvinism—a new worldview perspective emerged based on moral predestined superiority that would be evident by one's earthly successes. In its religious conception, the Protestant ethic, a predestined individual would be identified by certain virtues: elevated social status, private wealth, and asceticism. The element of social status and private wealth provided the seeds for capitalism, according to Weber. Soon the sacred element of asceticism was greatly diminished, paving the way for a secular mode of capitalism along with its new virtues of material wealth, social privilege, and conspicuous consumption. High social status also took on a secular flavor, along with connotation of social superiority.[2]

While it could be argued that initially there were few differences between the religious doctrines of the Church of England and those of the Roman Catholic Church, this was not the case of the new republic, the United States of America, where the Anglican Church was accepted but Catholicism was not. Protestantism in England under King Henry VIII basically retained the tenets of Catholicism with the exception of recognition of the pope as head of the church. When parliament made King Henry the head of the church (Submission of the Clergy) in 1533, he reaffirmed his commitment to the practices of Catholicism with passage of the Six Articles in 1539. While attempts were made by Henry's son and successor, Edward VI, to institute the more conservative Calvinist Protestantism in England, his short tenure obviated this movement. His sister, Queen Mary ("Bloody Mary"), went to the other extreme of reinstating Catholic doctrine within the Church of England. It was, however, her sister, Elizabeth I, who repealed Mary's Catholic doctrines creating a compromise between Catholicism and the foundations of Protestantism. Thus, by the late 1500s the foundations of the Church of England were laid and have survived to this day despite Oliver Cromwell's Calvinist conservative Protestant revolt, which was, in fact, inspired by the works of John Cotton, the Puritan leader in the Massachusetts Bay Colony during the mid-17th century.[3]

As the British Empire expanded so did the acceptance of cultural and religious differences, allowing for the forging of the complex nature of the British Commonwealth we see today. The Church of England also transformed into the Anglican Communion with two closely related branches, the Anglican Church of England and Canada, and the Episcopal Church in the United States and other commonwealth nations. The more conservative Puritans, in turn, split into two branches as well—the Congregationalists (conservative Puritans) and the more liberal Presbyterians. These were the predominant denominations in the New England colonies and were reconciled by the Cambridge Synod of 1648. Other conservative branches of Calvinism in the colonies included the Methodists and the Baptists. These denominations emerged primarily in the southern colonies.

Conservative Calvinistic Protestantism and its belief in predestined moral superiority existed from the beginning in the New World colonies in both New England and Canada. Max Weber noted that American capitalism, as espoused by Benjamin Franklin, went beyond secular capitalism by attaching a moral ethos as justification for its expansionistic designs: "Now, all Franklin's moral attitudes are coloured with utilitarianism."[4] This sense of religious and ethnic superiority, supported by the colonists self-proclaimed Covenant of Divine Providence (Manifest Destiny), paved the way for the moral justification of expansionism and ethnic cleansing.[5]

A myth often cited in justification of U.S. interventionism and territorial expansionism was that of religious tolerance illustrated by the Mormons' westward expansion and the Texas rebellion—the same justification cited as the impetus for British Empire settlements in the New World. The emerging United States had its auspicious beginning as a business endeavor contracted with the British government. The Massachusetts Bay Colony was chartered as a business corporation with legal authority to exercise law and order among its inhabitants. Charters were managed by a governor, deputy governor, and a board of 18 stockholders, also known as *freemen*. The latter constituted the general court that met four times a year to admit new members, elect officers, and make regulations. This governmental model was carried over into the new republic especially in the northern states. A similar process was in effect when Anglos settled portions of New Spain (Mexico).

What was lacking in the Massachusetts Bay Colony was religious freedom. Indeed, the Puritan leaders held an elitist view of Protestantism. In the New England colonies only church members were enfranchised, and membership was strictly limited so that most colonists were not part of the ruling elite. Until 1630, church membership required a minister's endorsement. Hence, there existed a strict social stratification even among free whites. Indentured whites and people of color (blacks and Indians) suffered even more within this social milieu. Erikson articulated this theocratic philosophy in his work *Wayward Puritans*: "God had chosen an elite to represent Him on earth and to join Him in Heaven. People who belonged to this elite learned of their appointment through the agency of a deep conversion experience, giving them a special responsibility and a special competence to control the destinies of others."[6] Intolerance against fellow Anglos occurred as they became more isolated from their home base in England. Cromwell's Puritan forces not only defeated the King of England, it also split the group into two general groups, the Scottish Presbyterian moderates and the Congregational Independents. The latter eventually represented the New England colonies, becoming the recognized church of state. Before this came bloodletting against challenges to the New England Puritan theocracy, notably the Quaker persecutions of 1656–65. Essentially the anti-Quaker law carried the death penalty for anyone professing to be a Quaker within the Puritan colonies.

Other forms of religious intolerance occurred in New England following their Declaration of Independence from Great Britain. The legislation of morality was a common practice in the colonies. These restrictions on public and private behavior, most notably on the Christian Sabbath (Sunday), were known as the *blue laws*. While the name is obscured by history, some sources attribute the name to the color of the paper on which the laws were written or to the cover of the statutes. These laws clearly established the New England colonies as Puritan theocracies.[7]

Anti-Catholicism Movement in the New Republic

While article 6 of the U.S. Constitution stated that religion is not to be considered as a qualification to any office or public trust in the United States, it allowed individual states to reserve the right to discriminate against certain religious sects and also to establish a state church. From the beginning these state statutes excluded Roman Catholics from holding state and local offices. Initially these sanctions pertained to the French Canadians, the northern neighbors of northern New England. However, the anti-Catholics soon found a new target in lower New England and New York and New Jersey with the onslaught of new Irish immigrants following the Irish Potato Famine of the 1840s. Indeed, at the time of the annexation of Texas and the beginning of the war with Mexico, the floodgates of non-Anglo Protestant immigration began to open in the United States. It is estimated that from 1846 to just prior to the Civil War over three million immigrants came to the United States, a number equal to 15 percent of the country's total population at the time. Part of the incentive was to populate the new territories east of the Mississippi gained through both the 1803 Louisiana Purchase and the spoils of the Mexican War.[8]

The white Anglo-Saxon Protestant (WASP) anti-immigrant movement fostered the nativist parties and secret societies as well as new political parties, leading eventually to the creation of the Republican Party in the late 1850s. Nonetheless, the effort to exclude non-Protestants (mainly Catholics and Jews) continued, with Massachusetts eliminating these restrictions in 1833, New Jersey in 1844, and New Hampshire not until 1877. New Hampshire was unique in that its anti-Catholic sentiments were directed mainly toward French Canadians and not to the Irish or other Catholic ethnic groups per se. In 1848, the New Hampshire legislature passed restrictive laws directed toward the Shakers, prohibiting the boarding of minor children within the sect. Ironically, it was Franklin Pierce, then a state senator, who represented the Shakers in this matter and who was able to kill the law in the state senate.[9]

The temperance and anti-Catholic and anti-Jewish immigrant movements, born in the 1840s, manifested themselves in other modes as well. The major platforms of the newly created Republican Party in the 1850s were its antipolygamy stance—one clearly directed toward the new Mormon religion (Latter Day Saints, aka LDS). In 1862, President Lincoln signed the Morrill Act, which not only created the land grant state university system in the United States but also made bigamy a felony in the territories, notably the lands gained from Mexico in the treaty of 1848, which were widely populated by Mormons. In 1879, the antipolygamy law was challenged in a case in Idaho Territory and upheld by the U.S. Supreme Court in *Reynolds v. United States*. Because it was difficult to prosecute these crimes as felonies given that subsequent wives were often not recorded as such in a territory dominated by Mormons, the Edmunds Act was enacted so as to prohibit bigamous cohabitation. The Edmunds Act resulted in the misdemeanor conviction and incarceration of some 1,300 Mormon males. Additional resistance was met by Mormon women who refused to testify against their husbands, resulting in the Edmunds-Tucker Act of 1887 allowing prosecutors to force wives to testify against their husbands. This act also disenfranchised LDS women who up to that time could vote in the Mormon dominated western territories. However, admittedly this was a shallow right given that Mormon women voted as directed by their male superiors—a status extended to any LDS male aged 14 or older.[10]

Calvinistic Protestantism continued to manifest its anti-immigration influence well into the 20th century. Prohibition, the 18th Amendment to the U.S. Constitution, represented the most significant blue law. Ostensibly, its imposition on a diverse ethnic and racial mix of Americans was the WASP's last-ditch effort to legislate morality. The new non-English immigrants were mainly Catholics and Jews from religious sects that used alcohol in their sacraments. Outlawing the manufacture, sale, or transportation of intoxicating liquors, as prescribed by the 18th Amendment in 1919, established the legal and moral superiority of those religious sects derived from the Calvinists.[11]

A dire failure, one fostering the emergence of organized crime (Mob, Mafia, drug cartels. . .), Prohibition was repealed by the 21st Amendment in 1933. However, Prohibition continued to exist at the state and local level until the 1970s especially in the South. Canada, on the other hand, outlawed its blue laws in 1985 when the Supreme Court of Canada ruled against the 1906 Lord's Day Act. Religious ultraconservatism continues to the present with such organizations as the John Birch Society. They see the United States as a Protestant white nation and are anti-immigration, against civil rights and the United Nations, as well as being staunchly against Catholics and Jews. Prior to the election of neocon George W. Bush, their closest attempt at national influence was during the 1964 presidential campaign when their candidates were Republican Barry Goldwater and retired Rear Admiral Chester Ward.[12]

Collectively, this section clearly dispels the myth that the United States always promoted religious tolerance. This is especially significant when the issue of religious intolerance is used to intervene forcefully in international matters under the guise of spreading "freedom" and "democracy."

STRAINS OF RACISM AND U.S. EXPANSIONISM

Historical Antecedents of Manifest Destiny

America's westward expansion from "sea to shining sea" has long been portrayed in history books as the divine rights of a chosen people to occupy what is now the continental United States. Another key element of the "American myth" is that of a fair and representative democracy. This myth is often used to contrast the United States from its "lesser" neighbors south of its borders—those described as inferior and corrupt third world dictatorships. The implied moral superiority of the United States has provided the justification for unilateral interventions, whether for the purpose of ethnic

cleansing or for regime change. The two guiding principles for these interventions are Manifest Destiny and the Monroe Doctrine. Despite its view
of other societies in the region, the United States struggled with its own internal disputes for two centuries—from its declaration of independence up
until the end of its own colonial wars in the 1970s. And these controversies
continue today with the expansion of Manifest Destiny with its promotion
of Christian capitalist democracy in the Middle East and former Soviet societies. Inherent in the history of this mechanism of influence is the complex relationship of religious intolerance, blatant racism, and secular white
Anglo-Saxon ethnocentrism.

The emerging United States republic came about after another protracted
colonial war, one involving not only the colonists, loyalists, and Britain but
also France, Spain, Holland, and Prussia. The Revolutionary War began on
April 14, 1775, when British troops were used by Massachusetts governor
Gage to suppress rebellion among the colonists and ended nearly nine years
later on January 14, 1784, when the newly created United States of America's Congress ratified the Treaty of Paris. Even then inter-Anglo conflict
with Britain regarding border disputes continued into the 1870s.

The irony of the European colonial wars is that both France and Spain,
components of the Catholic colonial empires, supported the rebellious colonists, providing the incentive for the Continental Congress to wage a full-
fledged war with Britain over its declaration of independence. Spain had
its own agenda. Seeing the Revolutionary War as a distraction in the East,
providing them with a better opportunity to seize control of the West Coast,
it hence established missions in October 1776, on the California coast of
what is now the United States. France, on the other hand, provided another
resource in the person of the 19-year-old aristocrat Marquis de Lafayette,
who soon became a trusted general in Washington's army. France formally
recognized the United States in October 1777. The next month, the U.S. Continental Congress adopted the Articles of Confederation and sent this out
for ratification by the individual states. The articles established the U.S. Congress as the sole authority for the new government, a process that would
greatly impact upon the independence of Indian tribes within the United
States to the present.

Many of Britain's battles were fought from their Canadian Territory. They
also employed American Indian tribes in their battles, a practice that served
to complicate the nature of the war. Moreover, France's increasing involvement in the Revolutionary War led to France and Britain declaring war in
1778, and Spain entering the fray on the side of France in 1779. Britain also
declared war on the Dutch, leading to battles far from the colonies and
Canada. Indeed, battles between these colonial powers were subsequently
fought in Africa, India, the Mediterranean, and the West Indies, giving the
European colonial wars of the 18th century the distinction of being the first
world war, preceding the 1914–18 colonial wars by over a century.[13]

In North America, the colonial wars took on a racial element with both
black slaves and American Indians abused by the combatants. The British

engaged American Indians in guerrilla war tactics against U.S. settlements, notably the torching of villages in New York and Pennsylvania. In retaliation, American troops from North Carolina and Virginia attacked the Chickamauga Indians in Tennessee in April 1779, and later defeated a Loyalist and Indian force at Elmira, New York in August 1779. American troops then went on and destroyed dozens of Cayuga and Seneca Indian villages in Iroquois country. These raids continued throughout the conflict, with army and militia often attacking more passive tribes in retaliation for raids by more aggressive tribes. Indeed, the last battle of the Revolutionary War, on November 10, 1782, involved an attack by the U.S. forces against Loyalist and Shawnee Indians forces in the Ohio Territory.[14]

The U.S. Congress officially declared an end to the war on April 11, 1783, and the Treaty of Paris was signed on September 3 of that year and ratified by the U.S. Congress on January 14, 1784. The black slave issue emerged six weeks after Congress's ratification of the Treaty of Paris, when Thomas Jefferson proposed a ban on slavery in the newly acquired western territories. Although narrowly defeated, this issue would fester until the 1860s and the U.S. Civil War. Another revolt by a disgruntled military officer, Captain Daniel Shays, was attempted in the fall of 1786. Put down in February 1787, Shays fled to the Republic of Vermont, an independent country from 1777 until it joined the United States in 1791. Indeed, Silverstone in his 2004 book, *Divided Union: The Politics of War in the Early American Republic*, noted that while the U.S. initiated wars of expansionism twice prior to the Civil War (War of 1812 and the Mexican-American War of 1846), there were seven other "near misses" that could easily have resulted in yet another armed conflict:

While our attention is naturally drawn to these two wars initiated by the United States, another important observation about U.S. foreign relations in this period is largely ignored: The United States was involved in a much larger set of "near miss" international crises, disputes in which the use of military force was a serious option, yet which were resolved short of armed conflict.[15]

Some of these situations merely postponed eventual conflict. Crises in 1807 and 1809 concerned similar conflicts with Great Britain, eventually resulting in the War of 1812. During this same time, President Madison and Secretary of State Monroe engaged U.S. forces in Spanish Florida from 1811 to 1813 under the pretense that Spain would relinquish east Florida to the British, allowing them a southern base for assaults on the United States. Florida was also seen as a haven for disgruntled displaced American Indians and escaped black slaves. These covert actions never rose to the level of a formal declaration of war with Spain.

And during the war with Mexico, the United States was again on the brink of war with Great Britain, this time over the Pacific Northwest. Here, the United States wanted to occupy the entire Oregon Territory, denying Britain any territory along the Pacific coast of North America. However, fighting on two fronts in 1846 was not feasible, resulting in international negotiations eventually refereed by Germany's Kaiser Wilhelm in 1872. Hence, a compromise initiated by President Polk in 1846 was finalized by President Grant in 1872, establishing the current U.S./Canadian border and solidifying U.S./British relationships. The resolution of this 26-year compromise set the stage for the resulting strong U.S./British relationship that was a significant requisite for the numerous conflicts in the 20th and 21st centuries, including the war on terrorism and the Iraq occupation. The 26-year conflict that put the United States on the brink of war with Great Britain has been called the Pig War in reference to its only casualty—a pig shot by the British forces for crossing over the then-disputed line separating both nations' forces on San Juan Island.[16]

War with Mexico in 1853 over the Mesilla Valley in southeastern New Mexico was avoided by President Pierce, who resisted the U.S. congressional and military leaders' call for another war with Mexico. Instead, Pierce convinced Mexican president Santa Anna to sell the disputed region to the United States in what resulted in the Gadsden Purchase. President Pierce also had to quell efforts to go to war with Spain over the acquisition of Cuba during this same era. His predecessor, President Buchanan, on the other hand, was unsuccessful in his attempts to go to war with Mexico due to the fear of European intervention and a resulting European monarch.[17]

As these conflicts attest, the newly recognized United States of America embarked upon its own colonial quest under the banner of Manifest Destiny, the moral and ethnocentric justification for exploitation of others for the purpose of territorial expansionism. Even though the United States also was willing to fight the British and its Anglo neighbors to the north, critical to this justification for expansionism was the concept of white supremacy. When the census was being developed for the determination of representation to the House of Representatives in July 1787, black slaves in the South were to be counted only as three-fifths of a person. And when the Census Act passed Congress in March 1790, American Indians were not counted at all. And as stated earlier, elected political positions were restricted to Protestants.[18]

Clearly, the white-dominant United States of America intended, from the outset, to become yet another European-style colonial power. A formal policy of ethnic cleansing soon became apparent. Manifest Destiny, the U.S. rationale for ethnic cleansing, emerged with President Jefferson and his plans for territorial expansion and an empire on the North American continent. He clearly articulated four obstacles to U.S. expansionism as being (1) the British in Canada, (2) the Spanish in the southeast and Mexico, (3) the French in New Orleans, and (4) the Indian Problem.[19] Consequently, President Thomas Jefferson was the architect of Manifest Destiny; President James Monroe articulated its mandate with the Monroe Doctrine; President Andrew Jackson implemented ethnic cleansing; and General Winfield Scott enforced Jackson's mandates. General Scott also played a prominent role in the war with

Mexico and the ensuing acquisition of lands extending the United States to the Pacific Ocean. The Monroe Doctrine of December 2, 1823, gave notice to European governments, including the Russian imperial government, that future colonial designs or intrusion into the Americas would be challenged by the United States.

It was under Jefferson's administration that the territory of the United States doubled with the Louisiana Purchase in 1802 (ratified by the U.S. Senate on October 20, 1803). Interestingly, Spain gave France sole guardianship of this territory in the hopes that it would provide a buffer from U.S. expansionism. Instead, France, an ally of the United States since losing Canada to Britain in 1763, sold the land to the United States in order to finance Napoleon's European battles. This action eliminated the French as a colonial competitor in North America while, at the same time, providing the United States access to Spanish colonial territories in the West via the major waterways: the Mississippi, Ohio, and Missouri Rivers. This newly acquired territory provided land necessary for the forceful removal of the tribes east of the Mississippi River. Thus began the United States' novel vehicle of ethnic cleansing, the forceful removal of Indian tribes, a marked departure from European colonial policies.[20]

The first U.S.-led colonial war had its roots with the war hawks led by John C. Calhoun of South Carolina and Henry Clay of Kentucky. The war hawks wanted to declare war on Great Britain under the guise of punishing them for impressing U.S. seamen but with the ultimate purpose of conquering Canada. On June 18, 1812, a divided Congress declared war on Great Britain in order to expand into British-held Canada. President James Madison signed the war measure, marking the first time the United States had declared war on another nation. It was also the narrowest vote to declare war in U.S. history. While any hopes of annexing Canada were quickly dashed, the war did end European liaisons with North American tribes, providing the U.S. the opportunity to further its wars with the Indian tribes it wanted eliminated or removed. The war with Britain and Canada ended in a stalemate three years later with the signing of the Treaty of Ghent in 1815 while the Indian fighting continued in the swamps of Florida until 1818.[21]

During the war, General (and later U.S. President) Andrew Jackson made a name for himself at the Battle of New Orleans and as an Indian fighter. The War of 1812 had two other significant consequences that played a role in later events, including the war with Mexico and the Civil War. One was the realization of the need for a full-time military, resulting in General Winfield Scott creating the U.S. Army and the United States Military Academy at West Point. The second factor resulted from the British blockade of the U.S. East Coast during the war, resulting in a greater reliance on domestic resources—slave labor in the South and the establishment of textile mills in New England.

The War of 1812 ended the use of armed conflict in order to expand northward to Canada but this issue was not settled until boundaries were finalized in the 1870s. It also provided the embarrassment of Washington, DC, being attacked, a feat not accomplished again until the September 11, 2001, terrorist attack on the Pentagon. Yet, the major positive colonial outcome of the War of 1812 was its justification for a continuation of the protracted Indian wars that would last until the 20th century. The United States used the War of 1812 to assert itself as an international force taking on Great Britain. However, Great Britain was otherwise disposed with the Napoleonic Wars and viewed the conflict with the United States as a mere distraction. Essentially, the War of 1812 aided Canada in developing its own sense of self-determination given that they provided the greatest number of forces in the conflict. The United States invasion of Canada also served to forge a sense of nationalism in Canada, uniting an otherwise divided country. With the United States as a common aggressor, both Upper Canada (Anglo-Canada) and Lower Canada (French-Canada) united in repulsing U.S. forces. Indeed, many of the Anglo Canadians fighting the United States were U.S. born loyalists who fled during the American Revolution. This war stopped future U.S. efforts to take Canada from Great Britain and set the stage for the process of Canadian Confederation.[22]

Now that it was clear that Canada would remain under the control of Great Britain, the United States focused on the Spanish territories and the Indian nations. General Jackson expanded the conflict justified by the War of 1812 to include Spanish holdings in what is now Florida. In 1817–18, Jackson ignited what became known as the First Seminole War where he unilaterally deposed the Spanish authorities and executed British subjects. These actions led to the U.S. acquisition of Spanish Florida in 1819, thus eliminating the Spanish from the Florida peninsula and leading to the eventual war with Mexico. Spanish holdings in the Caribbean would not become subject to U.S. expansionism until the late 19th century during the Spanish-American War.

Nonetheless, Jackson's bold actions during the Seminole Wars followed him into the White House where, as seventh president of the United States, he chose to ignore the U.S. Supreme Court's ruling relevant to the sovereign status of established Indian tribes. Instead, he authorized the forceful removal of the Five Civilized Tribes (Cherokee, Choctaw, Chickasaw, Creek, and Seminole) west of the Mississippi River to Indian Territory that was carved out of the Louisiana Purchase (currently the state of Oklahoma). It was during President Jackson's first term that the U.S. Congress passed the Indian Removal Act on May 28, 1830. The de facto federal police force used to undertake this task was the U.S. Army under the leadership of Winfield Scott. This was the first and last time that the United States assembled a national police, a requisite for ethnic cleansing.[23]

The long history of forced removal of tribes, using the U.S. Army, included the 1838 Cherokee removal ("Trail of Tears"), the 1863 Navajo removal ("Long Walk"), the 1886 removal and imprisonment of the Chiricahua Apache (Geronimo's tribe), and the 1890 massacre of the Sioux leader Big Foot and his followers in their flight to the Pine Ridge reservation ("Wounded Knee I"). In these incidents, and numerous others, harsh conditions and summary executions accounted for the deaths of thousands of American Indians under the auspices of the U.S. government, including a high percentage of the elderly, women, and children. The practice of broken treaties, forced removal, and both physical and cultural genocide continued into the 20th century with the last major armed conflict occurring on the Pine Ridge Sioux Reservation in South Dakota in the 1973 "Wounded Knee II" battle between the American Indian Movement (AIM) and the federal government. Moreover, American Indians did not receive legal recognition as "persons" until May 12, 1879, when federal judge Elmer Dundy ruled in the case of Standing Bear's writ of habeas corpus. It took the U.S. Congress another 45 years to enfranchise American Indians, doing so in 1924. And today the U.S. government stands accused of stealing and/or mismanaging tens of billions of dollars from Indian Country trust funds. Although the Spanish and later the Mexican government have had troubled relationships with Mexico's indigenous peoples, in the mist of the Civil War and the U.S. Indian Wars, Mexico had a full-blooded Indian as its president when Pablo Benito Juárez led from 1861–63 and again from 1867 until his death in office in 1872.[24]

Of course, the treatment of black slaves was yet another blight on the new American republic. Mexico outlawed slavery in its original constitution in 1820 while Britain did so in 1834 leaving the United States as the only slave nation in North America at the time. It took a costly civil war to end slavery in the United States but harsh treatment of blacks did not end with emancipation in 1865. The period of Reconstruction led to a double standard for blacks in the United States, subjecting them to harsh punishments including de facto executions in the form of lynchings. This system of abuses continued for another century until passage of the civil rights laws of the mid-1960s. A brief review of these circumstances includes legitimization of Jim Crow laws by the executive branch, Congress, and Courts.

Jim Crow America

In *Plessy v. Ferguson* (163 U.S. 537, 1896) the separate-but-equal Jim Crow laws in the South were upheld by the U.S. Supreme Court when it stated that racial segregation did not violate the 14th Amendment's equal protection clause. The Jim Crow separations were later found not to be equal at all, resulting in not only the forced integration of schools in *Brown v. Board of Education* (347 U.S. 483, 1954), but by congressional action with passage of the U.S. Civil Rights Acts of 1964.[25]

The problems leading to the landmark civil rights decisions of the 1950s and 1960s were clearly instituted under President Woodrow Wilson whose presidency did more to legitimize segregation in practice at the federal level than any southern state, including banning blacks from attending Princeton

University when he was the school's president. He viewed blacks in conde-
scending and paternalistic terms. Interestingly, his view of African Americans did not vary considerably from that of his opponents in the presidential
election of 1912—former presidents Theodore Roosevelt (1904–08) and William Howard Taft (1908–12). The main difference is that Wilson formally instituted segregation at the federal level, transcending the mostly parochial
practice of the southern United States. Once elected, Wilson appointed five
conservative Southerners to critical cabinet posts: Secretary of the Treasury
William McAdoo, Secretary of Agriculture David F. Houston, Attorney
General James C. McReynolds, Secretary of the Navy Josephus Daniels, and
Postmaster General Albert S. Burleson. These men were willing agents of
white supremacists, notably the National Democratic Fair Play Association.
The end result was the segregation of federal workers along with the removal
of any blacks who held supervisory positions over whites. These efforts not
only relegated blacks to inferior federal jobs but also officially segregated
the work place. Wilson's international academic and intellectual reputation
made this movement all the more dangerous.[26]

Wilson's antiblack sentiments were expressed on February 18, 1915, when
he held a private viewing for his cabinet members and their families of the
inflammatory film *The Birth of a Nation*. This film was the product of two of
Wilson's friends from his days at Johns Hopkins University, Thomas Dixon
and D. W. Griffith. Considered a technological marvel, the movie aired on
the 50th anniversary of the end of the Civil War with its clearly racial con-
tents. It celebrated the Ku Klux Klan as the saviors of Aryan culture while
treating blacks as grossly inferior (whites in blackface played African Americans in the film since it was felt that black people were incapable of acting). The NAACP called for a ban of the film.

The movement for more progressive black education began in the 1930s
when the National Association for the Advancement of Colored People
(NAACP) filed suits before the U.S. Supreme Court challenging the Jim
Crow segregation laws of the South. In these cases, the NAACP argued
that the Jim Crow laws restricted the quality of professional education for
blacks. Many felt that these early efforts against the University of Maryland
Law School (1935) and the University of Missouri Law School (1938) set the
stage for the landmark decisions in 1954 and 1955 (*Brown v. Board of Education*). The NAACP was also successful in its legal challenges against *Plessy v.
Ferguson* and the creation of integrated regional university centers following
the Second World War in the areas of professional education (law, medicine,
and education). The original *Brown v. Board of Education* (1954) addressed
the issue of integrated public schools. The appeals relevant to this decision
were filed from four states: Kansas, South Carolina, Virginia, and Delaware.
Here the U.S. Supreme Court reviewed and rejected *Plessy v. Ferguson* on
the grounds that studies had shown that the segregation of white and black
children resulted in a disproportionately inferior quality of education for
black students.[27]

Two other related cases address the issue of capital punishment in the United States. In *Furman v. Georgia* (408 U.S. 238, 345, 1972) the U.S. Supreme Court, in a narrow 5 to 4 decision, held that the imposition of the death penalty constituted cruel and unusual punishment in violation of the 8th and 14th Amendments of the U.S. Constitution. Indeed, the death penalty was a form of de facto segregation, especially in the South. However, the public sentiment for the death penalty prevailed, and in reviewing three cases in 1976 the U.S. Supreme Court allowed the reinstatement of capital punishment as long as it was for serious offenses, notably first-degree murder, and consisted of a two-stage process. The first stage is the guilty phase while the second phase requires the presentation and review of mitigating versus aggravating circumstances prior to a determination of a death sentence (*Gregg v. Georgia*, 428 U.S. 153, 96 S. Ct. 2902, 49 L.Ed.2d 859, 1976; *Jurek v. Texas*, 428 U.S. 262, 96 S Ct 2950, 1976; *Proffit v. Florida*, 428 U.S. 242, 252, 1976). The death penalty in the United States is a critical human rights issue given that minorities are most likely to be executed and that the mentally retarded and juveniles are death-qualified. In both phases the decision needs to be unanimous.[28]

Amnesty International cites the United States on human rights abuses for its use of the death penalty. The United States had a chance to eliminate the death penalty in 1972 but instead made a few changes and continued with its capital-punishment practice. Today Texas leads the nation in capital deaths while sharing the longest portion of the U.S./Mexico border, hence having more people of Mexican descent processed within its criminal justice system. The reintroduction of the death penalty at the federal level, as part of Racketeer Influenced and Corrupt Organizations Act (RICO) and the Anti Drug Abuse Act of 1988, has caused concern for both Mexicans and Mexican Americans (*United States v. Pitera*, 1992). Interestingly, in his five years as governor of Texas, George W. Bush sanctioned 152 executions, a modern record. He also reinstated the federal death-penalty practice as president.[29]

However, with the advent of DNA testing more death row prisoners are being released, again raising the question of racism and discriminatory justice in the U.S. courts. This exposure to past abuses in the death-qualifying process has raised considerable interest in the death-penalty issue. The most significant capital-punishment decision by the U.S. Supreme Court since its 1972 *Furman v. Georgia* (408 U.S. 238, 345) decision occurred on June 20, 2002. In *Daryl Renard Atkins v. Virginia* (536 U.S. 304; 122 S.Ct 2242) it found that the executions of mentally retarded criminals constitutes "cruel and unusual punishment" prohibited by the Eighth Amendment to the United States Constitution. In another landmark case, the U.S. Supreme Court, on June 24, 2002, overturned 168 death sentences in five states (Arizona, Idaho, Montana, Colorado, and Nebraska) where judges, and not the jury, death qualified convicted felons. This practice was in violation of the 1976 U.S. Supreme Court decision reinstating the death penalty in the United States.

Here the Court stated that there had to be a two-step process in death-qualified cases—a petit jury trial to determine guilt and then a second stage where mitigating versus aggravating evidence would be heard. Moreover, the Court stated that both steps needed to be heard by a jury and not determined by the bench.[30]

The U.S. Supreme Court is currently considering the status of foreigners on death row—those apparently adjudicated without the benefit of legal assistance from their national consulates. Of the118 death row foreigners in this class, 51 are from Mexico, most convicted in Texas, and a major source of contention between Mexico and the United States. Mexico has on its side a 2004 ruling from the International Court of Justice (ICJ} in The Hague. The ICJ ruled that the 51 Mexican convictions violated the 1963 Vienna Convention. To date the U.S. Supreme Court has not sufficiently addressed the fact that the United States ratified the Vienna Convention in 1969 requiring consulate access for Americans detained abroad and for foreigners arrested in the United States.[31]

Congressional Apology for Slavery

The discriminatory treatment of minorities in the United States, notably those of color, has long been a contentious issue with its neighbors in the Americas, the European Union, the United Nations, and its economic allies. Only since the 9/11 terrorist attacks and the United States' increased reliance on international support for its war on terrorism have significant changes come about. Interestingly, these changes stem from U.S. Supreme Court challenges and Senate proclamations and not from the former Bush Administration.

On June 13, 2005, the 109th Congress, U.S. Senate passed resolution 39 "apologizing to the victims of lynching and the descendants of those victims for the failure of the Senate to enact anti-lynching legislation." The resolution details the long history of these de facto abuses, including nearly 5,000 documented deaths, primarily of African Americans, and a dereliction of duty that resulted in only 1 percent of perpetrators being held accountable by the state. Essentially the apology noted that lynching succeeded slavery as the ultimate expression of racism in the United States following Reconstruction, lasting until the middle of the 20th century and involving all but four states. The resolution also noted the fact that 99 percent of all perpetrators of lynching escaped punishment. With this acknowledgement, the Senate resolved to:

1. apologize to the victims of lynching for the failure of the Senate to enact anti-lynching legislation;
2. express the deepest sympathies and most solemn regrets of the Senate to the descendants of victims of lynching, the ancestors of whom were deprived of

> life, human dignity, and the constitutional protection accorded all citizens of the United States; and

3. remember the history of lynching, to ensure that these tragedies will be neither forgotten nor repeated.[32]

Only 13 senators voted against the antilynching resolution. Mississippi, New Hampshire, Texas, and Wyoming were the four states that did not cosponsor the resolution.

On the same day, June 13, 2005, in a 6–3 ruling delivered by Justice David Souter, the U.S. Supreme Court overturned the death sentence of Thomas Miller-El, a black man, due to the historical practice in Texas courts of excluding qualified blacks from jury selection in capital cases. In the ruling Justice Souter noted that:

The prosecutors used preemptory strikes to exclude 91% of the eligible black venire panelists, a disparity unlikely to have been produced by happenstance. . . .The selection process was replete with evidence that prosecutors were selecting and rejecting potential jurors because of race.[33]

Clearly, the United States has been slow in addressing the brutality associated with its era of slavery. Recognition of those involved with the struggle leading to the Civil Rights Acts of the 1960s was exemplified with federal and state recognition of Martin Luther King Jr. Day. The last major holdouts for a nationwide recognition of the Nobel Prize winner and assassinated civil rights leader were the border states of Arizona in 1990 and New Hampshire in 2000.

CHAPTER 2

Myths and Realities of the Annexation of Texas and the War with Mexico

TEXAS—MYTHS AND REALITY

The Alamo is an old mission in San Antonio, Texas, where a small band of Texans held out for 13 days against the centralist army of General Antonio Lopez de Santa Anna. Although the Alamo fell in the early morning hours of March 6, 1836, the death of the Alamo defenders has come to symbolize courage and sacrifice for the cause of liberty. The memories of James Bowie, David Crockett, and William B. Travis are as powerful today as when the Texan Army under Sam Houston shouted "Remember the Alamo!" as it routed Santa Anna at the battle of San Jacinto on April 21, 1836.[1]

This is the most common myth justifying Texas's secession from Mexico, one perpetuated by the Daughters of the Republic of Texas who have managed the Alamo as a sacred shrine since 1905. The story is more complex than this simple portrayal of freedom-loving American émigrés fighting against a brutal dictator. Actually, the story began when Mexico was still a Spanish colony and at a time when the United States was challenging both the Spanish to its south and the British to its north in an effort to expand its territory. A critical factor in this formula was the issue of black slaves.

New Spain had a long colonial history extending to the early 1500s. The Spanish, more so than their British and French colonial counterparts, had a highly structured stratification based on laws of the Indies. And like the fledging United States, the newly independent Mexico patterned its legal, social, and economic structure on that of its colonial parent. One major difference was that the Spanish colonial system (Spanish America) was highly centralized with the top echelon in the military, Catholic Church, and civil service system occupied by Spanish-born officials. In the British colonies, on the other hand, the congregational structure of the quasi-official churches (Congregationalists in the northern colonies and English Episcopal in the South) allowed for local independence and responsibility with many governmental positions held by locally born men. Silverstone argues in his book, *Divided Union*, that this division of authority and the power of home rule saved the United States from the numerous military coups and other political disruptions that characterized Latin America.[2]

The basic rationale for independence from European colonialism differed significantly between the United States and Mexico, a schism that played a major role in the Texas Revolution. The 13 English colonies fought for control from the elite of Great Britain, while the 1810 Mexican Revolution was one for freedom from the Spanish feudal system. Canadian social philosopher John Ralston Saul, in his recent book on the collapse of globalism, views the early U.S. experience as negative nationalism, one where the United States was eager from the beginning to rival the European colonial powers in its pursuit of expansionism. Ralston Saul coined this "spread-eagleism"— a process eventually resulting in a 10,000-mile wingspan of U.S. influence from Manila to Puerto Rico.[3] Negative nationalism, or Manifest Destiny, a process whereby nationalism becomes synonymous with ethnicity, and supports elitism at the expense of others while justifying harsh actions against those standing in their way, also motivated the Texas revolt. The Daughters of the Republic of Texas's "cause of liberty" is Jefferson's "empire of liberty." It is also a process rooted in a perverse social/political system based on elitist ethnicity and ambition. In this sense genocide and ethnic cleansing are justified under the guise of doing God's work. This philosophy justified both U.S. expansionism at any cost and also fueled the Texas Revolution by disgruntled Anglo Americans seeking better fortunes in New Spain.

On the other hand, the colonial experience in New Spain was one of strict stratification, a caste system with the Spanish-born elite, the Peninsulares, occupying most of the important positions in government, the church, and the military. Historical records indicate that only three Criollos (Mexicans born of Spanish parents) held the position of viceroy of Mexico in the three centuries of Spanish rule. During this same period only 18 out of 754 high civil and military positions in all of Spanish America were held by local born Criollos (Creoles).[4]

The feudal system of New Spain evolved from the *encomiendas* system where large land holdings, including the Native inhabitants, were given by the Spanish Crown to the early Spanish explorers (Conquistadors). This system included a provision to educate and convert the American Indian population to Catholicism. The Native Americans, in turn, would serve as vassals to their Spanish lords. The encomiendas system lasted from 1521 until 1550 when it was replaced with the *repartimiento* system. The change was in response to the aging population of the original Conquistador Pennisulars. Again Spanish-born Peninsulars held large tracks of land where the Native Americans, Mestizos (those of mixed Indian/white and or black heritage), and rural *indomestizos* served as indentured sharecroppers. This feudal system then evolved into the hacienda system of large estates where the lower strata of society were dependent on the large landholders for their subsistence. It was a variation of the hacienda system that attracted slave-holding émigrés from the United States to New Spain just prior to the Mexican War for independence from Spain.

The new settlers to New Spain (Mexico) were given land grants termed *empresarios*—a form of hacienda. The empresario was essentially a land agent who would then provide settlers for his land grant. Spain, seeking to protect its northeastern territory known then as Coahuila and Tejas from intrusions from the United States and other European colonial forces, attempted first to entice other Mexicans and immigrants from other locations within Spanish America to settle this area. De León in his 1993 book, *Mexican Americans in Texas,* details the early settlement picture. He noted that Mexico City sent troops to what is now east Texas in 1716 in response to French activity in the area. The expedition force established the San Antonio settlement, home to the Alamo. In 1731, immigrants from the Canary Islands arrived in San Antonio, and more settlements were established along the Rio Grande in the 1740s and 1750s, including Laredo. A census in 1777 showed over 3,000 *pobladores* (settlers) resided in the area, most in San Antonio. Voluntary migration from the interior to the northeastern frontier was thwarted mainly by resistance on the part of hacienda owners fearing a labor shortage if sufficient numbers of rural Mexicans migrated north. Moreover, relaxation of foreign competition in the New World allowed for a more relaxed settlement plan.[5]

The Adams-Onís Treaty of 1819

The role of Anglo settlers from the United States had its beginnings with the War of 1812. While the major objective of the war was United States expansion into British Canada, Spain nervously watched as U.S. forces entered its territory in Florida and fought its last major battle in New Orleans. Stung by France's sale of its former buffer territory—the Louisiana Purchase—Spain was now compelled to populate its northeastern border as a protection from the encroaching United States. A major factor in this process was the Adams-Onís Treaty of 1819. The Treaty of Amity, Settlement, and Limits between the United States of America and His Catholic Majesty (aka Transcontinental Treaty of 1819; Florida Treaty; Adams-Onís Treaty) ended the Seminole Wars ceding Florida to the United States as well as establishing the Mexico/U.S. border at the Sabine River. Here Spain paid the United States five million dollars for Florida while relinquishing claims west of the Sabine River, finally ending its opposition to France's right to sell the Louisiana Purchase.[6]

The treaty ended the U.S. claim that the Louisiana Purchase included Spanish-held territory up to the Rio Grande and the Rocky Mountains, including what was then Texas and New Mexico. By selling Florida and forgoing its claims to Oregon Territory in the Northwest, Spain was able to establish its claim to Texas and the New Mexico territories (including what is now Arizona, Utah, and Nevada) maintaining a buffer between the United States and its California colonies. Unfortunately, while the Adams-Onís Treaty was signed on February 22, 1819, it was not ratified until three years later on February 22, 1821. Mexico's independence provided the United States another opportunity to break a treaty challenging its own border agreements regarding the U.S./Mexico border. Nonetheless, the Adams-Onís Treaty necessitated Spain's efforts to populate its territories along the U.S. border. This endeavor opened the door to empresario contracts with U.S. expatriates.

The Empresario Land Grants

Eight months prior to independence, a number of settlers from the United States petitioned for land grants. Moses Austin was granted the first empresario permit on January 17, 1821, allowing him to settle 300 families in what is now Texas. Moses Austin left Missouri for Mexico due to the better land deals offered by Spain. In the United States, two major events precipitated the migration south to Mexico. One was the economic panic of 1819 while the other was the high cost of public land. The economic panic of 1819 resulted in the loss of numerous holdings notably in the newly opened western United States, leaving many land holders destitute and bitter. Complicating this situation was the high cost of public land. The price per acre was set by Congress at two dollars payable in four installments. In 1820, the price was slashed to a dollar and a quarter per acre, but the bill had to be paid in full at the time of purchase, making these lands available only to the affluent. In Mexico good land was available at 12½ cents per acre with six years to pay. Much of this land was conveniently located in the eastern interior provinces close to the United States border. Texas/Coahuila was part of this territory. Mexico's independence from Spain on September 27, 1821, did not immediately alter these arrangements. But later difficulties arose due to the differences that existed between the Republic of Mexico and the United States of America. Two areas of contrast involved the issue of slavery and women's rights. Mexico outlawed slavery while continuing the Iberian legal tradition of recognizing women's property rights—events that would not occur in the United States for decades and after considerable internal conflict.[7]

The senior Austin died during the preparations for the settlement and his son, Stephen F. Austin, took over the responsibilities as empresario of the Austin grant. The empresario became the de facto lord or governor of his land grant, including the subcontracting families. However, neither the empresario nor the subgrantee settlers owned their land outright. Instead, empresarios were awarded a premium for each 100 families settled under their contract. Austin's premium was 23,000 acres per 100 settlers to his contracted lands. These land grants were interspersed with other elements of the Spanish frontier community which consisted of Catholic missions, presidios (frontier garrisons), ranchos, farms ,and towns. The empresario grants in Texas (Coahuila and Tejas) continued following the establishment of the Republic of Mexico on September 27, 1821, with the largest owners, including Austin, Green de Witt, and Haden Edwards.[8]

Under the Imperial Colonization Law immigrants had to be Catholics or convert to Catholicism. Each married settler family potentially received one league (*silio*) of 4,428 acres of combined pastureland and farmland. The family received one labor (177 acres) of farmland and if the new settler desired to raise cattle, then he could get 24 labors of pastureland (4,251 acres) as well. Unmarried settlers were granted one-fourth this amount. Mexico held the deed to the settler's land for six years. Title transfer was contingent upon all conditions being met. The Republic of Mexico continued this practice stipulated in its national decree of August 18, 1824. These conditions were then enacted by the Legislature of Coahuila and Texas on March 24, 1825. The limit of a single empresario was 800 families. The conditions of the empresarios were as follows. They were required to:

- establish boundaries of the proposed colony;
- respect the legal titles already existing in their proposed colony;
- settle the required number of families within six years;
- settle Catholic families of good moral character;
- prohibit criminals;
- organize and command a national militia force;
- make all official and public communications in Spanish; and
- after April 6, 1830, bar immigrants from adjoining countries, notably the United States of America.[9]

While the Anglo American immigration into Texas began with the Austin empresario during Spanish rule, the vast majority of expatriate Americans came with the Mexican Republic law of August 18, 1824, and state colonialization law of March 24, 1825. A month following passage of the state colonialization law in 1825, the governor of the combined state of Coahuila and Texas contracted for 2,400 American emigrant families. Two empresarios, Haden Edwards and Robert Leftwich, each contracted for the maximum 800 families. The flood of Anglo Americans continued until 1832. Mexican empresarios joined this movement to populate Coahuila and Texas as is evident by the listing of the other land contractors of this time: de Witt, Thorn, de León, Purnell, Lovell, Milam, Wavell, Wilson, Woodbury, Vehlein, Burnet, Cameron, Exeter, Hewetson, Power, McMullen, McGloin, Vehlein, de Zavala, Dominguez, Padilla, Chambers, Filisola, Beales, Royuela. The Beales and Royuela's empresarios were the last granted under the law of March 24, 1825.[10]

The Austin contracts were the most successful empresarios. The census of 1827 indicated the Austin colonies to be about 2,000 and 5,600 in 1831. Also successful were the empresarios of de Witt and de León. Others that had varying degrees of success were those of McMullen and McGloin, Robertson, Milan, Hewetson, Power, Zavala, Burnet, and Vehlien. And those that established no permanent settlements include: Wavell, Wilson, Wilson and Exeter, Woodbury, Cameron, Dominquez, Filisola, Padilla and Chambers, Thorn, Purnell and Lovell, Bales and Royuela, Campos, Beales and Grant. It is estimated that the predominant Anglo American empresarios totaled 30,000 at the time of the Texas Revolution in 1836.[11]

Mexico soon became wary of the growing Anglo American emigrants especially following the Fredonian Rebellion when the Edwards brothers led an uprising and declared independence in 1826. The Edwards brothers (Haden and Benjamin) were granted empresarial grants in April 1825 entitling them to settle up to 800 families in the Nacodoches area just north of the Austin grant. Their authoritarian methods of governance alienated many of the original residents in the region, which led to a probe by the regional political leader, José Antonio Saucedo. Haden Edwards and his political machine were investigated for oppression and corruption leading to the dispatch of a Mexican military force into the region led by the military commander of Texas, Lieutenant Colonel Mateo Ahumada. The Edwards brothers mustered their own militia and declared their empresario an independent republic called Fredonia. They even appealed to the United States for assistance in their rebellion. However, their neighbors in Texas, including Anglo Americans, Hispanics, and Native Americans, opposed the Edwards brothers' rebellion and assisted Ahumada in putting it down. The short-lived rebellion and independent Republic of Fredonia ended on January 31, 1827, when the remnants of the revolutionists fled across the Sabine River to the United States.[12]

Anglo American emigrants benefited from the chaos during the Mexican fight for independence (1810–21) and the aftermath of forging a viable republic. During this transitional decade Spanish policy endured, extending the status quo for the empresarios. During the first decade of postcolonial rule, Mexico, like its neighbors to the north, encountered contravening political perspectives on how to govern the new country. The main battles were between factions supporting a monarch, a decentralized federation, or a centralized government. During the early years of independence, Mexico went from being a short-lived monarchy with Augustín de Iturbride as emperor and to a republican federalist's state in 1824 only to succumb to a centralized regime in 1830. With the latter came efforts to enforce the dictates of the Mexican Constitution, including in the Anglo-dominated colony of Texas.

Following Iturbide's abdication and the emergence of a federal republic, Guadalupe Victoria became Mexico's first president. It was during his term that the new nation became leery of Anglo American aggression in Texas as illustrated by the Fredonian revolt. Indeed, the impact of the Mexican Congress's curtailment of Anglo American immigration was felt in New Mexico Territory as well. Here, the bulk of Anglo Americans were traders without empresario status. Even then, the New Mexico delegate to the Mexican Congress, Manuel de Jesús Rada, encouraged the establishment of foreign empresarios to create factories and mines in the territory. The worsening crises in Texas obviated goodwill endeavors initiated between the United States and Mexico relevant to expanding travel and trade in New Mexico.

The Mexican Constitution and the Slavery Issue

Serving his full term, Victoria was succeeded by his secretary of war—Gómez Pedraza. While Pedraza won the vote he was quickly overthrown by a military coup, making Vincent Guerrero the actual ruler. Inaugurated in April 1829, Guerrero issued his decree abolishing slavery throughout the Republic of Mexico in September, sending a shock wave throughout the Anglo settlers in Texas. Texas, however, was successful in avoiding Guerrero's decree due to a clause in the colonialization laws guaranteeing the settlers security of their property, including their slaves. Another military coup in January 1830 replaced Guerrero with his vice president, General Anastacio Bustamante.[13]

President Bustamante was instrumental in getting Congress to pass a decree on April 6, 1830, that would fuel the Texas Revolution. Four of the 18 articles of the Bustamante Decree, as it came to be known, were points of contention. Article 3 proposed closer oversight of the colonies while articles 9 and 11 were designed to curb further immigration from the United States, and article 10 enforced Mexico's antislavery laws.

Article 3. The government is authorized to name one or more commissioners who shall visit the colonies of the frontier states and contract with the legislatures of said states for the purchase, on behalf of the Federal government, of lands deemed suitable for the establishment of colonies of Mexicans and other nationalities; and the said commissioners shall make, with the existing colonies, whatever arrangements seem expedient for the security of the republic. The said commissioners shall supervise the introduction of new colonists and the fulfilling of their contract for settlement, and shall ascertain to what extent the existing contracts have been completed.

Article 9. The introduction of foreigners across the northern frontier is prohibited under any pretext whatsoever, unless the said foreigners are provided with a passport issued by the agent of the republic at the point whence the said foreigners set out.

Article 10. No change shall be made with respect to the slaves now in the states, but the Federal government and the government of each state shall most strictly enforce the colonialization laws, and prevent the further introduction of slaves.

Article 11. In accordance with the right reserved by the general congress in the seventh article of the law of, August 18, 1824, it is prohibited that emigrants, from nations bordering on this republic shall settle in the states or territory adjacent to their own nation. Consequently, all contracts not already completed and not in harmony with law are suspended.[14]

Ironically, in 1822, Bustamante had been a strong advocate of the Austin colony and the empresario system. Moreover, Stephen Austin continued to support Bustamante despite his 1830 decree. Bustamante's reign ended in December 1832 when Gómez Pedraza finally ascended to the presidency he had originally won in 1828. This action allowed Pedraza to serve the final three months of this constitutional four-year term.

More significant, however, was the ascendance of the Criollo Antonio López de Santa Anna to the presidency on April 1, 1833. He was the Mexican leader most intricately involved with Texas independence, the Mexican War, and the Gadsden Purchase. He subsequently served five terms as president within a 22-year span. Tejas Anglo American settlers despised Santa Anna, mainly for his enforcement of Mexico's antislavery laws. Clearly, Santa Anna's efforts to consolidate his authority by changing sides once duly elected as president upset many of the Anglo American immigrants. Santa Anna supported Pedraza's return to the presidency and used this as a vehicle for becoming the leader of the Liberal Republican Party and rising to the presidency himself. But once president, Santa Anna switched allegiances and supported the conservative Centralist Party—the party of the military and ecclesiastical aristocracy. With support of both the military and the Catholic Church, Santa Anna held considerable powers. During this chaotic time Austin was incarcerated in Mexico City and awaited trial on charges of disaffection. However, with no court willing to prosecute, Austin was released on bond on Christmas Day in 1835. He returned to Texas, and the stage was set for the Texas Revolution.[15]

Slavery and Catholicism were the two main objections of Anglo American emigrants in Texas, a sentiment noted by Stephen Austin in correspondence with Erasmo Sequin, a Texas representative to the federal Congress:

There are two obstacles that retard emigration to this province and to the whole nation; one is the doubt that exists concerning the admission of slavery, and the other is religion. Many Catholics would come from Louisiana if they could bring their slaves here, but, as the greater part of their capital consists in slaves, they cannot emigrate unless they take the slaves with them.[16]

Indeed, the main reason for the separation of the Texas colony from Coahuila was the Anglo emigrants desire to forge their own slavery laws. Austin saw the slave prerogative from an international perspective—one that favored the U.S. southern sentiments. These views were articulated in an 1835 correspondence to a friend in New Orleans:

Texas must be a slave country. It is no longer a matter of doubt. The interest of Louisiana requires that it should be, a population of fanatical abolitionists in Texas would have a very pernicious and dangerous influence on the overgrown slave population of that state [Louisiana]. Texas must, and ought to, become an outwork on the west, as Alabama and Florida are on the east, to defend the key of the western world—the mouths of the Mississippi.[17]

Seeds were sowed for the Mexican War following Texas's independence. Daniel Tyler noted that events such as the Adams-Onís Treaty and the Fredonian revolt forced Mexico to place their attention on events in Texas setting the stage for a weakened defense in its New Mexico Territory. These circumstances led to an increased illegal encroachment into this region. According to Tyler, when the Mexican Congress curtailed the activities of all immigrants from the United States with its stringent anti-immigration laws this action ultimately contributed to the rebellion in Texas, adding to the impoverishment and isolation of New Mexico.

THE EMERGING TEXAS REPUBLIC

The Anglo American colonists had their opportunity for rebellion when other Mexicans actively protested Santa Anna's rule throughout the country. Initially, a combination of Tejanos (Mexican Texans) and Anglo Texans participated in this protest. Leading the Tejanos faction was Austin's friend, Captain Juan N. Sequín. The majority of the Tejanos, however, remained neutral during the rebellion. Actions leading to the revolt began on December 10, 1835, when the Texans convened a General Council to select delegates to an assembly being held on March 1, 1836, at Washington-on-the-Brazos. The consultation sent Branch T. Archer, William H. Wharton, and Stephen F. Austin to the United States to solicit money, equipment, men, and support for their cause. The March convention at Washington-on-the-Brazos consisted of 41 delegates—39 Anglos and 3 native Mexicans (José Fransisco Ruiz, José Antonio Navarro, and Lorenzo de Zavala). On March 2, 1836, the convention signed their Declaration of Independence.

President Santa Anna exercised his constitutional authority to put down the rebellion and subsequently took a poorly trained and armed force north to quell the rebellion in San Antonio de Béxar. The Mexican army had outmoded smoothbore muskets and a force comprised of poorly trained conscripts, political prisoners, and even Mayan Indians who were impressed into the military, few of whom understood Spanish. With this force President/General Santa Anna laid siege to the rebels' outpost in San Antonio (the Alamo) on February 23, 1836.

The Alamo was well fortified with 21 cannons, 8- to 9-foot walls, and men armed with the best firearms of the time—Kentucky long rifles. Hence, the Alamo was considered to be the best-fortified military installation between New Orleans and Monterrey, Mexico. Santa Anna's army took the Alamo but with considerable losses—estimated to be between 500 and 600 men. All 186 Alamo defenders were slain with the exception of surviving family members of Tejanos, an Anglo American woman and her child, and one African American slave owned by defender William Barrett Travis. The Alamo fell four days following the Texas Declaration of Independence. The Mexican army was also quelling another revolt southeast of San Antonio at Goliad. Some 400 Texicans (rebels) surrendered with 342 of them executed while prisoners of war.

Santa Anna left San Antonio with his weakened forces to battle the main forces of the rebel army at San Jacinto. History tells us that Santa Anna's army of 1,500 was defeated by General Sam Houston's force of 900 men, including a small Tejano force led by Juan N. Seguín. Following a short battle, Santa Anna's forces were decimated. The Anglo forces continued to hunt down and slay retreating members of the Mexican force, resulting in some 600 deaths compared to Houston's force with only eight casualties. Three weeks later the Treaty of Velasco was negotiated with President/General Santa Anna conceding Texas independence. The Mexican Congress never confirmed the treaty. Nonetheless, given that Mexico was never able to retake Texas, it enjoyed de facto status as an independent nation.[18]

Slavery and the Texas Constitution

The constitution of the Republic of Texas was based on that of the United States and certain southern states, notably Tennessee. Sam Houston, former U.S. congressman and governor of Tennessee and close friend of President Andrew Jackson, was selected as commander in chief of the revolution while David G. Burnet became Texas's first president, leading the interim government. A Tejano, Lorenzo de Zavala, became vice president; Samuel P. Carson, secretary of state; Thomas J. Rusk, secretary of war; and David Thomas, attorney general. The constitution of the Republic of Texas had a few caveats addressing its anti-Catholic/anti-Spanish and pro-slavery stance.

ARTICLE I: Section 7. The senators shall be chosen by districts, as equal in free population (free negroes and Indians excepted), as practicable; and the number of senators shall never be less than one third nor more than one half the number of representatives, and each district shall be entitled to one member and no more.

ARTICLE IV: Section 13. The congress shall, as early as practicable, introduce, by statute, the common law of England, with such modifications as our circumstances, in their judgment, may require; and in all criminal cases, the common law shall be the rule of decision.

ARTICLE V: Section 1. Ministers of the gospel being, by their profession, dedicated to God and the care of souls, ought not to be diverted from the great duties of their functions; therefore, no minister of the gospel, or any priest of any denomination whatever, shall be eligible to the office of the executive of the republic, nor to a seat in either branch of the congress of the same.

GENERAL PROVISIONS: Section 6. All free white persons who shall emigrate to this republic, and who shall, after a residence of six months, make oath before some competent authority that he intends to reside permanently in the same, and shall swear to support this constitution, and that he will bear true allegiance to the republic of Texas, shall be entitled to all the privileges of citizenship.

Section 9. All persons of color who were slaves for life previous to their emigration to Texas, and who are now held in bondage, shall remain in the like state of servitude; provided, the said slave shall be the bona fide property of the person so holding said slave as aforesaid. Congress shall pass no laws to prohibit emigrants from bring their slaves into the republic with them, and holding them by the same tenure by which such slaves were held in the United States; nor shall Congress have power to emancipate slaves; nor shall any slave holder be allowed to emancipate his or her slave or slaves without the consent of Congress, unless he or she shall send his or her slave or slaves without the limits of the republic. No free person of African descent, either in whole or in part, shall be permitted to reside permanently in the republic, without the consent of Congress; and the importation or admission of Africans or Negroes into this republic, excepting from the United States of America, is forever prohibited, and declared to be piracy.

Section 10: All persons (Africans, the descendants of Africans, and Indians excepted) who were residing in Texas on the day of the Declaration of Independence, shall be considered citizens of the republic, and entitled to all the privileges of such. . . .

DECLARATION OF RIGHTS: First. All men, when they form a social compact, have equal rights, and no men or set of men are entitled to exclusive public privileges or emoluments from the community.

Third. No preference shall be given by law to any religious denomination or mode of worship over another, but every person shall be permitted to worship God according to the dictates of his own conscience. . . .

Eight. No title of nobility, hereditary privileges or honors, shall ever be granted or conferred in this republic. No person holding any office of profit or trust shall, without the consent of congress, receive from any foreign state and present, office, or emolument of any kind.[19]

The pro-United States, anti-Spanish influence is most evident in the Texas Constitution with article 4, section 13, article 5, section 1, and first, third and eighth items of the Declaration of Rights. Antiwhite sentiments, notably toward blacks and American Indians, are clearly articulated in article 1, section 7, and sections 6, 9, and 10 of the General Provisions. Although the vast majority of Tejanos absorbed into the new Texas Republic remained neutral during the conflict, they too would suffer considerable injustices at the hands of the Anglos.

Although the Alamo and the Texas revolt have been celebrated in U.S. history books, not all American leaders at the time viewed the Texas Revolution in a positive light. Former president John Quincy Adams, coauthor of the Adams-Onís Treaty of 1819, saw it as a blatant act of self-interest for slave owners and land speculators. These divided sentiments in the United States of America caused considerable unrest, which would lead eventually to the annexation of Texas, the war with Mexico, and the War between the States (Civil War). Texas's decade as an independent republic (March 2, 1836–February 18, 1846) was equally turbulent internally with sentiments oscillating between sovereignty and allegiance to the United States. This was exacerbated by the fact that from the beginning the Texas Republic had difficulty being recognized as an independent nation in its own right. Two factors played significant roles here—Mexico's congressional refusal to recognize the Treaty of Velasco and the slave issue.

Presidents Sam Houston and Mirabeau B. Lamar's contradictory political philosophies added greatly to the republic's short history. Like the United States to the north and Mexico to the south, these turbulent years were threatened by a military takeover by its own army. The human rights issue involving black slaves, Native American tribes, and the peasant Mestizos, perhaps more than anything denied Texas the recognition it sought among the world leaders at the time. This was despite the efforts of Texas's most influential statesman during this era—Secretary of State Stephen F. Austin. The internal conflict even resulted in the republic's first chief justice, James Collinsworth, committing suicide. In addition to the controversy around slavery, the Texas Republic continued to claim territory well beyond that agreed upon by the Treaty of Velasco.

The United States' intervention was considerable during this time, and the eventual annexation of Texas is widely attributed to the influence of Sam Houston, former governor of Tennessee, U.S. congressman, and friend and ally of Andrew Jackson. Indeed, the United States stood ready to protect the Texas Republic in the event of an invasion by Mexico. Even then, the Texas problem played itself out in the United States contributing to two wars— the war with Mexico and the War between the States, the latter being the bloodiest conflict in the 19th century.[20]

PRELUDE TO THE U.S. CIVIL WAR: TEXAS ANNEXATION AND THE WAR WITH MEXICO

The annexation of Texas began with Sam Houston's second term as president of the republic in 1841. Even his arch rival, former president Mirabeau B. Lamar, eventually came to support annexation to the United States mainly for the purpose of protecting the institution of slavery and to keep Texas from becoming a British protectorate. Annexation was initially rejected by the U.S. Senate in June 1844 but became a major issue in that year's presidential elections. James K. Polk won election by supporting the annexation issue, and Congress followed suit by passing the annexation resolution on February 28, 1845. Texas, under President Anson Jones, accepted annexation in October 1845, and Texas formally became part of the United States on February 19, 1846.

Annexation sowed the seeds of war with Mexico. Following years of diplomacy, Great Britain convinced Mexico to acknowledge the independence of Texas under the proviso that it not annex itself to any country—notably the United States. The manifested cause of the Mexican-American War was the border dispute between Texas and Mexico with Mexico claiming the Nueces River, as stipulated by the Treaty of Velasco, and the United States the Rio Grande. In January 1846, President Polk sent General Zachary Taylor across the Nueces River for the purpose of establishing military posts along the Rio Grande. In April of that year, Mexican troops crossed the Rio Grande, clashing with U.S. troops. President Polk reacted quickly, requesting Congress declare war with Mexico. Congress concurred and war was officially declared May 13, 1846. Mexico reciprocated 10 days later, initiating the two-year conflict known as the Mexican War in the United States and as the War of Northern Aggression or the United States War against Mexico in Mexico.[21]

Polk's War and a Divided Nation

Clearly the United States was divided over this blatant act of American imperialism under the guise of Manifest Destiny. It became clear that the United States was willing to forcefully take what it could not obtain through negotiations—a process already in place with the forceful removal of Indian tribes in the southeastern states. Mexico rejected offers to buy the adjacent northern Mexican territories of New Mexico and California. This followed the failure by the United States to expand its northern perimeter to the 49th parallel of the Alaskan border under the Buchanan-Parkenham Treaty of 1846 that awarded Great Britain all of Vancouver and the U.S. the Puget Sound—concessions that avoided yet another war with Great Britain. Polk's administration figured it was easier to fight a struggling third world country like Mexico instead of one of the colonial superpowers of the time. Connor and Faulk attributed the Mexican-American War to blatant imperialism:

The origins of the war between the United States and Mexico, 1846–48, remain controversial even today (1971). To most Mexicans the issue is simple—the United States fought Mexico in order to acquire the territory now called the American Southwest, including both Texas and California. Simple imperialism. To many Americans it is the same—the late Robert Kennedy once referred to the war as one of the most disgraceful episodes in the American past.[22]

Clearly, what the acquisition of this new territory did do was ignite the slave debate in the United States and pave the way for the more devastating conflict—the Civil War. Slavery and expansionism were the predominant issues that split U.S. support for the war with Mexico. Slavery exploded in Texas following statehood, increasing from 30,000 in 1845 to 182,566 in 1860. At the time Texas succeeded from the Union, black slaves comprised over 30 percent of the state's population. Indeed, the slave issue reflected the deep divisions in the United States at the time of Polk's presidency. Of the two major parties, the Democrats were proponents of Manifest Destiny, providing strong support for the annexation of both Texas and Oregon Territory. The Whigs, on the other hand, held a more conservative and cautious view on expansionism, supporting the status quo of strong federalism and local autonomy. These differences were played out in the election of 1844. Henry Clay, the Whig candidate, lost to James Knox Polk, the dark horse Democratic candidate, who ran on a platform of territorial expansionism under the guise of Manifest Destiny. Imbedded in this dilemma was the slave controversy. Hence, the Democrats came to be seen as being pro-slavery and pro-expansionist while the Whigs were viewed as being leery of rapid expansion, fearing that it would ultimately lead to a stronger centralized form of government and expand slavery into the newly acquired territories. Yet, Polk's expansionist interpretation of Manifest Destiny found support in both his cabinet and the Congress with the Democrats holding a 144 to 77 majority in the House and a 30 to 24 lead in the Senate. With this mandate, the war with Mexico soon followed as did a major reconfiguration of U.S. political parties.

Even with congressional support for territorial expansionism, slavery and the war with Mexico, the Democrats themselves were divided, as was the country. Serious factions emerged between the North and South. The Wilmot Proviso attempted to bridge these differences. Initiated by northern Congressmen and presented by David Wilmot, a freshman Democratic congressman from Pennsylvania, the amendment was attached to a war appropriation bill. It was designed to make Texas the last slave state:

Provided, territory from that, as an express and fundamental condition to the acquisition of any the Republic of Mexico by the United States, by virtue of any treaty which may be negotiated between them, and to the use by the Executive of the moneys herein appropriated, neither slavery nor involuntary servitude shall ever exist in any part of said territory, except for crime, whereof the party shall first be duly convicted.[23]

The Wilmot Proviso subsequently passed the House of Representatives in both 1846 and 1847 but never was approved by the Senate. The provision was negated by the Compromise of 1850 and was ultimately struck down by the U.S. Supreme Court in the 1857 *Dred Scott* case.

The war with Mexico spelled the demise of the Whig Party and the emergence of the Republican Party. The Whigs were heavily represented in the Northeast with Boston the center for its Conscience Wing, which viewed war, slavery, and the southern political structure as obstacles to both democracy and Christianity. Schroeder noted that these reformers: "interpreted the Mexican War in moral terms as an aggressive, unjust, and unholy war to extend the heinous institution of slavery." Nonetheless, the Whigs nominated Zachary Taylor, a southern slaveholder, as their candidate for the 1848 presidential contest. Although Taylor won the election, it further alienated the northern Conscience Whigs and some northern Democrats leading to the proliferation of break-off political parties, ultimately welded into the Free-Soil Party. The Free-Soil Party was initiated by the Wilmot Proviso and drew its membership from abolitionists from both the Whig and Democratic parties. The party believed in slave-free territory, free labor, free speech, and freedmen. They held their first party convention in 1848 with their leaders, Salmon P. Chase and John P. Hale.

John P. Hale, and his fellow New Hampshire native and former college roommate, Franklin Pierce, played significant, yet contravening, roles in the ensuing slave and expansionism debate leading up to the Civil War. Franklin Pierce was the son of Revolutionary War general and later, governor of New Hampshire, Benjamin Pierce. From this privileged background, Franklin entered Bowdoin College in Brunswick, Maine, at age 15 in the fall of 1820. It was here that Franklin Pierce forged a strong friendship with another scion of the state's aristocracy, John Parker Hale. Due to his family's strong political connections, young Pierce began studying law immediately following his graduation from Bowdoin and soon began practicing law from an office established for him by his father in their hometown of Hillsborough. The beginning of his law practice coincided with his father's election as governor of New Hampshire in 1827. Riding on his father's coattails, Franklin joined the New Hampshire legislature as a Democrat in 1829. In 1831, he became the youngest person to be made speaker of the house. A year later, in 1832, John Parker Hale entered the New Hampshire legislature as a Democrat representing Dover. Pierce helped Hale by appointing him to prestigious committees, but Hale failed to win reelection to his seat in 1833.[24]

In 1833, Pierce won a seat in the U.S. Congress and was instrumental in getting President Jackson to appoint Hale as the federal district attorney for New Hampshire. Hale reciprocated by helping Pierce win his appointment to the U.S. Senate in 1837. While in Washington, DC, Pierce was a staunch supporter of President Jackson's agenda including the right of Southerners to own slaves. With his wife, the daughter of the president of Bowdoin College, unhappy with Washington, DC, Pierce resigned his Senate seat in 1842, returning to New Hampshire to head the state's Democratic Party organization. In this capacity, Pierce was instrumental in getting John P. Hale elected to the U.S. Congress.

The split between Pierce and Hale came about with the 1844 election of James Polk as U.S. president. While the New Hampshire Democratic Party supported Texas annexation, Hale went against the state Democratic platform by proposing a resolution in the U.S. House of Representatives urging the creation of two states out of the former Texas Republic, one slave and one free. The resolution was soundly defeated and upset the state's Democratic Party chairman, Franklin Pierce, who set the stage for Hale's expulsion from the Democratic Party. This action effectively ended the close personal and political relationship between Pierce and Hale. Thus, the annexation of Texas raised the issue of slavery to a prominent level in U.S. politics with Franklin Pierce siding with the South and John P. Hale becoming the first U.S. Senator to speak against slavery. Hale is credited with the following pronouncement:

The measure of my ambition will be full if when my wife and children shall repair to my grave to drop the tears of affection to my memory they read on my tombstone, "he who lies beneath surrender office, place, and power rather than bow down and worship slavery."[25]

These same issues were driving a wedge between the two-party system of the time—the Whigs and the Democrats—and fueling the emergence of third-party alliances. John P. Hale won a full term to the U.S. Senate in 1846 under the New Hampshire legislative alliance of Independent Democrats and Whigs.

Franklin Pierce and John P. Hale also differed on the war with Mexico. While Pierce initially turned down a military cabinet position offered by President Polk, he enlisted in the militia as a private knowing that he would rapidly advance in rank due to his political stature and his father's previous military status. He quickly advanced to the rank of colonel and made brigadier general within a year's time. General Pierce served with General Winfield Scott and was wounded at the Battle of Churubusco, hence earning the needed national recognition for his eventual nomination as the Democratic presidential candidate in the election of 1852. Pierce was nominated on the 49th ballot running against both his former commanding general, Winfield Scott, and his Bowdoin classmate, John P. Hale, as well as Sam Houston, twice elected president of the Republic of Texas. Pierce won by supporting the Compromise of 1850. He was seen as a northern candidate with southern sympathies.

John Parker Hale, on the other hand, not only opposed the annexation of Texas, he opposed the war with Mexico. He was adamantly opposed to Polk's war, making his sentiments known in a January 6, 1848, speech in the U.S. Senate:

[W]hen we speak of the causes of this war, I must avow my conviction, beyond a cavil of doubt, to be, that it lies in the avowed policy of the American Government—a policy which was avowed four years ago—to make the extension of human slavery one of its primary motives of action. And when I say this, let me not be misunderstood. I refer to the principle avowed in the diplomatic correspondence which preceded the annexation of Texas to the United States. . . . Was not annexation itself an act of War? War was existing between Mexico and Texas at the time. By the very fact of annexing to ourselves one of the belligerent nations we incurred the responsibility of fighting her battles; although, even after that, subsequent history has demonstrated that, owing to the feeble and distracted state of Mexico, the most ordinary prudence on the part of the Executive might and probably would have avoided flagrant war. . . . The taking possession of Texas was of itself an act of War.[26]

The war with Mexico (Mexican-American War) of 1846–48 led to the signing of the Guadalupe Hidalgo Treaty on February 2, 1848, and proclaimed July 4, 1848. Santa Anna, in his fourth term as president of Mexico, was another casualty of the war, fleeing the country once again. The terms of the treaty formally ended Mexico's claim to Texas while expanding United States territory to the Pacific Ocean with the acquisition of New Mexico and upper California territories. In all, Mexico was forced to cede 55 percent of its territory, what is now the states of Arizona, California, New Mexico, and parts of Colorado, Nevada and Utah. The United States, in turn, paid Mexico 15 million dollars in compensation for damages incurred during the war. The treaty of 1848 also established the Rio Grande as the official southern border for the state of Texas.[27]

The war with Mexico provided the Mormons' legitimacy for their future colonies in Utah, Arizona, and Nevada. They had provided a battalion early in the war (First Iowa Volunteers) and patrolled the western Mexican territories. Apparently, the United States welcomed any assistance in its westward expansion and the Mormons provided a willing group to explore this region. While never engaging in any battles, they gained acclaim for their grueling 2,000-mile patrol from Council Bluffs, Iowa, to the coastal cities of San Diego and Los Angeles in California. Ostensibly, the Mormons used this trek as a reconnaissance for their future homeland, quickly laying claim to Utah and considerable portions of Arizona, Nevada, and even New Mexico, and providing for a political/religious/economic monopoly that exists to the present. However, their attempt to create a separate autonomous state out of this territory, Deseret (Mormonese for honeybee), was unsuccessful. This territory was to include all the lands surrendered by Mexico in 1848 between California Territory and New Mexico Territory (current states of Arizona and New Mexico).[28]

The war with Mexico also provided the United States with a fresh crop of military leaders, many of whom went on to fight in the Civil War: Ulysses S. Grant, Ambrose Burnside, Stonewall Jackson, George Meade, and Robert E. Lee. It also established a generation of U.S. presidents and presidential candidates, including Zachary Taylor, Franklin Pierce, Winfield Scott, Ulysses S. Grant, and Jefferson Davis. Andrew Jackson could be added to this list given his intrusions into Spanish Florida during the War of 1812. Indeed, the United States political leadership for much of the 19th century had a strong military component, a factor in its aggressive expansionism and interventionism under the guise of Manifest Destiny. Mexico had little choice but to militarize its own political leadership as a defense against the United States. Indeed, the U.S. Civil War threatened the stability of all North America at that time. The constant threat of U.S. intervention made the situation in Mexico so grave that its long-serving president during this time, Porfirio Díaz (1877–1911), expressed this dilemma as such: "Probre México! Tan lejos de Dios, y tan cerca de los Estados Unidos [Poor Mexico! so far from God, and so close to the United States]."

The Unresolved Slavery Issue

The Treaty of Guadalupe Hidalgo did not resolve all outstanding issues existing between the United States and Mexico. If anything, it exacerbated the unresolved slavery issue in the United States, ultimately leading to the U.S. Civil War (War between the States). Certainly the treaty did not provide adequate protection to either Mexican residents or Native Americans who traditionally inhabited the former Mexican territory ceded in 1848. Mexican Americans were regulated to second-class status much like blacks while some of the most intense Indian wars and ethnic cleansing occurred in the former Mexican territory under United States possession. New Mexico Territory was especially problematic to the U.S. expansionists in that it was the exception to the overall plan of getting the most land from Mexico with the fewest number of Mexican inhabitants. Texas and California fit this format with Anglo Americans readily outnumbering their Mexican counterparts, thereby making the white supremacy component of Manifest Destiny an easy doctrine to impose and enforce.

To many expansionists, New Mexico Territory (Arizona and New Mexico north of the Gila River) was merely an obstacle to reaching the riches of California. Texas had already attempted to include the eastern portion of the state into its territory. New Mexico Territory was problematic in that it had a substantial number of Mexican colonists along with an established Spanish/Catholic form of governance. The territory had some 60,000 Indian/Spanish Mestizo settlers along with 15,000 Pueblo Indians—long recognized as first Spanish and later Mexican citizens. It is estimated that there were fewer than 1,000 Euro Americans in the territory in 1848. This meant that the United States was responsible for nearly 100,000 colonial subjects in this territory alone. Not counted in this mix were the numerous unrecognized Native American groups, collectively labeled as "savages" (Apaches, Navajos, Utes, Comanches, Cheyenne, Cayugas, and Arapahos).[29]

Under the Treaty of Guadalupe Hidalgo, those colonial residents recognized by Mexico at the time as citizens had to be protected and provided for. Reluctant to transfer U.S. citizenship to those holding Mexican citizenship at the time of the treaty signing, three options were offered the captured residents of New Mexico Territory. One, the Mestizo population could elect to relocate to Mexico south of the newly established border. Only about 4,000 chose to do so, and even then they may have again been in a difficult position with the 1854 Gadsden Purchase. A second choice was that of de facto dual citizenship by formally retaining their Mexican citizenship by proclaiming such before a local judge (these were Mestizo judges). Finally, all others would presume to be U.S. citizens. The fact that so many colonized Mestizos chose the option of retaining their Mexican citizenship provided the small Anglo American faction with greater power proportionately to their numbers. And federally recognized U.S. citizenship is a far weaker legal status than state citizenship.

Laura E. Gómez provides an interesting thesis on how the United States avoided protracted guerrilla war in New Mexico Territory by allowing the existing ruling Spanish/Indian Mestizo leaders to claim off-white status, equating them politically, but not socially or morally, with the white supremacy dictum of Manifest Destiny. In doing so, the United States was able to break the coalition of Mestizo/Pueblo Indian resisters to U.S. occupation. According to Gómez's research, the Mexican empresario land grants in New Mexico Territory went to light-colored (off-white) people. The workforce also consisted of Mestizos. The upper-class Mestizo also had a tradition of keeping captured Native American women and children, mostly Navajo, as domestic servants, doing so in spite of the 1821 Plan de Iguala declaring all inhabitants of the new Mexican Republic as "equal citizens" and the specific tenets of 1829 abolishing black slavery in Mexico. There were fewer than two dozen blacks in the entire territory at the time of federal territorial recognition in 1850. At any rate, a well-established form of civil and religious order was operating in New Mexico Territory at the time it was declared an U.S. federal territory in 1850.

Moreover, the numerous Pueblo tribes in what is now New Mexico and Arizona (Hopi) were also granted Spanish land grants, a status that the Mexican Republic recognized. This special status came about after the Pueblo Indians (with the exception of the Piros Pueblo) were successful in driving the Spanish from New Mexico and Arizona in 1680. The Spanish colonists were allowed to return peacefully in 1692 in exchange for tribal land grants and protection from attacks by Utes and Apaches. Close alliances were forged between the Spanish and Pueblo Indians in the ensuing 158 years. Indeed, it was a Pueblo/Mexican alliance that actively resisted U.S. military forces during the Mexican War, instilling fear on the U.S. side that it would prove to be an expensive and protracted military engagement that would impede the U.S. military war with the other indigenous nomadic tribes—notably the Apache, Ute, and Navajo. Given the cost of the Mexican War itself, the U.S. government was not financially fit to attempt a costly regime change in the New Mexico Territory. Instead, it used its successful Indian policy of divide and conquer, devising its plan of providing the ruling Mestizos political parity with U.S. congressional oversight. This quid pro quo arrangement for "near white" status was contingent upon the disenfranchisement of the Pueblo Indians, thus dividing the Pueblo/Mestizo resistance.

Gómez makes it clear that the "off-white" status afforded the existing ruling Mestizos in the New Mexico Territory was not to be confused with social recognition as whites or even as being on par with the status of other white citizens of the United States. The Mestizos' main purpose was to maintain calm among the existing Mexican populace. And for the remainder of the 19th century, the Mestizo elite represented the majority of all legislative and elective positions especially in what is now the state of New Mexico. By providing order among the significant Mestizo population, the U.S. government could more effectively wage its wars on the non-Pueblo tribes, quelling the Navajo in 1863 and the Apache in 1886. Anglo American oversight kept the Mestizo elite under tight control, limiting their power and authority in order to maintain peace and harmony among the Hispanic population while suppressing the Pueblo tribes. Indeed, the most powerful territorial positions were presidential appointments, which included the territorial governor, territorial secretary, and the three justices of the territorial supreme court. For the most part, these positions were filled by outside Anglos. While Anglos eventually came to comprise the majority of the populace in New Mexico, the state still has the highest proportion of Hispanics (of Mexican descent) in the United States (estimated to be between 40 and 45 percent). And it continues to discriminate against its 22 Native American tribes (2 Apache tribes, a portion of the Navajo Nation, and 19 Pueblos). And while the U.S. Congress extended federal citizenship to all Native Americans on June 2, 1924, New Mexico did not provide state citizenship to its first residents until 1965—53 years after statehood.[30]

THE ROAD TO POLITICAL DISORGANIZATION FOLLOWING THE MEXICAN WAR

Whigs Exit—Republicans Emerge

In the United States, a divided nation weakened the traditional Democratic Party and wiped out the Whigs while, at the same time creating a new political party—the Republicans. The antiwar Whigs had their last candidate elected president in the elections of 1848. Antislavery Conscience Whigs bolted from their party, along with disenchanted northern Democrats, forming a new, third party—the Free-Soil Party. The Free-Soil Party chose the former Democratic candidate, Martin Van Buren, as their candidate. Their platform was based on an opposition to the expansion of slavery to the newly acquired western territories. Southern Whig, slaveholder, and Mexican War hero Zachary Taylor won the 1848 election. However, Taylor soon lost much of his southern support when he allowed New Mexico and California to draw up their own constitutions and both territories chose to prohibit slavery.

Dissatisfaction over the prohibition of slavery in New Mexico and California strained the delicate balance established by the 1820 Missouri Compromise with Southerners clamoring for secession. Added to the turmoil was Texas's claim to all lands extending to Santa Fe. In an attempt to salvage the Union, a number of influential congressional leaders, notably Henry Clay, Daniel Webster, John C. Calhoun, and Stephen Douglas, forged a compromise that got Texas to fall back into its original boundaries while the territories of New Mexico, Arizona, and Utah agreed to suspend the slave issue until statehood. California, on the other hand, would preserve its slave-free status and the slave trade would be abolished in the District of Columbia while preserving its slave-holding status.

The most controversial element of the Compromise of 1850 was the Fugitive Slave Act. This act attempted to curtail the Underground Railroad for slaves attempting to escape north. Under the law, all U.S. citizens were required to assist in the recovery of fugitive slaves. Without proper judicial oversight, even free blacks were captured and sent south to be enslaved. The compromise was only a temporary solution—one that actually served to widen the gap between slaveholders and abolitioners.[31]

The slave issue, exacerbated by the annexation of Texas and the subsequent War with Mexico, also accentuated festering religious biases stemming from newly arrived immigrants, leading to the emergence of the American Party. A number of (Protestant) nativist political parties emerged during the early years of the U.S. republic that were openly anti-immigrant, especially toward Catholics. One, the Order of the Star Spangled Banner, took on the moniker, the Know Nothing Party, due to its pat response when inquiries were made concerning its political platform and mandate. The Know Nothing Party initially targeted Irish Catholics following their mass migration to the United States after the potato famine in Ireland. Clearly, this situation merely exacerbated the long-held anti-Catholic sentiments held in the northeastern United States toward the French, in general, and French-Canadians, in particular.

The Know Nothing Party adapted as its influence spread to the newly acquired western territories following the Treaty of Guadalupe Hildago. Fueling the anti-Catholic, anti-Irish sentiments of the Know Nothing Party was the role of the Irish conscript who joined the Mexican forces during the war with Mexico. Most notable was the Saint Patrick Battalion, comprised of mainly Irish immigrants who deserted from the U.S. Army to fight on the Mexican side. Most were killed at the Battle of Churubusco with rumors of surviving POWs being tortured and executed by U.S. forces.[32]

Franklin Pierce—New England Advocate for Slavery and Imperialism

The Know Nothings also became known as the nativist American Party, which viewed established white Anglo-Saxon Protestants (WASP) as the only true Americans. The American Party played a significant role in the 1852 presidential elections. Here, the combined effects of the Free Soilers and American Party forced serious fractures in the traditional Democratic and Whig parties, resulting in a diverse slate of candidates including Thomas Hart Benton, Generals William O. Butler and Winfield Scott, and even Sam Houston. When the dust settled, the Free-Soil Party candidate was John Parker Hale while the Whig Party candidate was General Winfield Scott and the Democratic Party candidate was Franklin Pierce. Pierce won and the Free-Soilers merged into a new political party—the Republicans. Interestingly, Franklin Pierce won the Catholic vote and became the first U.S. president to have a Catholic in his cabinet. James Campbell, a second-generation Irish-American, became postmaster general in the Pierce administration. Pierce's former friend turned political nemesis, John Parker Hale, went on to serve in the U.S. Senate for another decade (1855–65) and then became U.S. minister to Spain. Wallner noted that Pierce's declining popularity as president contributed to Hale's political rebirth. The Kansas-Nebraska Act was unpopular in the North contributing to the growth of nativism and the Know Nothing Party, which resulted in the defeat of New Hampshire Democrats in state elections in 1855, allowing Hale to again return to Washington as a U.S. senator.[33]

During the Pierce presidency, United States expansionism continued with the purchase of more Mexican territory and tacit support for armed intervention in Latin America. The gunboat diplomacy initiated by Pierce's predecessor, President Millard Fillmore, came to fruition with the signing of the U.S./Japan Treaty of Kanagawa on March 31, 1854, forcing Japan to open its ports to American and European trade. This action inadvertently introduced yet another player into the fierce colonial wars that continued to rage during the 19th and 20th centuries, culminating in World War II. Pierce's support of white supremacy, Manifest Destiny, and the God-given mandate for forceful expansionism is evident in his message before Congress imploring them to maintain the Union.

Our forefathers of the thirteen united colonies, in acquiring their independence and in founding this Republic of the United States of America, have devolved upon us, their descendants, the greatest and the most noble trust ever committed to the hands of man, imposing upon all, and especially such as the public will may have invested for the time being with political functions, the most sacred obligations. We have to maintain inviolate the great doctrine of the inherent right of popular self-government; to reconcile the largest liberty of the individual citizen with complete security of the public order; . . . to harmonize a sincere and ardent devotion to the institutions of religious faith with the most universal religious toleration . . . to preserve sacred from all touch of usurpation, as the very palladium of our political salvation, the reserved rights and powers of the several States and of the people; to cherish with loyal fealty and devoted affection this Union, as the only foundation on which the hopes of civil liberty rest; to administer government with vigilant integrity and rigid economy, to cultivate peace and friendship with foreign nations, and to demand and exact equal justice from all, but to do wrong to none; . . . never to shrink from war when the rights and the honor of the country call us to arms, . . . whilst exalting the condition of the Republic, to assure to it the legitimate influence and the benign authority to a great example amongst all the powers of Christendom. Under the solemnity of these convictions the blessing of Almighty God is earnestly invoked to attend upon your deliberations and upon all the counsels and acts of the Government, to the end that, with common zeal and common efforts, we may, in humble submission to the divine will, cooperate for the promotion of the supreme good of these United States.[34]

Pierce's sentiments toward slavery, for the sake of the Union, was also evident in his presidential messages to Congress.

If a new State, formed from the territory of the United States, be absolutely excluded from admission therein, that fact of itself constitutes the disruption of union between it and the other States. But the process of dissolution could not stop there. . . . It is necessary to speak thus plainly of projects the offspring of that sectional agitation now prevailing in some of the States, which are as impracticable as they are unconstitutional, and which if persevered in must and will end calamitously. It is either disunion and civil war or it is mere angry, idle, aimless disturbance of public peace and tranquility. Disunion for what? If the passionate rage of fanaticism and partisan spirit did not force the fact upon our attention, it would be difficult to believe that any considerable portion of the people of this enlightened country could have so surrendered themselves to a fanatical devotion to the supposed interests of the relatively few Africans in the United States as totally to abandon and disregard the interest of the 25,000,000 Americans; to trample under foot the injunctions of moral and constitutional obligation, and to engage in plans of vindictive hostility against those who are associated with them in the enjoyment of the common heritage of our national institutions. . . . I know that the Union is stronger a thousand times than all the wild and chimerical schemes of social change which are generated one after another in the unstable minds of visionary sophists and interested agitators. I rely confidently on the patriotism of the people, on the dignity and self-respect of the States, on the wisdom of Congress, and, above all, on the continued gracious favor of Almighty God to maintain against all enemies, whether at home or abroad, the sanctity of the Constitution and the integrity of the Union.[35]

Pierce's presidency witnessed continued raw expansionism under the guise of Manifest Destiny with armed interventions into Mexico and Latin America by American filibusters. Most notable was William Walker, a medical doctor and lawyer from Nashville, Tennessee, whose forces first raided Baja, California, and Sonora State in an attempt to carve another independent republic out of Mexico with Walker anointed president of the Republic of Sonora. Mexican resistance forced Walker's regime to retreat, resulting in a brief trial for Walker followed by an acquittal. Walker's next adventure was to lead an American force of mercenaries in Nicaragua where he successfully defeated the Nicaraguan National Army and captured the capital of Granada in 1855.

With support from American business leaders who wanted to construct a rail link in Nicaragua connecting the Atlantic and Pacific oceans and pro-slave groups in the United States, Walker represented a group that wanted to expand slavery in Latin America by overthrowing the governments of Costa Rica, El Salvador, Guatemala, and Honduras and establishing WASP [white Anglo-Saxon Protestant] administrations. One of Walker's first acts as president of Nicaragua was to rescind the county's 1824 emancipation edict making slavery legal. Franklin Pierce readily recognized Walker's regime in Nicaragua, lending tacit support to this plan. Walker later crossed Cornelius Vanderbilt, curtailing his efforts to build the east/west rail link and leading to Walker's exit from Nicaragua. Walker was later captured by the British Navy entering Honduras (Belize) and instead of returning him to the United States, where he was seen as a southern hero, they turned him over to local authorities who executed him on September 12, 1860.[36]

The Ostend Manifesto and Gadsden Purchase

The Ostend Manifesto was yet another example of attempts at raw expansionism during the Pierce administration. The Ostend Manifesto represented a clandestine plot hatched by pro-slavery leaders in the Pierce administration, initiated by his secretary of state, William L. Marcy. Here, the U.S. diplomats to Britain (James Buchanan), France (John Y. Mason), and Spain (Pierre Soulé) met with Spanish officials in Ostend, Belgium, in an attempt to force Spain to sell Cuba to the United States for a sum of 120 million dollars. Once acquired it would then be added to the Union as a slave state. The United States delegation made it clear that Cuba would be taken by force if they did not agree to this plan. The document, along with its intention of Cuba becoming a U.S. slave state, was leaked and met with fierce opposition from the Free-Soilers who termed the clandestine plot, the Manifesto of Brigands. President Pierce and Secretary of State Marcy quickly backtracked and the manifesto offer was withdrawn.[37]

Pierce was successful, however, in purchasing additional lands south of the U.S./Mexico western border articulated in the 1848 Treaty of Guadalupe Hidalgo. This became known as the Gadsden Purchase. Named after Pierce's U.S. minister (ambassador) to Mexico, James Gadsden, the purchase's official name is the Treaty of La Mesilla of December 30, 1853. Ostensibly, the purchase of over 45,000 square miles at a cost of 15 million dollars was to settle the suspended Bartlett-García Conde Compromise designed to resolve errors in the original (Disturnell) map. The major boundary error following the Treaty of Guadalupe Hidalgo was the inclusion of the city of El Paso within the territory acquired by the United States. The purchase actually represented a continuation of the efforts to expand the slave-holding territory associated with the South. It was in effect a diluted model of the ill-fated Ostend Manifesto.

James Gadsden was an unabashed capitalist whose major interest was completing a southern east/west rail route. Born in South Carolina,

Gadsden's previous roles included being President Monroe's agent in charge of removing Florida's Seminole Indians onto reservations. His blatant conflict of interest in the Gadsden Purchase was his role as president of the consolidated South Carolina, Louisville, Charleston, and Cincinnati railroads, which wanted to construct a rail line to the Pacific Ocean in an attempt to beat northern rail efforts to connect the east with California. The purchase became necessary for Gadsden's plan when engineering studies indicated that the most efficient route was one south of the Gila River delineating the southern U.S./Mexico border emerging from the 1848 Treaty of Guadalupe Hidalgo. An additional gain was the rich Santa Rita copper mines that were originally mined by Native Americans before the advent of Europeans and continues to be mined today by Phelps Dodge Company.[38]

The Gadsden Purchase also gave the United States an opportunity to renege on one of the critical agreements in the 1848 settlement—that of providing Mexican residents protection from attacks from Indian tribes residing in the newly acquired U.S. territory. It also imposed upon Mexico provisions for a railroad across the Isthmus of Tehuantepec for mainly U.S. purposes. Here, article 2 of the Treaty of La Mesilla voided article 11 of the Treaty of Guadalupe Hidalgo; while article 8 gave the United States further rights of intrusion into Mexico for American self-interest.

Article II (Gadsden Purchase) The government of Mexico hereby releases the United States from all liability on account of the obligations contained in the eleventh article of the treaty of Guadalupe-Hidalgo; and the said article and the thirty-third article of the treaty of amity, commerce, and navigation between the United States of America and the United Mexican States concluded at Mexico, on the fifth day of April, 1831, are hereby abrogated.

Article XI (Treaty of Guadalupe-Hidalgo) Considering that a great part of the territories, which, by the present treaty, are to be comprehended for the future within the limits of the United States, is now occupied by savage tribes, who will hereafter be under the exclusive control of the Government of the United States, and whose incursions within the territory of Mexico would be prejudicial in the extreme, it is solemnly agreed that all such incursions shall be forcibly restrained by the Government of the United States whensoever this may be necessary; and that when they cannot be prevented, they shall be punished by the said Government, and satisfaction for same shall be extracted in the same way, and with equal diligence and energy, as if the same incursions were mediated or committed within its own territory, against its own citizens.

It shall not be lawful, under any pretext whatever, for any inhabitant of the United States to purchase or acquire any Mexican, or any foreigner residing in Mexico, who may have been captured by Indians inhabiting the territory or either of the two republics; nor to purchase or acquire horses, mules, cattle, or property of any kind, stolen within Mexican Territory by such Indians.

And in the event of any person or persons, captured within Mexican territory by Indians, being carried into the territory of the United States, the Government of the latter engages and binds itself, in the most solemn manner, so soon as it shall know of such captives being within its territory, and shall be able so to do, through the faithful exercise of its influence and power, to rescue them and return them to their country, or deliver them to the agent or representative of the Mexican Government. The Mexican authorities will, as far as practicable, give to the Government of the United States notice of such captures; and its agent shall pay the expenses incurred in the maintenance and transmission of the rescued captives; who, in the mean time, shall be treated with the utmost hospitality by the American authorities at the place where they may be. But if the Government of the United States, before receiving such notice from Mexico, should obtain intelligence, through any other channel, of the existence of Mexican captives within its territory, it will proceed forthwith to effect their release and delivery to the Mexican agent, as above stipulated.

For the purpose of giving to these stipulations the fullest possible efficacy, thereby affording the security and redress demanded by their true spirit and intent, the Government of the United States will now and hereafter pass, without unnecessary delay, and always vigilantly enforce, such laws as the nature of the subject may require. And, finally, the sacredness of this obligation shall never be lost sight of by the said Government, when providing for the removal of Indians from any portion of the said territories, or for its being settled by citizens of the United States; but on the contrary, special care shall then be taken not to place its Indian occupants under the necessity of seeking new homes, by committing those invasions which the United States have solemnly obliged themselves to restrain.

ARTICLE VIII (Gadsden Purchase)

The Mexican Government having on the 5th of February, 1853, authorized the construction of a plank and railroad across the Isthmus of Tehuantepec, and to secure the stable benefits of said transit way to the persons and merchandise of the citizens of Mexico and the United States, it is stipulated that neither Government will interpose any obstacle to the transit of persons and merchandise of both nations; and at no time shall higher charges be made on the transit of persons and property of citizens of the United States than may be made on the persons and property of other foreign nations, nor shall any interest in said transit way nor in the proceeds thereof, be transferred to any foreign government.

The Unites States, by its agents, shall have the right to transport across the isthmus, in closed bags, the mails of the United States not intended for distribution along the line of communication; also the effect of the United States Government and its citizens, which may be intended for transit, and not for distribution on the isthmus, free of customhouse or other charges by the Mexican Government. Neither passport no letters of security will be required of persons crossing the isthmus and not remaining in the country.

When the construction of the railroad shall be completed, the Mexican Government agrees to open a port of entry in addition to the port of Vera Cruz, at or near the terminus of said road on the Gulf of Mexico.

The two Governments will enter into arrangements for the prompt transit of troops and munitions of the United States which that Government may have occasion to send from one part of its territory to another, lying on opposite sides of the continent.

The Mexican Government having agreed to protect with its whole power the prosecution, preservation and security of the work, the United States may extend its
protection as it shall judge wise to it when it may feel sanctioned and warranted
by the public or international law.[39]

This landgrab added Yuma, California; Tucson, Nogales, Wilcox, and
Douglas in Arizona; and Lordsburg, Deming, Columbus, Mesilla, and Santa
Rita in New Mexico as well as numerous other villages and tribal homelands to the United States. The United States also added insult to injury with
article 8, for not only did the United States wage war on Mexico to steal more
than half of its territory, it now had the audacity to demand free passage
across the isthmus so that the eastern part of the country could trade and
communicate with the newly acquired western territories. The eventual
digging of the Panama Canal made this item moot in the long run. It did,
however, establish a precedent regarding free travel across the international
border for Americans while later, in 1929, making it illegal for Mexicans to
traverse the border to enter the United States without its permission.

Regarding local tribes, some of the fiercest Indian warfare occurred in
this newly acquired territory in violation of the 1848 treaty relevant to Mexico's confirmation of citizenship to Native Americans with its 1821 constitution. Instead, the United States raged a war of genocide on Indians in the
southwestern United States, treating them as less-than-human pests that
needed to be removed. These tribal wars raged on both sides of the border
and were not resolved until the surrender of Geronimo in 1886 and the
forced removal and imprisonment of the entire Apache band to a prison
in Florida. However, all three major players in this deal were eventually
discredited. James Gadsden was recalled as Minister to Mexico for his conflict of interest in the purchase. Moreover, he died in 1858 never realizing
his dream of a southern transcontinental rail route. Indeed, the Civil War
ended the efforts for a southern route to be the first transcontinental route.
Congress authorized funding in 1862 for a northern route going from
Omaha, Nebraska, in the East to Sacramento, California, in the West. The
Union Pacific and Central Pacific railroads met at Promontory Point, Utah,
on May 10, 1869, while the Southern Pacific line from New Orleans to California was not completed until 1883. Antonio López de Santa Anna again
disgraced his country, this time during his fifth, and last, term as president.
He was again exiled first to Colombia and, later, the Virgin Islands. He returned to Mexico in 1874 impoverished, and died in 1876. Franklin Pierce
served a single term as U.S. president, and became the only sitting president
to seek and not receive his party's nomination for a second term. Pierce
died an alcoholic in 1869 at age 64.[40]

Pierce was replaced with a true southern sympathizer, his minister (am-
bassador) to England, James Buchanan. Social conditions in the United
States continued to deteriorate with the 1857 *Dred Scott* decision, John
Brown's attack on Harper's Ferry in 1859, and South Carolina's ordinance

of secession from the Union. During this time the new Republican Party emerged, drawing from the many splinter groups for membership, most notably the American Party. The ensuing War between the States (U.S. Civil War) became the deadliest conflict of the 19th century, splitting the nation for over a century until the civil rights movement and resulting laws enacted in the mid-1960s. But the United States was not alone; conflict was contagious throughout North America. Conflict in Canada resulting from the 1849 Union Bill led to the establishment of its current form of government with the British North American Act creating the Dominion of Canada in 1867. This act attempted to resolve the wide cultural, social, and religious differences between Anglo Canadians and French Canadians.[41]

In Mexico with Santa Anna's despotic rule finally ended, Mexico turned to a full-blooded Native American as its leader. Benito Pablo Júarez assumed the presidency on January 19, 1858, following his release from prison and in his capacity as chief justice. Júarez's government was recognized by the United States in April 1859. He was elected as president of Mexico in the elections of 1861 and served until 1863. One of his major accomplishments in office was to challenge the role of the Catholic Church. This action plus his suspension of payments on the nation's national debt led to France declaring war against Júarez on April 16, 1862. Napoleon III's forces captured Puebla in May of that year, and Napoleon proclaimed his relative Maximilian von Hapsburg emperor of Mexico. This Catholic colonial force ruled from 1864 until 1867 leading to Mexico's own civil war known as the War of Reform with its most famous battle being the Cinco de Mayo battle against Maximilian's forces. Júarez's forces finally won, putting Maximilian and his principal followers before firing squads. Júarez was again elected president of Mexico in 1867, serving until his death in 1872. Júarez continues to be revered by Mexico's indigenous peoples and its substantial Mestizo population. Nonetheless, the emerging conflicts in both the United States and Mexico and between these two neighboring countries intensified along their borders up until the Second World War.[42]

CHAPTER 3

The History of Border Conflicts and Their Impact on Migration Trends and Policies

The longstanding conflict along the United States/Mexico border has its roots in the Texas Republic era. Internal conflicts, wars and revolutions, on both sides of the border, often exacerbated international border security. Race and culture need to be factored in to any analysis given the police and military resources directed toward the nearly 2,000-mile U.S./Mexico border vis-à-vis the virtually open 5,000-plus-mile U.S./Canada border. This situation continues even following the September 11, 2001, terrorist attacks on the United States and the ensuing war on terrorism. Despite the fact that Canada is the preferred route of entry into the United States, the United States has instead increased its security along the Mexico border.

THE TEXAS RANGERS

The Texas Rangers during the Republic Era

The law-enforcement force historically involved in Anglo/Hispanic border conflict is the Texas Rangers. Long lauded as a heroic force for justice in myth and in the media, a closer examination of their history paints a different picture. Contemporary analysis portrays the Texas Rangers as an extermination squad ridding Texas of Hispanics, Mestizos, and American Indians at the bidding of Anglo settlers. Indeed, the Texas Rangers trace their origins to 1821 and the Austin empresario in Mexico, where 10 men were hired as rangers to protect the Anglo settlers from Indian raids. Before the Texas revolution the term "ranger" often was synonymous with the militia, and numerous scrimmages occurred during this time between the Tonkawas,

Tawakonis, Karankawas, and Waco tribes. One incident indicates that in June 1824, 30 men were mustered by Captain Robert Kuykendall of the militia to pursue and punish a group of Karankawas, resulting in a treaty with the tribe. Again, in 1826 the record of the Austin empresario shows that a contingent of rangers/militia, under Captain James J. Ross engaged in another punitive expedition against Indians encroaching on the Anglo settlement. Following these incidents, Austin called for a standing ranger unit, comprised of 20 to 30 men, to be drawn from the six militia districts within the Anglo settlement.

During the Texas Revolution the Texas Rangers were expanded into three companies of 56 men each under the command of a major. During the formation of the revolutionary government the "permanent council" on October 17, 1835, promoted a resolution for the creation of a corps of Texas Rangers whose duties were to "range" and guard the new republic. Initially, the head of each Texas Ranger detachment was termed a "superintendent" and not a captain. When a more permanent military organization was developed in November 1835, the army, militias, and the Texas Rangers all fell under the authority of the commander in chief. Thus, the Texas Rangers became official with the third reading of the ordinance, providing their permanent status on November 24, 1835. This ordinance provided for three companies of 56 men led by a captain and two lieutenants. A major was designated as the superior officer for the entire force. And in times of war the Texas Rangers could be mustered into the Texas army as an autonomous battalion.[1] While placed under the authority of the new army, the Texas Rangers were an irregular force different from both the army and the militia, having no colors (flag), surgeon, or regular equipment. Indeed, the Rangers were expected to provide their own horses and weapons. During the Texas revolt, the Texas Rangers were not involved in any of the major battles but instead were assigned to protect the Anglo settlers from Indian attacks. Even then treaties with the Cherokee and Comanche prevented any outbreaks during the revolution. The Texas Rangers' main claim to glory was the capturing of three Mexican supply ships—the *Watchman*, *Comanche*, and the *Fanny Butler*—confiscating supplies worth over 25,000 dollars. For this feat, Captain Burton's Rangers were also know as *horse marines*. Even then their malevolence toward Mexicans was clear, as Weber noted:

Hatred of Mexicans had a long tradition among the Rangers. During the Mexican War they formed two special units of volunteers. Their atrocities in the Mexican northeast—the pillaging of farms and the shooting or hanging of innocent peons—led General Zachary Taylor to threaten to jail an entire unit. In Mexico City *Los Tejanos Sangrientes* killed children and old men and raped women, thereby infuriating General Winfield Scott who authorized a plan to get the Rangers out of the city.[2]

The Texas Rangers competed with the regular army during the nine years of the Texas Republic. Nonetheless, they were employed mainly as

Indian fighters. Sam Houston during his first administration attempted to make peace with the indigenous tribes. Toward this end he had forts and trading houses built to both protect the settlers and engage the tribes with economic opportunities. A force of "mounted riflemen" was authorized in December 1836 with the role of protecting the northern frontier. In June 1837 the Texas Congress authorized a corps of 600 "mounted gunmen" to serve for a six-month tour. While these terms of service are similar to those used to describe the Texas Rangers, the word "ranger" is absent in the records. The authorization for a permanent military force came in May 1838 when President Houston authorized a cavalry corps of 280 men to serve from one to three years. This force was not designated as Indian fighters but rather was designed to protect the southwest border from Mexican intrusions.

When Lamar became president he immediately unraveled Houston's plans for peaceful coexistence with the Indian tribes. Clearly, his policy was one of ethnic cleansing:

Nothing short of [absolute expulsion] will bring peace or safety. The Indians could not be handled by treaty or by a policy of moderation and forbearance. The United States had pursued that policy in vain. The white man and the red man cannot dwell in harmony together. Nature forbids it. The strongest of antipathies of color and modes of thinking separate them. Knowing these things, I experience no difficulty in deciding on the proper policy to be pursued towards them. It is to push a rigorous war against them; pursuing them to their hiding places without mitigation or compassion, until they shall be made to feel that flight from our borders without hope of return, is preferable to the scourges of war.[3]

President Lamar set out to establish a more permanent military force to carry out his ambitious ethnic cleansing program, leaving the irregular Ranger force out of the loop. On December 21, 1838, Lamar approved the creation of a regiment of 840 men comprised of 15 companies of 56 men operating within 8 detachments. The men signed on for a three-year term. A week later, authorization was provided for eight companies of mounted militias whose enlistment would be for six months duration. While the record is not clear, some of these men could have served as Texas Rangers, especially those serving on the northern and western frontiers. During Lamar's administration he negated the peace treaty the Mexican government made with the Cherokee and in 1839 sent the Texas army to forcefully remove them much like they were removed a year earlier in the United States. In a battle in July 1839 the Texans, including Rangers, attacked and drove out the Cherokee, Delaware, Shawnee, Caddo, Kickapoo, Boloxie, Creek, Muscogee, and Seminole, killing Houston's longtime friend, Cherokee Chief Bowles. In January 1840, the leaders of the Comanche came to San Antonio seeking peace and were instead massacred, including chiefs and their wives and children. Also killed were those designated as "renegade Mexicans."

Eventually, President Lamar's experiment with a regular standing army proved to be too costly, and Houston reversed this trend during his second term as president of the Republic of Texas. Houston disbanded the regular army and sold the Texas navy. The authorization for a militia survived his veto in January 1843 and became the foundation for the reemergence of the Texas Rangers. A year later John C. Hays led a company of Rangers along with other companies emerging during this time. Many of the mounted militia and mounted gunmen considered themselves to be Texas Rangers. Clearly, horsemanship and firepower were the two features that distinguished these paramilitants from regular soldiers and sailors. It was said at the time that a Texas Ranger "could ride like a Mexican, trail like an Indian, shoot like a Tennessean, and fight like a devil." Indeed, the Texas Rangers are closely linked with the Colt revolver—the only repeating weapon of the day. More significantly, the Republic of Texas became the proving grounds for this innovative weapon. Samuel Colt of Hartford, Connecticut, patented his repeating handgun in 1836—the same year Texas declared its independence from Mexico. Texas was Colt's first customer, ordering 180 .36-caliber Holster-model five-shot Paterson Colt revolvers for its navy in August 1839. Texas Rangers, on the other hand, had been ordering them individually since they first became available in 1837. Once Houston disbanded the navy the Paterson Colts were reassigned to the Texas Rangers.

Colonel John Coffee Hays made the Paterson Colt famous while fighting the Comanche at Plum Creek (August 1840) and later at the Pedernales River in July 1844. Here, the Texas Rangers grossly outnumbered Comanche warriors, effectively ending retaliatory raids on Anglo settlers. With single shot weapons the Comanche would send in a few warriors to draw the fire and then send in a larger force to decimate the troops while reloading. With the advent of the Paterson Colt repeating single-action revolver the Texas Ranger could continue to fire as long as he could fan the hammer which rotated the cylinder. Texas Rangers often carried three or more revolvers with loaded extra cylinders, greatly increasing their firepower. This technique greatly enhanced the Texas Rangers' image as a deadly force. Consequently, in February 1845, during President Anson Jones's administration, a law was passed extending Captain Hays's authority and securing the Texas Rangers' role as Texas became part of the United States of America. During the Mexican War, the Texas Rangers again proved the superiority of the Colt revolver. The Texas Rangers not only field-tested the Colt revolvers, they also offered practical adaptations to make the weapon more efficient. Captain Samuel H. Walker ordered 1,000 new modified Colt revolvers that now were six-shot weapons with a fixed trigger with guard and a loading lever beneath the barrel. This order and its success in the Mexican War saved Colt Firearms from bankruptcy, making it the largest producer of revolvers during the U.S. Civil War and the most popular weapon (the Peacemaker) in the West during the 19th century.[4]

The Texas Rangers following Statehood:
A Sordid History Continues

During the Mexican War, the Texas Rangers served as a voluntary irregular cavalry under both General Taylor and General Scott. They soon earned their distinction for brutality during this time. Hays and Walker led the Texas Rangers in the Mexican War, making them responsible for the Rangers' ruthless behavior and their derogatory image as *los diablos Tejanos*— Texan devils. Harris noted: "From the Rangers' point of view, the war was a splendid opportunity to kill Mexicans and get paid for it."[5] Johnson noted in his 2003 book: "(A)ccording to one American soldier, the land was 'strewed with the skeletons of Mexicans sacrificed by these desperadoes.' Similar violence in occupied Mexico City prompted General Zachary Taylor to threaten to imprison an entire Ranger unit."[6] The Texas Rangers continued their anti-Mexican initiatives in blatant violation of international law, conducting cross-border raids that included the 1855 destruction of the Mexican town Piedras Negras.

The Texas Rangers lost favor during the Reconstruction Era but re-emerged in 1874 when the old pro-confederate Democrats again took over the mantle of power in Texas. For the rest of the 19th century, the Texas Rangers served as the private police for the governor of Texas and big Anglo ranchers. Apparently, the Texas Rangers had carte blanche when it came to maintaining Anglo financial interests in the area, doing so by deploying their Special Force and Frontier Battalion. Interestingly, special forces still connote military and police forces that operate with a license to kill outside the restrictions of military or civil justice. Clearly, the Texas Rangers were to Mexicans, Mestizos, and American Indians what the Ku Klux Klan was to blacks until they were brought under the authority of the Texas Department of Public Service in 1935. The Texas Rangers could no longer be used merely as the private police force for the governor of Texas. They were now accountable to the general statutes applicable to all law enforcement agencies within the state.[7]

THE PORFIRIATO: SETTING THE STAGE
FOR THE MEXICAN REVOLUTION

The long reign of Porfirio Díaz, known as the Porfiriato, lasted from 1872 until he was exiled to Paris on May 25, 1911, in the midst of the Mexican Revolution that began in 1910. Díaz, a general under President Júarez during the rebellion against Archduke Maximilian, first made a name for himself as part of the May 5, 1862, defeat of Napoleon III's troops at Puebla—a major event in Mexican history celebrated to this day as Cinco de Mayo. Díaz was also involved in the final defeat and execution of Maximilian in 1867. Díaz and Júarez later had a falling out over the 1871 presidential elections won by Júarez, which paved the way for his administration following the death of Díaz on July 9, 1872. Confirmed as president in 1877, Díaz begins his long tenure as de facto head of Mexico.

The United States' Favorite Despot

Díaz had support from the United States because of the lessening of border tensions and the opening up of Mexican resources and markets for U.S. capitalist endeavors. During the Porfiriato era, Mexico had the semblance of political stability and economic growth. The national debt was paid and the national treasury had some 70 million dollars worth of cash reserves at the end of Diaz's tenure in 1911. This prosperity for big business and the upper classes came at a price, one that eventually led to the revolution of 1910. The indigenous Indians and poor lower-class Mestizos suffered under the classist and racist policies of the Porfiriato era. These practices, however, further endeared Díaz to U.S. political and business interests.

Essentially, Díaz was an ideal partner for both U.S. and European capitalists opening up Mexico's resources for their exploitation and profit. This economic environment included cheap labor, significant tax breaks, and favorable judicial responses that favored foreign interests as well as those of the elite *cientificos*. Consequently, notable capitalists like William Randolph Hearst invested heavily in mines (gold, silver, zinc, lead, and copper), petroleum, and textiles while amassing large land holdings along with the elite Mexican cientificos. The Díaz administration facilitated these foreign endeavors by constructing a rail system from southern Mexico to the United States, providing a means of transporting minerals and products out of Mexico. The rail system also provided greater access to low-cost Mexican laborers by allowing for the better distribution of this available labor resource. Toward this end of appeasing foreign interests, peasant lands and Indian collectivities were taken for these enterprises or in order to create massive haciendas. Taking a chapter from United States Indian policy, Díaz abrogated Spanish laws protecting Indian lands and peasant collective farms. This process forced Indians and peons to continue to live on their former land and compelled them to work for the new landowners. This bondage of the impoverished peasants was further welded by forcing the peons to purchase all essentials from the hacienda store, thereby forcing them into debt—a debt passed on from generation to generation and among hacienda owners, making these workers virtual slaves. Another facet of cientifico control was maintained by keeping the peons ignorant by denying them any education—a model borrowed from the American slave plantations. At the time of the revolution in 1910, 3 percent of the population owned 95 percent of functional land in Mexico.

An outgrowth of the Díaz administration was the emergence of a middle class comprised of clerks, teachers, small businessmen, and legal and clinical practitioners. While creating a wedge between the elite cientificos and the large peon/peasant class, this group by virtue of its limited influence also felt alienated by the government. During the Díaz administration a class ceiling was in effect where the upper echelons of loyal cientificos continued to hold all important and profitable positions in Mexican society. Clearly, the prosperity of the Díaz era did little to increase the quality of life for the rank-and-file Mexican worker and his/her family. Even in foreign-based enterprises, Mexican workers earned less than workers from the United States employed at the same facility. Concern over the double-wage system led to strikes in mines and to the bloody suppression of the Mexican workers. Borrowing techniques from the Texas Rangers these strikers were brutally suppressed by government goon squads called *rurales*. Garner, in his book on Porfirio Díaz, noted that in the Cananea mining strike of 1906 the Mexican government allowed the mine's U.S. owners to bring in U.S. police and vigilantes to quell the strike and attack Mexican workers doing so under the pretense of protecting U.S. lives and property. This became a common Manifest Destiny theme later played out numerous times in U.S. interventions in Central America and continued to the present. The harsh responses to labor strife were precursors to the Mexican Revolution:

The first flashpoint was the mining town of Cananea in Sonora, which was, in effect, a US company town belonging to the Cananea Consolidated Copper Company. A protest over wage differentials between the 6,000 Mexican employees and their 600 US counterparts led to a riot in which company guards fired on the workforce. The excessive use of force was compounded by the permission granted to the company by the governor of Sonora, Rafael Izábal, to allow 260 Arizona rangers to cross the border to restore order, in what was widely criticized at the time as an open violation of Mexican sovereignty.[8]

A year later, strikes at Mexico's textile mills were also brutally suppressed by troops and rurales, resulting in striking workers killed and five union leaders executed. These actions merely solidified the solidarity of the workers and their membership in the Great Circle of Free Workers—comprised mainly of female workers—a force to be reckoned with in the festering revolution. These were workers in the textile mills of Puebla, Tlaxcala01, and Veracruz who called for a number of strikes over pay and working conditions. Their actions were met with lockouts and firings. Harsh treatment by the government extended beyond striking workers. Manzanarez noted that law and order under the Díaz administration came at a high price. Civil liberties and rights were suppressed for the majority of Mexicans, especially for those of Indian descent. This double standard of justice was based upon the cientificos' belief that the indigenous and the poor lower-class Mestizos were morally inferior. From this, Manzanarez concluded: "The *Porfirian* society was not only classist, but racist too."[9]

GEOPOLITICS AND THE MEXICAN REVOLUTION

Ironically, Harris noted that Diaz's effectiveness in controlling crime along the border led to the disbanding of the Texas Rangers' notorious Frontier

Battalion and to the relegation of the Rangers to a state police force providing assistance to local law enforcement agencies. The Mexican Revolution changed the status quo when the war threatened the borderland area. By 1901, the Texas Rangers had become the personal police force for the reigning governor, serving to protect the large landowners and the railroad tycoons. In this sense, they served a similar function as their counterparts in New Mexico and Arizona, intervening in labor disputes and quelling strikes.[10] Díaz's administration inadvertently helped set the stage for further U.S. expansionism—an extension of Pierce's interpretation of Manifest Destiny and the Monroe Doctrine. Following Maximilian's defeat, Díaz postponed Mexico's revolution by toning down the anti-Catholicism fervor initiated by Benito Juárez, thus giving the impression of appeasing the Indian and Mestizo who held their lands in communal holdings. Nonetheless, Díaz shared the United States' view of American Indians—that they were racially inferior and a significant burden to modernization and progress. Díaz's policies of the 1880s and 1890s included harsh penalties against protests as well as the revision of colonialization laws allowing the Mexican elite and white foreigners, notably Protestants, to obtain large tracks of land that formerly were held by the Catholic Church and peasant communities. Hence, some two million acres of communal Indian lands went to large landholding corporations.

With a peaceful northern border, one heavily policed by friendly Díaz forces, the United States was again free to strike against Spanish holdings in the Americas and beyond. The pretense for the Spanish-American War was the mysterious sinking of the gunboat USS *Maine* in Havana harbor on February 15, 1898. It set the stage for U.S. military intervention against the remaining Spanish holdings in the Americas and beyond. This intervention included Cuba and Puerto Rico, as well as Spanish holdings in the Pacific—the Philippines, Carolina, and the Marshall and Mariana Islands, which included Guam. President McKinley's war concluded with a treaty with Spain, signed in Paris on December 10, 1898. The Spanish-American War made McKinley a national hero along with his Assistant Secretary of the Navy, Theodore Roosevelt, who both agitated for this conflict. When war appeared inevitable, Theodore Roosevelt resigned his administrative position for the brevet military rank of lieutenant colonel and command of a volunteer regiment comprised of cowboys, Texas Rangers, and Ivy League friends. His unit was coined the First United States Voluntary Cavalry, also known as the Rough Riders.

Nonetheless, the Teller Amendment to the congressional approval for the war in April 1898 precluded the United States, or any other foreign country, from colonizing Cuba. The exception was that section captured in the first military action in Cuba by U.S. Marines—Guantanamo Bay. The United States has held a perpetual, irrevocable lease on this portion of Cuba since 1903. The Paris treaty expanded U.S. holdings to include Puerto Rico, Guam, and the rest of the Mariana, Carolina, and Marshall Islands. And the

United States forced Spain to relinquish the Philippine Islands for 20 million dollars, much like it did in the Gadsden Purchase nearly a half-century earlier. The purchase of the Philippine Islands, however, was contested by its indigenous peoples, leading to the Philippine-American War of 1899–1900. The new acquisitions in the Pacific, including the annexation of Hawaii in 1898, led to considerable resentment among the Japanese, who felt that Asia was its own to colonize, as well as the eventual U.S. involvement in the Second World War. Moreover, as with the war with Mexico, this latest episode of U.S. imperialism provided the proving ground for a number of military and political leaders during the 20th century, notably, Theodore Roosevelt, who used his Rough Rider fame to become governor of New York, vice president, and president; brevet Major John Pershing, who rose to the highest U.S. military rank of general of the armies after a career that included leading a regiment of black "Buffalo Soldiers" (hence his nickname—"Black Jack") and heading the Punitive Expedition into Mexico in 1916–17 and the American Expeditionary Force in the First World War; and Douglas MacArthur, who served as second lieutenant under his father, Major General Arthur MacArthur, in the Philippine-American War, and who became a highly decorated general in the First World War and a five-star general during the Second World War.[11]

Seeds of Mexican Discontent

While most Mexicans were probably not much interested in the geopolitics of the time, United States imperialism in Spanish-held territories had to worry some of the elite within Mexico. Ai Camp, in his book *Politics in Mexico* offered more compelling grassroots reasons for the anti-Díaz revolution. While Díaz did much to improve the overall Mexican economy, the wealthy elite, both at home and abroad, were the main benefactors. Conspicuously absent from these capitalistic gains were the laboring Mestizos and the native Indians. These were the same groups that strongly supported Díaz when he succeeded the popular indigenous President Juárez. His political machine included executive control of the national police and the army, a brute force governing mechanism that was an integral part of Mexican politics until the 1940s. The political manipulation of national elections existed until the 21st century. By placing increasingly more power in the hands of the elite, Díaz managed to reverse the decentralization trend begun by President Juárez. Indeed, over its 30 years of influence, the Porfiriato reverted back to the old Spanish authoritarian and paternalistic model that excluded the masses from meaningful enfranchisement.

After three decades of abuse, Mexicans revolted over the exploitations of Mestizo and Indian peasants as well as the restrictions placed upon the new, emerging middle class, notably their being shut out of top echelon positions in the government and businesses.[12] The Maderista Revolt against the Díaz régime was launched on November 10, 1910, by Francisco Madero, a Mexican of high status and wealth. Francisco Madero ran against Díaz in the 1910 elections and was subsequently arrested, escaped from jail, and fled to the United States. On November 10, 1910, Madero and his forces crossed into Mexico from the United States at Piedras Negras in the state of Coahuila. Two popular revolutionary leaders emerged during the early years of the revolution—Emiliano Zapata, a Mexican Indian, and Francisco Pancho Villa, a Mestizo. In May 1911, Madero's forces took Ciudad Juarez, the critical border town linking El Paso, Texas, with Mexico. This event led to the Treaty of Juarez in which Díaz agreed to resign and leave the country. On May 25, 1911, General Victoriano Huerta escorted Díaz to a German ship for exile to France, leaving his vice president, Francisco Leon de la Barra, to take over as interim president, and setting the stage for Madero's election as Mexico's president in November 1911. Madero's reign was short-lived. He and his vice president, Pino Suarez, were assassinated in a coup d'etat led by General Victoriano Hureta in 1913. In July 1914, Huerta was forced into exile and the revolution took on new dimensions with the forces of Generals Carranza and Obregón (Constitutionalists), now fighting the popular forces of Emiliano (Emilio) Zapata and Francisco (Pancho) Villa (Conventionists). The Constitutionalists represented a strong Mexican federal government free of U.S. controls but one that maintained the status quo of a highly stratified social structure, while the Conventionists wanted an autonomous country but with a redistribution of the land and a return to the communal village system. Zapata was assassinated under orders of General Pablo Gonzalez while Pancho Villa's forces raised havoc in northern Mexico, finally lending his support to President-elect Adolfo de la Huerta in 1920.[13]

Border Disruption: From Roosevelt's Corollary to the Wilsonism Critique

An extension of the Spanish-American War and a precursor to the Mexican Revolution were the aggressive actions of President Theodore Roosevelt, who held a paternalistic view of Latin America. Critical here was the Roosevelt Corollary of 1904 whereby President Roosevelt established the right of the United States to unilaterally intervene in the Caribbean and Central America in order to prevent foreign nations from intervening relevant to unpaid international debts. This policy authorized the subsequent use of U.S. Marines as de facto international police in order to protect U.S. business interests. The policy resulted in interventions in Cuba, Nicaragua, Haiti, and the Dominican Republic before it was replaced with President Franklin D. Roosevelt's Good Neighbor Policy in 1934. The Good Neighbor Policy was a friendlier approach to U.S. protectionism in the Americas with the intention of ending the era of U.S. unilateral interventions into Mexico. It was seen as a revision of the Monroe Doctrine. A U.S. general's public criticism in 1931 likely influenced this change in policy. A speech by Major

General Smedley Butler condemned the use of the Marine Corps as an international police force to protect U.S. business interests in Latin America:

War is a racket. Our stake in that racket has never been greater in all out peace-time history. It may seem odd for me a military man, to adopt such a comparison. Truthfulness compels me to. I spent 33 years and 4 months in active service as a member of our country's most agile military force—the Marine Corps. I served in all commissioned ranks from a Second Lieutenant to Major General. And during that period I spent most of my time being a high-class muscle man for big business, for Wall Street and for the bankers. In short, I was a racketeer for capitalism. . . . Thus, I helped make Mexico and especially Tampico, safe for American oil interests in 1914. I helped make Haiti and Cuba a decent place for the National City Bank boys to collect revenues in. I helped in the raping of half dozen Central American republics for the benefit of Wall Street. The record of racketeering is long. I helped purify Nicaragua for the international banking house of Brown Brothers in 1901–12. I brought light to the Dominican Republic for American sugar interests in 1916. I helped make Honduras "right" for American fruit companies in 1903. In China in 1927 I helped see to it that Standard Oil went its way unmolested. During those years, I had, as the boys in the back room would say, a swell racket. I was awarded with honors, medals, promotions. Looking back on it, I felt I might have given Al Capone a few hints. The best he could do was to operate his rackets in three city districts. We Marines operated on three continents. . . . We don't want any more wars, but a man is a damn fool to think there won't be any more of them.[14]

Clearly Roosevelt's big stick tactics in Latin America coupled with his support of the Philippine-American War led to unrest among Hispanics, contributing to intrigue along the international border between Mexico and the United States. A consequence of the Mexican Revolution was the migration of hundreds of thousands of Mexicans to the United States. It is estimated that nearly 900,000 immigrants crossed the border between 1910 and 1920. Fearful of border conditions during this time, Roosevelt's hand-picked successor, President William Howard Taft, ended the United States' long-held nonintervention policy with the Díaz regime, instead creating a Maneuver Division of Buffalo Soldiers (blacks) to patrol the U.S. side of the border, beginning in March 1911. These soldiers were stationed in San Antonio, Texas, as a readiness force to counter any cross-border attacks.

Taft's successor, President Woodrow Wilson, took an even more active military approach toward border security and Mexican politics with his paternal Wilsonism critique. Wilson's intent was to side with the Constitutionalists like Carranza and those he thought would protect U.S. oil, mining, and manufacturing interests in Mexico. When Mexicans objected to Wilson's intervention in their internal affairs, the United States reacted by using gunboat diplomacy in April 1914 in reaction to the Tampico Incident, where nine U.S. sailors from the USS *Dolphin* were arrested ashore in Tampico, Mexico. President Wilson used this minor incident as a pretext for invading and occupying Veracruz from April until November, again raising the U.S. flag over Mexico. During the U.S. Marines Corps' occupation some 400 Mexicans died compared to 4 U.S. deaths. Wilson's involvement in the Mexican Revolution also involved his support of General Francisco (Pancho) Villa during the first years of the Mexican Revolution.[15]

The popular stereotype of Pancho Villa, born Doroteo Arango, in U.S. society is that of an impulsive, dangerous bandit. In reality, Francisco "Pancho" Villa was a successful general during the Mexican Revolution, who once controlled all of Mexico north of Mexico City. In 1913, Villa became a leading general under Carranza and the Constitutionalists. At this time the United States sided with the Constitutionalists and were opposed to the federal forces of Huerta, who they perceived were receiving support from Germany. Consequently, Villa was also considered an ally of the United States. When General Villa seized the major northern cities of Chihuahua and Juarez in late 1913 and early 1914 he became popular with both the Wilson administration and the U.S. general public, with the *New York Times* calling him the "Robin Hood of Mexico."

Indeed, Villa's attack on Ojinaga in January 1914 forced Huerta's forces to cross over into the United States and surrender to the U.S. Army instead of face punishment from Villa's forces. This voluntary surrender showed early involvement of the United States military in the Mexican Revolution. Now the United States was responsible for the care of 5,000 Mexican combatants including 1,000 women, 500 children, and some 3,000 horses and mules. They were first held at Fort Bliss in El Paso and later transferred to Fort Wingate in New Mexico near the Navajo Reservation. The victory at Ojinaga gave Villa's forces control of northern Mexico, including the Mexican/U.S. border—a factor that became more significant with the onset of the First World War in Europe. Both U.S. General Hugh L. Scott and Secretary of State William Jennings Bryant became confidants and strong supporters of General Villa. With northern Mexico in the seemingly safe hands of General Villa, President Wilson felt secure in intervening in Veracruz in an attempt to send a message to Germany to cease interference in Mexico on the pretense of providing support to Huerta's forces.

It was General Villa's break with Carranza that eventually led to his falling out with the United States, although it appears that both General Scott and William Jennings Bryant continued to support him until Wilson's declaration of support of Carranza in October 1915. Now Villa's forces were fighting the Carranzitas under General Álvaro Obregón with tacit assistance from the U.S. military along the border. Indeed, the United States first alienated Villa in April 1915 in the battle for Matamoros when it allowed the Carranzitas to cross over into the protection of Brownsville while at the same time stopping Villa's forces from hot pursuit. Brigadier General "Black Jack" Pershing and his Buffalo Soldiers played a major role in border military politics at this time. With the United States now taking sides, providing support for Carranzitas, Villa's forces suffered a number of losses in northern Mexico in the spring and summer of 1914. The final blow came with President Wilson's formal recognition of the Carranza regime as the de facto rulers of Mexico on October 9, 1915. Ten days later the Conference of Latin American Countries followed suit. And Villa's status changed from respected military general to U.S.-designated renegade bandit.

President Wilson's recognition of Carranza over Villa was probably an effort to end the internal strife within Mexico, which many in the United States felt was being fueled by Germany in its effort to draw the U.S. military into the Mexican Revolution, thereby keeping them out of the European war. Evidence of the German motive came later with the Zimmerman communiqué of May 3, 1916. Most likely Germany saw Villa's March 9, 1916, raid on the U.S. Army base in Columbus, New Mexico, as the likely catalyst for full U.S. involvement in Mexican affairs. Clearly, the resulting Punitive Expedition had the opposite effect, mobilizing the National Guard for the first time and transforming the U.S. military from the 19th century horse tactics to a mechanized force in the form of the highly successful Rainbow Division led by Brigadier General Douglas MacArthur under the overall leadership of the army chief of staff, General "Black Jack" Pershing. Harsh reactions to the Plan de San Diego by the United States, notably the use of the Texas Rangers, also aggravated these issues, contributing to General Villa's cross-border raids.[16]

The Plan de San Diego: A Failed Attempt to Regain the Homeland

U.S. interventions and interference in the Mexican Revolution helped precipitate the Plan de San Diego, a manifesto initiated January 16, 1915, by a small radical element of the Mexican revolutionaries calling for a bloody revolt by both Mexicans and Mexican Americans in order to regain territory lost to the United States since 1848. It represented the Mexican answer to the Aryan supremacy associated with the United States' Manifest Destiny and called for a coalition of Mexicans, African Americans, Japanese immigrants, and eventually Indians to free southwestern states from the grip of the United States. Evidently, the Plan de San Diego's radical mandate did not represent the sentiments of either major group involved in the Mexican Revolution—the Constitutionalists or the Conventionists, although there is some evidence that followers of General Venustiano Carranza were involved. Even then the Plan de San Diego underwent second and third versions and actually involved some 30 cross-border raids during its year-long existence, but resulted in only 21 U.S. deaths.

Nonetheless, President Wilson's strong endorsement of the widely disseminated propaganda film *The Birth of a Nation* in the United States in 1915 justifying the brutal suppression of blacks by the Ku Klux Klan and the portrayal of the KKK as the protectors of Aryan white supremacy only added fuel to this marked division in North America between white Anglo-Saxon Protestants (WASP) and those considered to be lesser humans—blacks, American Indians, Mexicans, ethnic Catholics, and Jews. These sentiments fueled a vicious race war along the Rio Grande Valley in south Texas where outnumbered whites, in an overreaction to the Mexican raids of those associated with the Plan de San Diego, killed over 300 Mexicans or Mexican Americans, many summarily executed by the Texas Rangers. These actions were supported not only by the U.S. and Texas governments but also by the whites with large land holdings like the King Ranch.[17]

The Texas Rangers' Reign of Terror

Benjamin Heber Johnson, in his 2003 book *Revolution in Texas,* documented the Texas Rangers' active involvement in vigilantism directed against Tejanos:

Tejanos paid a high price for the newfound unity of Anglo south Texans . . . Those suspected of joining or supporting the raiders constituted the most obvious of targets, as they had from the uprising's beginning. Ethnic Mexican suspects were lynched after nearly every major raid in 1915. Shortly after the attack on the Norias ranch house, for example, unknown assailants killed three Tejanos . . . presumably for suspicion of aiding or participating in the attack. The Texas Rangers who had arrived after the fight might have been responsible. In any event, the Rangers' actions encouraged such measures: the next morning, they posed with their lassos around the three corpses, and the picture soon circulated as a postcard.[18]

U.S. soldiers, who were not permitted, by military law, to execute their prisoners, often turned Mexican or Tejanos suspects over to local sheriffs or the Texas Rangers, knowing that they would execute them without a trial. In a battle on September 28, 1915, Texas Rangers and raiders fought near Ebenoza, in Hidalgo County. Following the clash the Texas Rangers took and hanged over a dozen prisoners, leaving the bodies to rot with empty beer bottles stuck in their mouths. Relatives did not dare to bury their dead because of the fear of being targeted for death themselves by the local sheriff or Texas Rangers. Many felt that the 300 death count was low. A local paper, the *Regeneración,* put the count closer to 1,500. U.S. Army scout Virgil Lott noted: "How many lives were lost can not be estimated fairly for hundreds of Mexicans were killed who had no part in the uprising, their bodies concealed in the thick underbrush and no report ever made by the perpetrators of these crimes."[19]

The Texas Rangers' reign of terror in south Texas had its effect on the Tejanos with many fleeing across the border never to return. This was what the large Anglo landowners wanted. Indeed, Robert Kleberg, manager of the King Ranch, wanted martial law enforced in south Texas with Mexicans and Tejanos placed in concentration camps. He further suggested that: "When a certain man [who] is discovered to have taken part in a bandits' raid is captured or killed in such a raid, his brothers, half-brothers, and brothers-in-law are assumed to be guilty and are immediately arrested or killed." It should be noted that the King Ranch increased its holdings under Kleberg from 500,000 acres in 1885 at the time of the death of founder Richard King to nearly 1.25 million acres. Much of this land was stolen from Mexican and Tejanos owners at the time of the 1848 Treaty of Guadalupe Hidalgo and given to Anglos like King by white-run courts. The King Ranch was run with sharecropper labor and its owner had a keen interest in keeping the former Hispanic owners as subservient laborers indebted to the company store. Toward this end, the Texas Rangers acted as the King Ranch's private police force, harshly punishing any uppity Mexican. Interestingly, this program of ethnic cleansing and the forced displacement and elimination of Mexicans and Tejanos in south Texas has only recently been widely discussed despite an investigation by the Texas legislature in 1919 looking into the deaths of some 5,000 people of Mexican descent by the Texas Rangers and local law-enforcement officers doing the dirty work of Anglo landowners. A positive outcome was that this extreme action of targeting Hispanics resulted in an effort to organize Mexican Americans into a viable political entity, leading to the creation of the League of United Latin American Citizens (LULAC).[20]

VILLA'S 1916 RAID ON COLUMBUS, NEW MEXICO, AND THE PUNITIVE EXPEDITION

The massacre of Mexicans and Mexican Americans (Tejanos) by the Texas Rangers in south Texas and across the border had a negative impact in Mexico itself with United States residents targeted by Mexican forces. These actions were often sanctioned by General Pancho Villa who dominated the revolutionary forces in northern Mexico. Ironically, General Villa was the only revolutionary leader not to openly condemn President Wilson's action of sending U.S. troops into Mexico and seizing Veracruz in 1914. Nonetheless, the harsh treatment of Hispanics following the ill-fated Plan de San Diego soured Villa. As a result, he engaged in cross-border raids—the most notable being the 1916 raid on the U.S. Army base at Columbus, New Mexico. Villa, long alienated from the Carranza administration, was also upset that President Wilson now formally recognized Carranza as the legitimate leader of Mexico. General Villa believed that Wilson had made an agreement with Carranza allowing Mexico to become a de facto U.S. protectorate, thus allowing for a return to the Díaz status quo. Two months before, on January 11, 1916, Villa's troops stopped a train at Santa Ysabel, Chihuahua, Mexico, and executed 17 Texas mining engineers who were invited by President Carranza to reopen the Cusihuiriachic mines in Mexico. In reaction to this act, U.S. vigilantes killed another 100 or so Mexican Americans.

On March 9, 1916, Villa and 485 troops made an early morning raid on the 13th U.S. Cavalry at Camp Furlong near Columbus, New Mexico, former Mexican territory until the Gadsden Purchase. The raid had a dramatic effect on U.S./Mexican relations because of its audacity and not due to

U.S. casualties with only 10 enlisted men and 8 civilians killed. The aftermath of the raid had far more devastating consequences for Mexicans and Mexican Americans. James Hurst, in his work on the Villista prisoners, indicated that some scholars contend that abuses occurred immediately following the raid with U.S. soldiers indiscriminately killing anyone who looked Mexican during the so-called hot pursuit led by Major Frank Tompkins' forces. Tompkins justified the "hot pursuit" into Mexico and the slaughter of up to 100 Mexicans by claiming that these casualties were part of the raiding party. President Wilson's reaction was one of intervention into Mexico under the United States' unilateral authority inherent in the Monroe Doctrine.

President Wilson sent in up to 12,000 army troops under Brigadier General John J. (Black Jack) Pershing in an 11-month Punitive Expedition. In listing all U.S. forces involved in the Punitive Expedition two National Guard units, the First New Mexico Infantry National Guard and the Second Massachusetts Infantry National Guard, were among the forces mustered for this action. While the Posse Comitatus Act restricted the National Guard for use only by the authority of the governor of a state unless authorized by the president pursuant to the Insurrection Act, this represented a new era in U.S. national defense. These two National Guard units remained on the U.S. side of the border during the Punitive Expedition, providing a supportive function. The concept of a federally mobilized National Guard greatly aided in the expansion of the U.S. Army for the First World War via the Defense Act of 1916. This also put an end to volunteer regiments, like the Rough Riders, which were often poorly trained with allegiance only to their politically appointed leaders.

The expedition brought considerable hardships to Mexicans in the area but never completed its original mission of capturing General Villa. The Punitive Expedition not only raised havoc among the rural, poor Mexicans in northern Mexico, it clashed with Carranza'a government force on June 20, 1916, in the town of Carrizal where dozens were killed. Anticipating a full-fledged war with Mexico, Congress passed the National Defense Act in June 1916 authorizing doubling the size of the U.S. Army and authorizing the president to federalize the National Guard. Following its passage, President Wilson activated some 75,000 National Guardsmen into federal service to serve along the U.S./Mexico border.

Harsh Treatment of the Villista Prisoners

While Mexico showed compassion for U.S. Prisoners-of-War (POW), the United States did not reciprocate in kind. In the Columbus, New Mexico raid seven Mexican soldiers were captured, tried in civilian courts, and sentenced to death by hanging. Racial sentiments played a major role here as they did in south Texas. With anti-Mexican sentiments running high among Anglo Americans in New Mexico, especially in the southern part bordering Mexico, the Deming, New Mexico, courts labeled the captured prisoners bandits. Another 19 soldiers were captured by Pershing's troops in Mexico, and they also were charged with murder and tried in civilian courts. Six Mexican soldiers were executed (hanged) in June 1916 and six of the seven captured in the Columbus raid eventually received full, complete, and unconditional pardons from New Mexico governor Lorrazolo in November 1920. His decision was influenced by the 1907 Hague Convention concerning the laws and customs of war on land. These rules were adopted in response to the brutal treatment of the Boer (Dutch) by the British in South Africa during the Boer War and the atrocities attributed to U.S. troops in the Philippines in the aftermath of the Spanish-American War. But once freed by the governor, they were rearrested by the Luna County sheriff and again charged with murder. They were sentenced to prison terms in a violation of the U.S. constitutional guarantee against double jeopardy.[21]

From Unilateral Police Action to Diplomatic Border Politics

Relationships were already strained by World War I, which began in Europe in 1914. While the United States remained neutral until 1917, the ongoing Mexican Revolution exacerbated border tensions with Germany trying to sway Mexico toward its cause. Border surveillance relevant to terrorists and saboteurs filtering into the United States along with tens of thousands of Mexican immigrants was of great concern to the United States at this time. This situation became more critical following the disclosure of the Zimmerman telegram of 1917 in which the German foreign secretary enticed Carranza to help Germany by establishing an American front with the promise of the return of Mexican lands at the conclusion of the war. President Carranza remained neutral but did condemn the Punitive Expedition and Wilson's illegal invasion of Mexico. The United States entered the First World War five weeks following the interception of the Zimmerman telegram, pulling out its battle-tested forces from Mexico and elevating Pershing as Commander of the U.S. Expeditionary Forces in Europe.

Criticism of President Wilson's intervention in Mexico from both within the U.S. and throughout the world coupled with the United States entry into World War I on the side of the Allies led to the abrupt end of the Punitive Expedition. Furthermore, U.S. intervention into Mexico's internal affairs not only made General Villa a national hero, along with his martyred counterpart, Emiliano Zapata, but it also forced the Carranza administration to include many of the Conventionists planks into the Mexican Constitution of 1917. Article 3 called for compulsory secular, free public primary education (six grades) for all citizens. Article 27 called for land reform effectively eliminating large land holdings, as well as foreign and church ownership of lands and minerals. It allowed Mexican states to expropriate lands with compensation. It restored the *ejido* land system of 1856. Article 123 addressed labor reform, prohibiting child labor, establishing an eight-hour workday and equal pay for equal work. It also called for payment in legal tender, thus eliminating the hacienda credit system. Workers were now able to organize unions for collective bargaining and even to strike. And article 130 restricted religious influence in government, outlawing foreign-born religious leaders and greatly restricting church-owned property. Article 130 also made marriage a civil contract.

The Wilson administration and U.S. Congress were not pleased with Carranza's concessions to the Conventionists in the 1917 constitution, fearing an end of capitalist exploitation of Mexican human and mineral resources. The Wilsonism critique and unilateral intervention into Mexico under the guise of the Monroe Doctrine was again considered in the early 1920s following the De la Huerta rebellion. As mentioned previously, the elevation of Adolfo de la Huerta to provisional president of Mexico convinced General Villa, the last major military force in the revolution, to lay down his arms, disband his forces, and retire in July 1920. Another factor in Villa's retirement was the ouster and death of Carranza in May 1920 and the subsequent U.S. withdrawal of recognition of Mexico's postrevolutionary government. When Álvaro Obregón became President in November 1920, De la Huerta became finance minister and was successful in settling Mexico's international debt due to the nationalization of foreign interests. Apparently, Villa's assassination in 1923 was a precondition for U.S. recognition of Mexico's government. In the end, many of the major players in the Mexican Revolution died for this cause, notably Francisco Madero, Emiliano Zapata, Venustiano Carranzo, Obregón, and Pancho Villa.

This diplomatic crisis was not resolved until the Harding administration and the Bucareli Conference in August 1923. During the 27-month impasse, the petroleum interest pressured the United States to again forcefully intervene in Mexico. De la Huerta was opposed to the Bucareli Conference, fearing that it would undo all the reforms gained by the bloody 10-year revolution. He feared that Obregón would become another U.S. puppet government like the one proposed under the Wilsonism critique. In December 1923, De la Huerta and General Guadalupe Sanchez proclaimed their revolution against the Obregón/Calles administrations with their Plan de Veracruz. Under the plan, De la Huerta would be the supreme chief of the revolution. The dilemma later for the Coolidge administration was choosing between De la Huerta's opposition to special-claim reparations by U.S. firms and the Calles form of socialism (the U.S. labeled Calles a Bolshevik because of his socialistic plans). The Obregón/Calles faction won out with the added support from American labor union boss Samuel Gompers, president of the Pan American Federation of Labor. This international liaison served to quell armed intervention plans from the United States into Mexico. The fact that both Obregón and De la Huerta indicated support for the debt agreement spelled out by the Bucareli Conference further defused tensions between the U.S. and Mexico. Ratification of the Bucareli agreements by both the United States and Mexico also served to quell the De la Huerta revolt. President Coolidge's departure from Wilson's unilateral intervention into Mexican affairs, despite his distaste for the tenets of the 1917 constitution, eventually led to diplomatic resolutions to U.S./Mexican differences and the end of the De la Huerta revolt. Charles Evans Hughes, U.S. secretary of state under Coolidge, is credited for this diplomatic trend and the recognition of the elected regime in Mexico—no matter how distasteful to U.S. business interests. Thus ended the border wars of the early 20th century.[22]

MEXICO-U.S. TRADE CORRIDORS

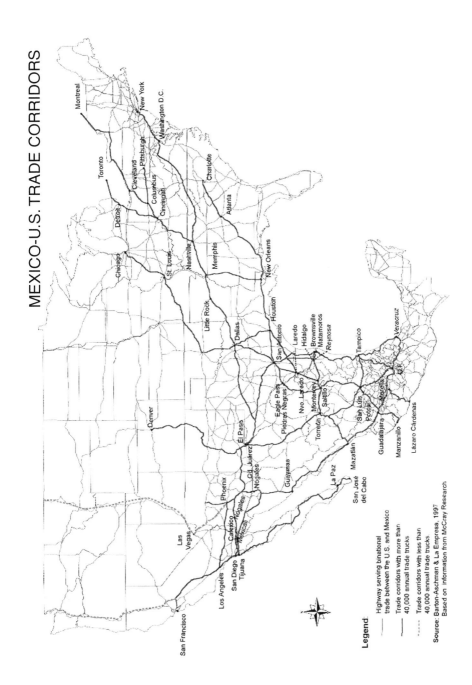

Legend:

— Highway serving binational trade between the U.S. and Mexico

— Trade corridors with more than 40,000 annual trade trucks

····· Trade corridors with less than 40,000 annual trade trucks

Source: Barton-Aschman & La Empresa, 1997
Based on information from McCray Research

STATE OF ORIGIN OF MIGRATORY AGRICULTURAL
WORKERS ENTERING U.S., 1942-1968*

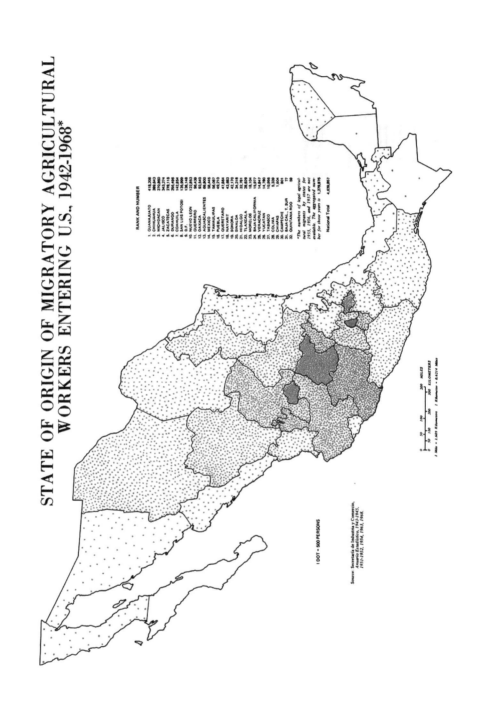

RANK AND NUMBER

1. GUANAJUATO 418,306
2. CHIHUAHUA 390,843
3. MICHOACAN 370,860
4. JALISCO 343,374
5. ZACATECAS 278,118
6. DURANGO 256,646
7. COAHUILA 142,866
8. SAN LUIS POTOSI 135,599
9. D.F. 126,318
10. NUEVO LEON 122,883
11. GUERRERO 95,439
12. OAXACA 83,640
13. AGUASCALIENTES 66,800
14. MEXICO 56,445
15. TAMAULIPAS 48,987
16. PUEBLA 45,210
17. QUERETARO 47,664
18. NAYARIT 43,983
19. SONORA 42,170
20. SINALOA 34,318
21. HIDALGO 32,391
22. TLAXCALA 28,029
23. MORELOS 18,151
24. BAJA CALIFORNIA 15,977
25. VERACRUZ 14,947
26. YUCATAN 14,760
27. TABASCO 10,896
28. COLIMA 5,339
29. CHIAPAS 1,604
30. CAMPECHE 901
31. BAJA CAL., E. SUR 77
32. QUINTANA ROO 59

National Total   4,630,867

*The numbers of legal agricul-
tural migrants by states for
1955, 1956, and 1957 are not
available. The aggregated number for those years is 1,270,976.

1 DOT = 500 PERSONS

Source: Secretaría de Industria y Comercio,
Anuario Estadístico, 1942-1945,
1951-1952, 1954, 1963, 1968.

0   50   100   300 MILES
0 50 100   300   KILOMETERS
1 Mile = 1.609 Kilometers   1 Kilometer = 0.6214 Miles

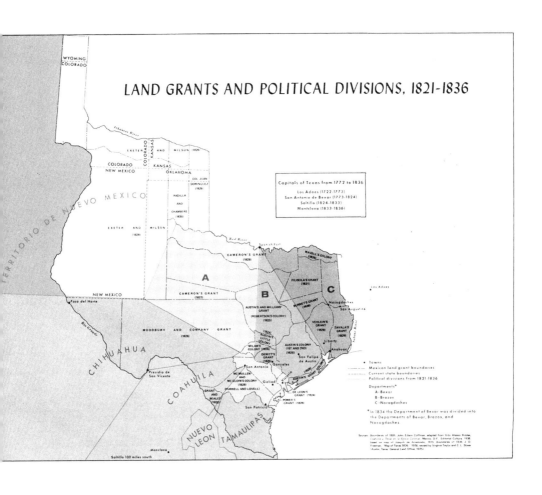

LAND GRANTS AND POLITICAL DIVISIONS, 1821-1836

WYOMING
COLORADO

Arkansas River

EXETER   AND   WILSON (1828)

COLORADO   KANSAS
NEW MEXICO   OKLAHOMA

COL. JUAN
DOMINGUEZ
(1829)

PADILLA
AND
CHAMBERS
(1830)

MEXICO

EXETER   AND   WILSON
(1829)

TERRITORIO DE NUEVO

NEW MEXICO

Paso del Norte

Rio Grande

CHIHUAHUA

WOODBURY   AND   COMPANY   GRANT
(1826)

Presidio de
San Vicente

COAHUILA

GRANT
AND
BEALE'S
(1832)

Red River

Spanish Fort

CAMERON'S GRANT
(1828)

A

CAMERON'S GRANT
(1827)

B

AUSTIN'S AND WILLIAMS'
GRANT
(ROBERTSON'S COLONY)
(1825)

AUSTIN'S
LITTLE
COLONY
(1828)
'MILAM'S
GRANT
(1826)
DEWITT'S
GRANT
(1825)

San Antonio

MC MULLEN
AND
MC GLOIN'S COLONY
(1828)

PURNELL AND LOVELL'S
(1828)

San Patricio

RAVELL'S COLONY
(1829)

FILISOLA'S GRANT
(1831)

C

BURNET'S GRANT
(1826)

VEHLEIN'S
GRANT
(1826)

ZAVALA'S
GRANT
(1829)

AUSTIN'S COLONY
(1ST AND 2ND)

San Felipe
de Austin

Gonzales

Goliad

AUSTIN'S COAST COLONY

DE LEON'S
GRANT (1824)

POWER'S
GRANT (1829)

Los Adaes

Nacogdoches
San Augustine

Liberty
Anahuac

Capitals of Texas from 1772 to 1836

Los Adaes (1722-1773)
San Antonio de Bexar (1773-1824)
Saltillo (1824-1833)
Montclova (1833-1836)

NUEVO
LEON   TAMAULIPAS

Monclova

Saltillo 100 miles south

•   Towns
——   Mexican land grant boundaries
——   Current state boundaries
——   Political divisions from 1821-1836

Departments*
A - Bexar
B - Brazos
C - Nacogdoches

*In 1834 the Department of Bexar was divided into
the Departments of Bexar, Brazos, and
Nacogdoches.

Sources: Boundaries of 1826; John Edsen Coffman adapted from Vito Alessio Robles,
Coahuila y Texas en la Época Colonial, Mexico, D.F. Editorial Cultura 1938,
based on map of Joaquín de Arredondo, 1819; Boundaries of 1836; J. D.
Freeman, Map of Texas 1836. 1936, revised by Virginia Taylor and C. L. Stiver
(Austin, Texas: General Land Office, 1965).

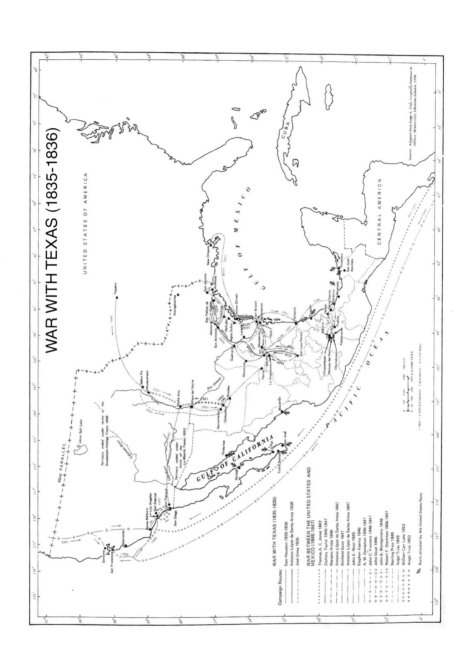

WAR WITH TEXAS (1835-1836)

Campaign Routes: **WAR WITH TEXAS (1835-1836)**

Sam Houston 1835-1836
Antonio López de Santa Anna 1836
José Urrea 1836

WAR BETWEEN THE UNITED STATES AND MEXICO (1846-1847)

Thomas A. C. Jones 1842
Zachary Taylor 1846-1847
Mariano Arista 1846
Antonio López de Santa Anna 1847
Winfield Scott 1847
Antonio López de Santa Anna 1847
John E. Wool 1846
Stephen Kearny 1846
A. W. Doniphan 1846-1847
John C. Frémont 1846-1847
John Sloat 1846
John B. Montgomery 1846
Robert F. Stockton 1846-1847
Sterling Price 1846
Ángel Trías 1846
William Carr Lane 1853
Ángel Trías 1853

Ports attacked by the United States Navy

UNITED STATES OF AMERICA

GULF OF MEXICO

CUBA

CENTRAL AMERICA

PACIFIC OCEAN

GULF OF CALIFORNIA

42nd PARALLEL

Territory ceded under terms of the
Guadalupe-Hidalgo Treaty 1848

Territory ceded under the
terms of the
La Mesilla Treaty 1853

Source: Adapted from Jorge A. Vivó, *Geografía Humana de
México*, México City, Ediciones Galatea, 1958.

PART II

Mexican Migration and Social Issues from 1917 to Present

CHAPTER 4

Labor and Migration Issues: 1917–64

The 1917 Mexican Constitution dismantled entire systems of power once enjoyed by a religious and political elite. The federalization of church lands, the establishment of the minimum wage, endorsement of national currency over private script, and so forth signaled a tremendous shift in social paradigms.

As scholars like Manzanarez have noted: "The 1917 Mexican Constitution became a testament to the accomplishment of the revolution. The hope was that under the new political system, justice would finally be achieved for those who had been neglected ever since the arrival of the Europeans on what became Mexican soil."[1] Ai Camp sees the ideology of Mexicanization as the major outgrowth of the Mexican Revolution. Mexicans, notably the middle class, were finally able to share in the incredible wealth the United States had invested in Mexico's economy. He has found that by 1911 foreign investment in Mexico rose to nearly three-and-a-half billion dollars.[2] Yet, any viable discussion of Mexican migration to the United States needs to take into consideration not only the influence of the Mexican Constitution of 1917, but also the labor shortages in the United States created by the First World War; and the impact of the 1917 Immigration Act.

MEXICANS AND EARLY IMMIGRATION LAWS

Indeed, it seems that U.S. anti-Asian sentiments helped foster the Mexican migration trend beyond that of the long-established travel routes between Mexican and Mexican American families in their former homeland, notably Texas, New Mexico, Arizona, and California. The United States passed a number of laws designed to restrict peoples from Asia and the Pacific Islands from entering the country. Laws designed to exclude Chinese immigrants specifically from entering the United States go back to the 1870s, culminating in the enactment of the 1882 Chinese Exclusion Act, which essentially barred Chinese immigration to the United States. These first immigration laws were expanded with the passage of the U.S. Immigration Act of 1917. Here, the U.S. Congress passed, over President Wilson's veto, a law expanding the exclusion of both Asians and Pacific Islanders from entry into the United States, including those peoples from their newly acquired territories in the South Pacific. A section of the 1917 act, known as the Asiatic Barred Zone Act, would (coupled with the Japanese Exclusion Act of 1924) set the stage for the large-scale introduction of Mexican workers. They would be called on to fill the void created by the exclusion of Asian workers and the millions of U.S. service personnel engaged in the First World War.

The Immigration Act of 1917 also barred entry to polygamists, anarchists, the mentally retarded, mentally ill, indigent, and those with physical defects. Individuals whose first language was not English were required to take a literacy test, another element designed to curtail continued immigration from Eastern and Southern Europe. Interestingly, the act initially exempted Mexicans from the literacy requirement, until this aspect of the immigration laws was changed in 1921. Consequently the Immigration Act of 1917 favored Mexican male laborers needed to work on the railroads and in the agricultural sector. This influx of Mexican laborers is often referred to as the first Bracero Program—formal agreements between the United States and Mexico regarding the use of temporary labor from Mexico in the United States. This influx of Mexican males into the United States allowed them to migrate to regions of the country not traditionally associated with Mexico's former territories. It made it more difficult to stem the flow of Mexican migrants as more restrictive immigration policies and quotas were eventually instituted.

Placing the Mexican migrant issue in proper perspective requires a brief review of the migratory trends in the United States from the colonial times to the 20th century. Migratory trends in the United States fall into four erratic waves according to John Isbister. He estimates that over 60 million immigrants came to the United States from the colonial period to the present, with the vast majority being of European descent. The first wave occurred during the colonial era and early years of the republic (1607–1820). Here most of the immigrants were English, followed by the Scots, Irish, Dutch, Germans, Swedes, French, and African slaves. The second wave includes the period of the Mexican War until the early period of Reconstruction (1840–79). During this period some 15 million immigrants entered the United States, with the majority again being from Europe and England and with the largest populations coming predominately from Ireland (Irish famine) and Germany. The United States also inherited hundreds of thousands of Mexicans following the acquisition of northern Mexico at the end of the Mexican

War in 1848. Also, a significant number of Chinese, mainly males, entered the United States at this time to work the gold fields of California and later to work on the transcontinental railroad. French Canadians began to cross the northern U.S. border in significant numbers to work in the textile mills of New England during this time as well.

The third wave, however, represented the largest immigration wave, some 25 million people entering the United States between 1880 until the borders were closed in 1930 due to the Great Depression. This group included more English, Irish, and German immigrants but also large numbers of southern and eastern Europeans, notably, Poles, Italians, Russians, Greeks, and Austria-Hungarians. This latter group differed from the white Protestant immigrant of the past in that most were either Catholic (Roman or Orthodox) or Jewish, augmenting the predominately Catholic French Canadians and Acadians also entering the United States from Canada. It was during this time that the first exclusionary legislation was enacted—the Chinese Exclusion Act of 1882. The fourth, and current wave, according to Isbister, began around 1965 and will be discussed in the next chapter.[3]

The immigration situation from the early 20th century until the Second World War was one where people of Mexican origin, living along the U.S./ Mexico border, either fled south to Mexico to avoid the harsh repercussions associated with the Plan de San Diego or they fled north into the United States to avoid the battles associated with the Mexican Revolution. Either way, this migration was mostly into the borderland region and, for many, was seen as being transitory until matters improved in their former homeland. Moreover, the male drain in the United States due to the First World War, coupled with both the newly enforced restrictions on Asian immigrants and the rapid growth of the economic revolution in the United States, led to a labor shortage especially in mining, railroads, and agriculture, opening these jobs to Mexican males willing to migrate. Soon the agricultural demands in the fertile fields of Texas, New Mexico, and California led to the black market practice of smuggling illegal Mexican laborers into the United States. Hence, the first informal Bracero Program set the stage for the program initiated during the Second World War. Van Nuys estimated that 10 percent of the Mexican population fled to the United States during the Mexican Revolution, enriching the borderland region by at least a million immigrants from south of the border. This coupled with the United States' stereotype of the Mexican peon as a docile, ignorant, hardworking entity immune to the harsh desert conditions of the West, and the distrust of Asian workers at this time led to the special waiver provisions of the restrictions of the Immigration Act of 1917, eliminating the literacy test, head tax (registration fee), and contract labor provisions for Mexican workers from May 1917 to March 1921.

De Leon, in his work *Mexican Americans in Texas* indicates that tens of thousands of Mexican-born workers entered Texas during the period of 1900–1930 with over 70,000 coming in 1900, 125,000 in 1910, over 250,000 in 1920, and some 266,000 in 1930. These migrations occurred during a time when the U.S./Mexico border was basically unpoliced much like the U.S./Canadian border at the time. These undocumented migrations occurred even though the U.S. Border Patrol was established in 1924. However, its initial function was enforcing customs laws against Asians as well as enforcing Prohibition smuggling laws—a function that involved the borders both north and south of the United States. De Leon noted that while most of these early immigrants stayed within the old territorial borders conceded to the United States in the 19th century, they were still perceived in racist terms. Speaking of what some termed the "Mexican Problem," even those advocating continued migration of Mexican laborers perceived them as being a degenerate people posing moral and political danger to the United States. But, they argued, this was outweighed by the fact that overall they were docile farmwork laborers who lived together in barrios and, therefore, could be easily controlled without posing a threat to the dominant white society. Restrictionists, on the other hand, worried that some of the Mexican laborers might leave the agricultural fields and migrate to the industrial centers where they would replace white workers. They also argued that the Mexicans represented an inferior people who would spread disease and crime in the United States. Though thousands did legally enter the country, the restrictionists did win the battle during the hardship years of the Great Depression when most foreign laborers were being restricted entry into the United States, even those from Canada.[4]

During the Great Depression, Mexican workers were displaced by unemployed white farmers and sharecroppers from the farm belt areas of the United States, which had been devastated by drought and severe economic conditions. Many of these were "Okies"—from Oklahoma—who drifted to the West Coast, notably California, to work the harvest seasons. Interestingly, the depression and drought also plagued Mexico's agricultural economy. Nonetheless, Mexico and the United States engaged in a repatriation program for Mexican workers stranded in the United States during these trying times. Mexico had its own works progress program (WPP) with jobs provided for improving its own agricultural economy by clearing land, building irrigation systems, and constructing reservoirs, notably in the states of Coahuila, Aguacalientes, Durango, Hidalgo, Chihuahua, and Sonora. Both the Mexican and U.S. governments aided the returning Mexican laborers by providing free rail passes to these project sites. The United States provided transportation from agricultural states to the major border crossings in Arizona and Texas. Crucial to this process was the Mexican Migration Service, which provided special trains that could accommodate up to two thousand *respatriados* at a time. Clearly, the Mexican government, through its Mexican Migration Service, provided better access for the respatriados than the U.S. State Department with the former providing service personnel at 26 border sites while the latter provided services at only 7 Mexican ports of entry.

During the Repatriation Program of the Depression Era, it is estimated that 90 percent of the Mexican laborers were located in the border states

that once comprised Mexico prior to the 1848 Treaty of Guadalupe Hidalgo—California, New Mexico, Texas, Arizona, and Colorado. Interior urban
populations of Mexican workers at this time included those in Detroit, Chicago, and St. Paul. Because of the sparse population along the California/
Mexican border, these workers had to first be transported to major border
centers such as Nogales in Arizona and El Paso and Laredo in Texas. In
Texas alone it is estimated that the Mexican/Mexican American population
was about 700,000 in 1930. Over 130,000 individuals of Mexican heritage
departed Texas during this program from 1930 to 1932, disappointing those
in the state that hoped this program would rid Texas of most of its Mexican-
heritage population. California, on the other hand, saw about 50,000 of its
Mexican migrant workers take advantage of the repatriation program during this same period. Arizona, with a very strong anti-Mexican element then
as today, had an estimated Mexican migrant population of over 114,000 in
1930 but only 18,520 were repatriated between 1930 and 1932. It was in the
northern industrial cities that significant numbers of Mexican migrant workers were repatriated, which provided relief to local welfare rolls and school
budgets in the communities they left behind. Mexican statistics reveal that
over 30,000 Mexicans were repatriated from Illinois, Michigan, Indiana, and
Ohio during the period of 1930–32.

   However, the program was not without controversy. An issue that arose
out of the repatriation program was the U.S. Bureau of Immigration's policy
of allowing its agents to unilaterally play the roles of investigator, judge, and
jury relevant to deportation actions. This situation did not change until 1934
when the bureau's policies changed forbidding the same agent from participating in both the preliminary and final hearings for a deportee client. This
change stemmed from President Franklin D. Roosevelt's executive order of
June 10, 1933 that merged the bureaus of immigration and naturalization
into the consolidated Immigration and Naturalization Service. This new organization resulted in new standards and procedures, as well as a change in
attitude toward migrants along the border. The INS now trained its personnel in ways to better deal with the public. During the repatriation program,
the Mexican Migration Service reported that 132,469 Mexicans returned to
the homeland, many skirting the U.S. Labor Department's scrutiny. The
program declined until around 1937 when significant numbers of migrants
returned. During this same time, some 27,000 Mexicans came to the United
States legally, most on student visas or in business and academic profes-
sions. Few laborers could enter the United States at this time without violating federal laws. Clearly, the economic incentive was no longer an attraction
for farmers and industry given the availability of cheap U.S. labor from displaced tenant farmers and other unemployed people.[5]

THE BRACERO PROGRAM

Following the Great Depression and increased border security, the corridor
north for Mexican "day laborers" (braceros) became a challenge, but one that

continued to thrive mainly due to the establishment of the immigrant press. Spanish-language publications kept the lifelines opened between Mexican Americans and their counterparts residing in old Mexico. One of the oldest daily Spanish-language paper, *La Prensa*, was distributed along the border region in both nations. Thus, a unique Hispanic culture took hold in the transborder region from California/Baja through Arizona/Sonora, New Mexico/Chihuahua, and all of Texas and the corresponding border Mexican states: Chihuahua, Coahuila, Nuevo Leon, and Tamaulipas. This border region established its own subculture with a distinctive lifestyle and economy different from the interior societies of either Mexico or the United States. In Mexico, the northern borderland region is known as the *frontier*. It is within this region that experienced internal migration within Mexico facilitated the movement of peoples and goods across the international border.

In the early 1940s conditions in the United States and internationally again precipitated a manpower drain in both the military and in industry, just as a rapid urban/industrialization was required to fuel the Second World War. These conditions again forced the United States to import a cheap, readily available labor source. Mexico, with its proven record earlier in the century, was again seen as providing this needed resource. Thus began the formal Bracero Program. The Bracero Agreement was signed on August 4, 1942, and revised in April 1943. The agreement stipulated the conditions for Mexican laborers legally working temporarily in the United States. These conditions were dictated mainly by the Mexican government in order to secure protection for its workers during their stay in the United States. Legal written contracts, sanitary living conditions, adequate wages without any unauthorized deductions, and transportation to the job sites as well as transportation during repatriation were issues Mexico insisted upon while the United States stipulated that these workers should not be employed in order to displace other U.S. workers or for the purpose of reducing the pay rate. Mexico also had a provision that these workers would be bonded by the U.S. employer with funds deposited in either the Bank of Workers or the Bank of Mexico. Lastly, these workers could not be recruited into the U.S. military.[6]

The Bracero Program, Public Law 45, did not initially include entry into the United States along the entire border region. Texas, with the longest section of borderlands, did not originally participate mainly because Texas farmers and ranchers felt that they could get illegal Mexican "wetbacks" (*mojados*) at a cheaper rate and without adhering to the humane conditions spelled out by Public Law 45. Mexico, on the other hand, was reluctant to contract with Texas farmers due to the state's long history of abuse toward Mexicans and Mexican Americans, especially at the hands of the Texas Rangers. Ironically, these actions by Texas ranchers and farmers to illegally hire Mexican day laborers led to the massive federal/state expulsion process coordinated by the Immigration and Naturalization Services and the U.S. Border Patrol, in conjunction with state law-enforcement agencies, to rid the nation of illegal Mexican workers beginning in the 1950s. This was known as Operation Wetback. Part of the irony of Operation Wetback was the active involvement and support of the expulsion of mojados by established Mexican American citizens of Texas, the Tejanos. Part of this process involved intra-ethnic racism, involving white Mexican Americans versus the Mestizo peons who entered the United States as laborers. What the Tejanos and their counterparts in New Mexico, Arizona, and California did not expect was that their elitism served to fuel the simmering prejudices that non-Hispanic whites held toward all people of Mexican descent, including them.

The Bracero Program of 1942 was unique in that it allowed Mexico to establish the minimum standards for its workers in the United States. And the United States, while refusing to provide similar standards for U.S. farmworkers, including whites, blacks, Mexican Americans and Filipinos, during the Great Depression, consented to Mexico's demands. During the period covered by the initial Bracero Agreement, from 1942 until 1947, some 200,000 braceros came to the United States as agricultural workers under these international provisions. They worked in agriculture in 24 states with the vast majority employed in California. Again, due to the Mexican boycott, Texas received no braceros during this contract period. Ill feelings toward Mexicans certainly brewed during this time given that foreign migrant workers were guaranteed wages and benefits denied U.S.-born farmworkers. With Texas boycotting the initial accord, its reliance on illegal Mexican migrant workers further fueled anti-Mexican sentiments, even among the rising Mexican American political class. While political opposition to the Bracero Program existed in the U.S. Congress, the fact that the program was under the auspices of the U.S. Department of Agriculture (USDA), and not Labor, gave the strong agricultural business lobby what it wanted—cheap labor.

Dissension from labor groups and the ensuing Korean conflict led to changes in the original Bracero Agreement for the period from 1948 until 1951. Again some 200,000 legal Mexican migrant laborers were recruited during this period with approximately twice as many undocumented workers (referred to derogatorily as illegal wetbacks) recruited as well. The major difference now was that the agricultural agents could directly contract with the Mexican workers, obviating many of the guarantees Mexico insisted upon in the original agreement. One major sector disenchanted with the original Bracero Program was the agricultural businesses in the Pacific Northwest who saw strikes among the bracero workers. Part of the problem was the cultural isolation of the Mexican migrant workers in communities alien to them and without a Spanish-speaking support system. White prejudices only compounded a tense situation. Mexican consuls reported numerous breeches of contract incidents where the Mexican migrant workers were not being paid or treated according to the original agreement stipulated in Public Law 45. It was reported that the braceros in this region were treated worse than Italian and German prisoners of war held in northwestern farm labor camps had been.[7] These prejudices led to harsh working conditions including a high accident and death rate. Both the Mexican migrants and the northwestern agribusinesses ended a five-year experiment with the latter thereafter recruiting Mexican American workers solely for their seasonal harvests. The Bracero Program existed in a state of flux during the 1948–51 period. The abuses were now directed toward American workers, while those Mexican citizens who crossed the border in search of work, found that their home country was increasingly disenfranchised from protecting its workers.

BRACERO REVISED, EMERGING MEXICAN AMERICAN ORGANIZATIONS, AND OPERATION WETBACK

The controversy over Mexican workers in the United States became heated in the 1950s with the conservative, anti-Communist McCarthyism movement headed by the Wisconsin U.S. senator Joseph R. McCarthy. A major target of McCarthyism was racial and ethnic minorities who were grouped together with political minorities—Socialists and Communists—and identified as threatening to the American way of life. This phenomenon led to the heated bracero debate of 1951, which eventually fostered Operation Wetback, as well as the subsequent backlash that emerged during the turbulent 1960s, where anti-immigrant sentiments abounded, spelling the eventual end of the Bracero Program. Notwithstanding the fear incited by the McCarthy witch hunt, Public Law 78 passed on July 12, 1951, establishing the first effort at legislating the Mexican guest workers program. This arrangement again placed the bracero contracts at a government-to-government level, eliminating the blatant abuses that abounded during the interim 1947–51 period. Despite the loud opposition from the conservative McCarthy camp, agribusiness in general supported this effort at congressional oversight, if only to guarantee needed seasonal laborers for planting and harvesting U.S. crops, the exception being the sugar beet farmers of the Northwest. The caveat offered those opposed to the Bracero Program was the built-in six-month renewal clause, which meant that the law had to be reconsidered twice each year. Even then, Public Law 78 continued to regulate the Bracero Program unopposed for the next 13 years.

In the 22 years of the official Bracero Program, Mexico was forced to reevaluate its own agricultural and rural communities—those from which guest workers originated. In the final analysis, while certain progress was being made, rural poverty persisted in Mexico while the campesino programs stalemated. In the end, over four-and-a-half million Mexican workers were involved in the exchange of labor sanctioned through the official Bracero Agreement. Ironically, the Bracero Program also contributed to a rush of undocumented Mexican workers into the United States. It is estimated that while a little over 200,000 guest Mexican workers were contracted for 1953, nearly 900,000 others that are known of also entered the U.S. workforce. Actually, the flow of undocumented Mexican workers began with Texas agribusinesses that openly skirted the rules of the Bracero Agreement in order to bring in workers at a lower cost and without the requirement of minimum housing and working standards. As a result, an underground business in transporting and finding employment for undocumented Mexican workers flourished during the entire 22 years of the official Bracero Agreement, often with a wink from the administration and U.S. Congress, which did not want to upset the powerful agricultural lobby at this time.

However, social events in the United States during the 1950s and early 1960s spelled the end of the Bracero Agreements. Increased mechanization in harvesting agricultural products, notably cotton, led to a reduced need for the guest worker. This, plus the efforts of the Kennedy Administration's New Frontier program followed by President Johnson's Great Society programs finally addressed the working conditions of America's own impoverished working classes. The fact that the guest workers program existed from 1951 until the end of 1964 was due mainly to the efforts of the Mexican government. The end of Public Law 78 did not, however, stem the flow of undocumented Mexican workers into the United States, now to work in any venue where cheap labor was needed. In the final analysis, the antibracero groups included both Mexican American workers and Mexican American political action organizations, including the Imperial Valley Farm Labor Contractors Association and the Mexican American Educational Conference Committee.[8]

As stated earlier, the emerging political activism among Mexican Americans following the Second World War had the unintended consequence of intensifying anti-Mexican sentiments in the United States especially in white communities in the border states, notably Texas, California, and Arizona. Ironically, newly charged Mexican American political action groups played a significant role in this latent process. The Mexican American identity, notably among the middle-class Tejanos in Texas, emerged following the deadly Anglo response to the Plan de San Diego of 1915. As mentioned earlier, the middle- and upper-class Hispanics of Mexican heritage attempted to assimilate into the larger U.S. society by forming ethnic organizations like the Order of Knights of America and the League of Latin American Citizens with the mandate of promoting U.S. citizenship and attempting to blend into mainstream America. These organizations merged in 1929 into the League of United Latin American Citizens (LULAC). LULAC provided a sense of cultural and political clout for middle-class Mexican Americans, and this process was rejuvenated with the return of Hispanic GIs during both World War II and the Korean conflict. No longer satisfied with the existing Jim Crow apartheid system operating in the United States, returning GIs, charged by their patriotism and worldly experience, abandoned the Jim Crow system for one that proudly promoted Mexican heritage. This new ethnic-pride focus extended to the working class, long ignored by LULAC, including documented and undocumented Mexicans living in the United States. Ell-wyn Stoddard captured this transitional movement in 1972 in his book *Mexican Americans*:

During World War II many Mexican Americans became aware of their former sub-ordinate status and exploited energies. Following the end of the war, they and their children spearheaded the organizational impetus to disengage from institutions fos-tering Anglicization and committed themselves to a doctrine of cultural pluralism, within which their ethnic identity, as determined by themselves, could be realized.[9]

Like their black American and American Indian counterparts, returning Mexican American service men and women found the same discriminatory practices existing as when they left—despite participating in the epic world war allegedly fought to end such prejudices and discrimination. One of the factors here was the denial of veterans of Mexican heritage entry into congres-sionally sanctioned veterans' organizations—the Veterans of Foreign Wars and the American Legion, the former established following the Spanish-American War and the latter after the First World War. When allowed to join, they had to become members of separate ethnic-specific units. The de-nial of federal benefits even extended to the denial of burial in local military cemeteries. Like the First World War, it seems America was restricting its military honors to only Anglo GIs. What the Mexican American GIs did get was access to the GI education bill. Now more Mexican American GIs were armed with college degrees, better preparing them for the civil rights bat-tles ahead. Concerned about social and educational equality for all Mexican American Hispanics, the returning GIs in Los Angeles formed the Council of Mexican American Affairs (CMAA) in 1954. Clearly, the 1950s was the decade of rapid political awareness among Mexican Americans, setting the stage for the collective activism to follow in the 1960s. Nonetheless, the estab-lished Mexican Americans contributed to the expulsion of undocumented Mexican nationals in 1954 in the program known as Operation Wetback.

The basic rationale for the strong opposition by both LULAC and the American GI Forum against Mexican laborers, both documented and un-documented, was that their presence in the workforce tended to keep Mex-ican American wages low. Thus, while their objections appeared to be basically economic in nature, once Operation Wetback went into effect the overwhelming negative reaction to all people of Mexican descent engulfed them as well. The term "wetback" pertained to all illegal Mexican workers, not only those in Texas where the international border is clearly defined by the Rio Grande (big river), but also to the dry land border separating New Mexico and Arizona and much of California as well.

Although short-lived, Operation Wetback was significant for a number of reasons. It established the border patrol as a viable agency while articulating the issues relevant to undocumented Mexicans that exist today: construction of a border fence, use of military-like operations, and legal arguments over who should be punished—businesses who employ undocumented workers or the illegal Mexican who is enticed to the United States for low-paying, often seasonal work. As for the border patrol, its mandate was greatly modified during Operation Wetback from its original objective at the time of its inception in June 1924. Placed under the Department of Labor, the border patrol's initial function was to keep out undesirables attempting to enter the United States, notably Asians and Eastern Europeans, restricted by the immigration laws of 1917 and 1924. They were also charged with curtailing the smuggling of alcoholic beverages during Prohibition. These activities were likely to occur at either the southern U.S./Mexico or the U.S./Canada borders as well as by sea into Florida and other coastal states. These activities, at the federal level, also involved the U.S. Coast Guard and coordination and cooperation with state and local law-enforcement agencies. The border patrol's function changed following repeal of the Volstead Act, ending Prohibition in 1933. Now their focus was on immigration control and as such they began to be transformed from law-enforcement officers to immigration officers. In 1940, the parent organization of the border patrol, the Immigration and Nationalization Service (INS), was transferred from the Labor Department to the Department of Justice, placing the border patrol under the U.S. attorney general.

This change came about mainly due to President Franklin D. Roosevelt's concern over Axis agents, notably German and Italian, attempting to enter the United States through its porous borders facing both Canada and Mexico. Obviously, this reflected the administration's slant toward Britain in the Second World War, months before the United States entered the fray. With this new emphasis, border-patrol agents were able to use considerable discretion in the enforcement of Mexican workers entering the United States. Essentially, their latent function often was to aid U.S. agricultural interests in obtaining sufficient cheap laborers when these resources were needed. This role continued among border-patrol agents stationed along the U.S./Mexico border until the Bracero Program was instituted in 1946. Even then, their role was often to transform an apprehended undocumented Mexican worker from his wetback status to that of a contracted bracero. But when the war ended and a new swing toward federal cost-cutting began, the border patrol was downsized from 1946 until 1954 and the initiation of Operation Wetback.

Operation Wetback emerged during the conservative era of McCarthyism of the Eisenhower administration. Texas, Arizona, and California officials complained about crimes committed by Mexican laborers, which were not readily substantiated by data, adding fuel to the antiminority inflammatory rhetoric already being spewed by McCarthyism. At the same time, President Eisenhower was attempting to enforce the recent 1954 U.S. Supreme Court decision in *Brown v. Board of Education*, as southern states refused to desegregate their public schools. Here, Eisenhower employed a new tactic in federal enforcement of unpopular laws; he federalized the state National

Guard, forcing them to protect the black students entering formerly all-white schools. This initiative was not lost on others in his administration who wanted to use the military to secure the U.S./Mexico border during this time of anti-immigration sentiments. After Attorney General Brownell's efforts at having legislation passed making it an offense to hire illegal Mexican workers failed due to the strong agribusiness lobbies, he attempted to get the secretary of defense to deploy an army division along the 250-mile-long border covering California and Arizona, thereby allowing the border patrol to concentrate on enforcing the New Mexico/Texas portion of the U.S./Mexico border. This plan was dubbed Operation Cloudburst.

The U.S. attorney general's idea of using the U.S. Army along the border was opposed by the military and by the State Department, which feared that this type of force would lead to worsening relations not only with Mexico but throughout all of Latin America, which already had bad memories of U.S. military interventions on behalf of U.S. businesses. Moreover, recriminations were already being made toward some of the brutal measures being employed in certain border-patrol sectors, including forcing Mexicans captured as they tried to enter the U.S. without papers to return back to Mexico through 45 miles of rattlesnake–infested desert as a de facto punishment for their illegal entry into the United States. These occurrences were reported in the region near Zapata, Texas.[10] Other accusations, supported by the Mexican consulate, included the border patrol shaving the heads of captured wetbacks as a means of humiliation. These incidents were reported in both the U.S. and Mexican press, forcing the United States to soften its attempts to militarize the U.S./Mexico border.[11] The United States realized that it needed the support of the Mexican government if Operation Wetback was to succeed, if only as a public relations program.

As an alternative to this opposition to Operation Cloudburst, Attorney General Brownell, with the strong approval of the president, instead appointed an army general to direct Operation Wetback. General Joseph M. (Jumping Joe) Swing, recently retired as commander of the Sixth Army in California, was a classmate of President Eisenhower at West Point, and was part of General Pershing's Punitive Expedition into Mexico in 1916. He also saw action in World War II and Korea, earning the Distinguished Service Cross and three Silver Stars, and got his nickname, Jumping Joe, after serving with the 101st Army Airborne. Swing was appointed commissioner of immigration in 1954 and placed in charge of Operation Wetback, where he could conduct his military-type campaign against illegal Mexican immigrants without fear of an international backlash. Eisenhower and Brownell chose Swing so as to circumvent the political and business influences on the border patrol at that time. In order to eliminate the border patrol's long-held dual role as purveyor of mojados for local agribusiness and ranching interests, Swing had those agents involved in this process transferred to the U.S./Canadian border, thus neutralizing the influence of politicians in Arizona, California, and Texas, including U.S. senator Lyndon Johnson, from interfering in Operation Wetback.

Swing then hired two other army generals, Frank Pattridge and Edwin Howard, as consultants to the INS providing direct planning for Operation Wetback. Toward this end, the border-patrol system was consolidated into four districts with the southwest region designated as that along the U.S./Mexico border. Swing, with the recommendations of his consulting generals, created the position of senior patrol inspector for each sector allowing for direct communication, data collection, and action within their section of operations. Swing also acted on a recommendation made by one of his agents and established mobile task forces, which were response teams designed to quickly descend upon an identified problem within the sector, including roundups of wetbacks. These concentrations of federal, state, and local agents aided in the quick roundup of those in the country illegally. Swing also employed other military-like tactics in Operation Wetback, including airlifts, buslifts, trainlifts, and boatlifts for the purpose of transporting captured mojados back to Mexico away from the border frontier where they could easily return to the United States. The use of tracking dogs was also implemented by the border patrol in the southwest region during this operation. This multifaceted method of rapid response coupled with quick deportation used another recent military innovation—that of air-to-ground and vehicle-to-vehicle communication systems, setting the stage for the system still employed today in law enforcement.

While short-lived and expensive, Operation Wetback set the stage for future border-enforcement endeavors. It significantly changed the border patrol while soliciting cooperation with the Mexican government in the control of illegal immigrant workers. A positive aspect was the encouragement of mojados to return to the United States as braceros, thus allowing the extension of the Bracero Accord for another decade. In the two-month life of Operation Wetback the INS is purported to have deported over a million illegal Mexican workers, mostly from California and Texas. In addition to the fear, and in some cases physical harm, generated among Mexican and Mexican American laborers as the roundup was executed, the negative impact of Operation Wetback—one that continues to resonate today—was the portrayal of the Mexican worker, regardless of legal status, as a subhuman, despicable character who was prone to crime and violence. Unfortunately, many U.S. citizens of Mexican descent were confronted and forced to prove their citizenship. Those who could not were arrested and deported to Mexico. Apparently President Eisenhower, Attorney General Brownell, and General Swing were not opposed to the public and media attention paid to Operation Wetback being played within the highly charged anti-WASP McCarthyism movement of the time.[12]

The backlash of anti-Mexican sentiments associated with Operation Wetback, an effort strongly supported by both the established LULAC and the

emerging American GI Forum (AGIF), forced Mexican Americans into political action designed to establish their credibility in United States society.
Political activism among Mexican Americans began with attempts for better working conditions and to improve the quality of education. The stated
aims of LULAC in 1944 including the following goals:

- To eradicate discrimination;
- To utilize legal means in obtaining equal rights, equal protection under the
  laws, and equal opportunity;
- To define our unquestionable loyalty to the ideals, principles and citizenship of
  the United States of America;
- To maintain a sincere and respectful reverence for our racial origin;
- To assist in the education and guidance of Latin-Americans using lawful
  means;
- To participate in all local, State and National political contests;
- To endeavor to secure equal representation for our people on juries and in the
  administration of Governmental affairs.[13]

Strikes by Mexican Americans and Mexican nationals were often short-
lived due to a lack of support from national labor organizations. This is
reflected in the Chino mine strike in the mid-1950s in the Silver City area of
New Mexico. Because the strike gained national, even international, attention with the movie *The Salt of the Earth,* Juan Chacon and his fellow Hispanic
workers did gain recognition as a viable labor force that could confront the
Anglo-run political apparatus which was obviously biased toward the mine
executives. It did put an end to the heavy-handed tactics long used by the
Anglo-dominated law-enforcement agencies and their use of excessive and
extra-legal measures commonly employed in the region for over half a century. In the Chino strike this included the jailing of the wives and children
of the striking workers, which was featured in the movie. The exposure provided by *The Salt of the Earth* spread to the Clifton-Morenci mines just across
the state border in Arizona, which had a long history of brutality toward its
workers of Mexican descent. Hence, in the mid-1950s, the mine executives
and the Anglo-dominated political apparatus of Arizona and New Mexico
were given notice that business-as-usual in regards to worker exploitation
was coming to an end.

Regarding education, Mexican Americans suffered under the same Jim
Crow segregation as black Americans but without the protection of law since
their segregation was of a de facto nature due to their "other white" status.
Nonetheless, both Hispanics and blacks were affected by the Supreme Court
decision in *Brown v. Board of Education.* Part of the problem was the intent of
LULAC to Americanize Mexican Americans as part of the larger dominant
society. Shortly following LULAC's establishment in 1929, and as a reaction
to the reemergence of white supremacist groups such as the Ku Klux Klan,

the 1930 *Del Rio ISD vs. Salvatierra* decision labeling Mexican Americans as the "other white race" was initially welcomed by LULAC, given that this classification separated them from the African American population. However, with the creation of the American GI Forum (AGIF) in 1948, educational inadequacies were again brought to the forefront. A major focal point for the Mexican American educational reform movement was San Antonio, Texas, where the Pan-American Progressive Association (PAPA) was initiated. LULAC, the AGIF, and the Ladies GI Forum Auxiliaries all joined the effort to end segregation in public schools. The education for Mexican and Mexican American children in public schools in Texas led to both LULAC and the AGIF challenging the inferiority of segregated schools in *Delgado v. Bastrop ISD*. Similarly, another case was working its way through the California courts. At this time, it was estimated that 27 percent of those of Mexican heritage in Texas had no schooling at all and that the separate schools for Spanish-surname children had minimal facilities with a poor curriculum restricted to domestic and vocational training.[14]

Mendez v. Westminster School District began in March 1945 when a number of Mexican American families filed suit in the U.S. District Court in Los Angeles claiming that thousands of children of Mexican ancestry were segregated into inferior schools within Orange County, California. The district court ruled in favor of the plaintiffs, rendering its decision on February 18, 1946. The school district then appealed the decision to the Ninth Circuit of Appeals in San Francisco which ultimately upheld the lower court decision. However, the decision did not settle the "separate-but-equal" issue addressed in the 1896 *Plessy v. Ferguson* case, mainly due to the "other-hite" status of Mexican Americans. Interestingly, Earl Warren was the governor of California when the case was determined and he signed into law the provisions outlined in the circuit-court decision. The NAACP, represented by Thurgood Marshall and Robert L. Carter, joined *Mendez v. Westminster* as amicus curiae (friends of the Court). Marshall and Carter are the attorneys who successfully argued the 1954 *Brown v. Board of Education* case before the U.S. Supreme Court then headed by Chief Justice Earl Warren.[15]

Neither the *Delgado* nor *Brown v. Board of Education* case immediately resolved the de facto segregation issues in Texas public schools. Again, the major issue here was the argument that Mexicans were not a colored minority and as other whites they did not benefit from the de jure ruling of the U.S. Supreme Court in their 1954 *Brown* decision. The rationale for the separate, and largely unequal, education offered to those of Mexican ancestry was due to the language barrier. Indeed, following the *Brown* decision, Texas school districts transferred black students into the inferior Mexican schools under the pretense that they were in compliance by integrating white, albeit, "other white," schools. The issue of desegregation of Mexican schools was not resolved until 1957 with the *Herminca Hernandez et al. v. Driscoll Consolidated ISD* case, which for all intents and purposes ended pedagogical and de jure segregation in the Texas public schools.[16]

These cases reflected the intra-group conflicts facing Mexican Americans at this time. The descendents of the Criollos, Mexican-born of Spanish heritage—those who considered themselves to be phenotypically Caucasoid (the "other whites"), pitted themselves against the mixed-blooded brown Mestizos. The issue facing Mexican American communities during the turbulent 1960s was which of these groups should provide the identity and leadership for Hispanics.

CHAPTER 5

Post-Bracero Migration Trends and Issues

THE "OTHER WHITES'" EMERGENCE SOCIALLY AND POLITICALLY

Clearly, the harsh reaction to the Plan de San Diego led to the politicalization of Mexican Americans, notably in Texas with the election of J. T. Canales to the legislature, as well as the resurgence of LULAC and the emergence of the American G.I. Forum. Indeed, in 1960 LULAC had over 150 councils in comparison to only 46 in 1932. Even then, the higher-status "light skinned" Mexican Americans continued to adapt to the challenges of the 1960s with the La Raza Unida Party (LRUP), spinning off into the Mexican American Youth Organization (MAYO) under the leadership of Jose Angel Gutierrez. By working within the system, MAYO was able to receive support from established organizations such as the Ford Foundation, and federal projects like VISTA (Volunteers In Service To America) and OEO (Office of Economic Opportunity). In this regard, Caucasoid-appearing Hispanics benefited from their status as "the other whites." Mestizos, on the other hand, suffered from the same discrimination associated with black Americans up until the 1960s. Benjamin H. Johnson noted this in his book, *Revolution in Texas:*

The wealthiest, lightest-skinned, and most influential of ethnic Mexicans could avoid some of this caste system. Much as they had forged alliances with incoming Anglos in the preceding generations, these Tejanos continued to enjoy social prestige and access to the Anglo-dominated world. . . . For example, several dozen Mexican Americans from the Valley attended the University of Texas at Austin in 1930, a time when the state completely excluded African Americans from the university.[1]

Even as a handful of Mexican Americans were advancing within the social hierarchy of the United States, Mexico's social hierarchy was being reordered completely. As discussed previously, the revolution resulted in the establishment of communal land grants known as *ejidos*. Here, the land is held by the community with tracts parceled out to individual families (campesinos). While the family occupied its parcel within the ejido, it could not sell, rent, or mortgage it. The redistribution of agricultural lands helped keep many Mestizos and Indians on the land in their villages. This actually helped stem the migration trends to the United States, even when the Bracero Program was in effect. The ejido system also helped maintain community ties for those workers who left to work seasonally in the Bracero Program. Even then, a sizable number of these migrants, both documented and undocumented, formed barrios in the United States in areas that once belonged to Mexico before the creation of the Republic of Texas, and 1848 and 1853 land grabs by the United States. This migration was due to the finite land available within each ejido and its subsequent subdivision among family members. As the family grew, more male offspring had to find work elsewhere within Mexico or in the United States, while, at the same time, maintaining their community (ejido) identity and their family plot (campesino). Hence, these Mexican migrants, unlike most other ethnic groups who migrated to the United States, maintained a de facto dual citizenship, rarely severing their family ties in the homeland. It was from this migrant population that the American Mestizo clambered for recognition as a viable Hispanic group—not the "other white," black, or Indian per se, but the brown Chicano/Chicana.

During the turbulent civil rights and antiwar era of the 1960s and 1970s, Cesar Chavez became the most prominent of these brown-power Mexican Americans, much like Benito Júarez, the first Mexican president of pure Indian descent, in Mexico a century earlier. Chavez got his start within the Mexican American middle-class-oriented Community Service Organization (CSO), which supported LULAC principles of getting Hispanics involved in language and citizenship classes and registered to vote in local and state elections. Together these efforts were termed La Causa during the 1950s, ostensibly sharing the same mandate of electing Hispanics in Texas, New Mexico, Arizona, and California.

However, Chavez took the CSO in California in a different direction, focusing on labor issues. Chavez essentially shifted the Hispanic focus away from middle-class, "other white" Mexican Americans to the brown Indian and Indian-mix (Mestizo). This departure led the CSO board to abandon Chavez in 1961, attesting to the intra-group prejudices existing among Mexican Americans themselves. Chavez's affiliation with farmworkers began in 1965 when he became strike leader for both striking Filipino Americans and Mexican Americans working in the vineyards of California. The prolonged strike gave Chavez and the National Farm Workers Organization national attention and support. Finally, in the fall of 1970, the last holdout agreed to the farmworkers' demands for a minimum wage. This attention also happened while numerous other groups were demonstrating across the country for civil rights for minorities and against the Vietnam War. These groups that came to rally with the Mexican American farmworkers included college students, African Americans, and those of draft age. With this support and notoriety, Chavez and his Mexican American United Farm Workers took their battle to the fruit and vegetable fields and orchards throughout California. Equally significant, the attention to the Mexican American farmworker spread to the barrios where many other Mexican Americans lived in substandard, ghetto-like conditions.

The riots of the 1960s and early 1970s drew attention to urban poverty especially among minorities of color. Los Angeles, originally a Mexican outpost prior to the 1848 treaty giving it to the United States, played a significant role in this unrest. Wheeler and Becker describe the effects of the LA riots on the American conscience in their book *Discovering the American Past*:

The Watts riot of 1965 in Los Angles shocked many Americans with its violence and revealed poverty and despair in the midst of what had appeared to be prosperity and optimism. . . . During the six days that the Watts riot lasted, it spread to adjoining areas, and the National Guard was called out to help contain it. Thirty-four people were killed, more than a thousand were injured, and $40 million worth of property was damaged or destroyed. In 1970, and again in 1992, more riots broke out in Los Angeles.[2]

Wheeler and Becker alluded to yet another factor that impacted urban dissent among Latinos. During the Vietnam conflict and following the end of the Bracero Program, the United States began to loosen its immigration restrictions, resulting in a new wave (fourth wave) of immigration with many coming from Latin America, especially Mexico, in addition to those migrating from Asia (the target of the original immigration laws in 1917) and the Pacific Islands. Wheeler and Becker claim that this opened the floodgate of immigration to Southern California with over one million new immigrants, mostly Hispanic and Asian, arriving in the Los Angeles area. With the crowding in the poorer inner-city areas already occupied by African Americans, interracial tensions heightened, forcing each subgroup to take action to assert its cultural identity within this conflicting ecosystem. Hence, the emergence of the Brown Power movement.[3]

It took a professional boxer from the barrios of Denver, Colorado, to ignite and activate the bronze element of the Mexican American community. Rodolfo "Corky" Gonzales was a fighter well known in the Hispanic community, and he was the catalyst that inspired the more radical elements of the Brown Power movement of the 1960s and 1970s. Gonzales broke away from his role with the Crusade for Justice Organization in Denver in 1965. His stance was not integration like those espoused by LULAC. Instead, he

advocated for a separate Chicano movement. In 1968, he advocated for a
Brown Power orientation for Chicanos in the larger dominant white society. The vehicle for the separatists-oriented Brown Power movement was
the La Raza Unida Party (LRUP), which aligned itself with the more radical
elements of social discontent at the time, including the Black Panthers.

The short fall of the LRUP was its failure to align with either Gutierrez's
or Chavez's organizations. This weakness came to light at the four-day
conference Gonzales called for in September 1972 at the El Paso del Norte
Hotel. During this time a campus-based movement was underway that was
much like the Anglo students' counterpart—the Students for a Democratic
Society (SDS). The Hispanic student movement was MECHA—El Movimiento Estudiantil Chicano de Aztlan. It was an outgrowth of the Chicano
Youth Liberation Conference held in Denver in March 1969 with the movement now designated the Plan de Aztlan. MECHA originally was an ally
of the more radical views held by Corky Gonzales but moderated by the
early 1970s. Even the Brown Berets, originally patterned after the Black Berets and Black Panther groups, began to lose their radical edge by the early
1970s. The cathartic event for the collective expression of Brown Power, collectively known as the La Raza Unida Party, was the National Chicano
Moratorium March of August 29, 1970, held at Laguna Park in Los Angeles with representation from Mexican American organizations across the
Southwest. Police reaction to the Moratorium March led to three people
being killed, including *Los Angeles Times* columnist Ruben Salazar. Corky
Gonzales was among the 70 arrested and jailed by the LAPD. Sixty-four
policemen were injured in the ensuing riot that they clearly aggravated.

It is with this history of the Chicano movement that Corky Gonzales
called for a national convention of the La Raza Unida Party in 1972. But at
this juncture, Corky Gonzales's dream of a strong separatist movement was
waning. Nonetheless, this was to be a test of who would direct the Mexican American Political Association (MAPA) within the larger Chicano movement. Three thousand delegates met in El Paso, Texas, to determine the
direction of the national La Raza Unida Party. Hispanics from the entire
Southwest as well as the Midwest were represented, and in the end the
moderates, those advocating peaceful change via the ballot box like that
demonstrated earlier in Crystal City, Texas, prevailed. Jose Angel Gutierrez, of the MAYO, with the support of Cesar Chavez and his UFW, beat out
Corky Gonzales for the position of party chairman. Gonzales was given the
largely ceremonial position of the presiding officer of the national convention, Congreso de Aztlan, as a token for his role in organizing the convention. The major outcomes of the La Raza Unida Convention were support
for a guaranteed annual income for Latino workers, national health insur-
ance, no land taxation, bilingual education, parity in employment, increase
in admissions to medical schools, parity in jury selection, support for organizing farmworkers, and enforcement of the land grant conditions of the

1848 Treaty of Guadalupe Hidalgo. Essentially, this outcome represented the synthesis of the "other white" thesis and the reactive antithesis Brown Power separatists.[4]

A more radical contemporary of the Chicano Movement of the 1960s and 1970s was Corky Gonzales's colleague—Reies Lopez Tijerina—leader of the Alianza land grant revolt. Reies Tijerina's most radical action was a June 5, 1967, courthouse raid in northern New Mexico. He was born in 1927 in Falls City, Texas, to a sharecropping family. Influenced by his religious mother, he went to a Bible school run by the Assembly of God and while he apparently did not complete the program, he eventually was licensed as a minister and first practiced in California. He later became the spiritual leader of a small group of followers establishing a commune called the Valley of Peace in Arizona. His involvement in the Alianza movement occurred in 1958 when he went to northern New Mexico to assist the Abiquiu Corporation of Tierra Amarilla, which was advocating for historic Spanish land grant rights.

Tijerina went to Mexico in early 1960 to research the land grant documents and found the 1570 authorization for land grants issued by King Philip II of Spain and promulgated in Spanish colonial laws. Armed with this evidence, Tijerina sought to restore over a million acres of land in New Mexico to descendants of the original land grants, which were ostensibly protected under a provision of the 1848 Guadelupe Hidalgo Treaty between Mexico and the United States. Toward this end, Tijerina formed the Alianza de Las Mercedes in February 1963, calling for the return of the land to the Mexican American people, using force if necessary. His rhetoric quickly raised his status within the growing Chicano civil rights movement, but he did not gain the national attention he sought. The idea of a revolution came following the second Alianza convention in August 1964 where advocates for action like that taken by blacks in the Watts, LA, riots outweighed the more peaceful methods employed by Cesar Chavez and the United Farm Workers. The fiery "King Tiger," Tijerina advocated arson, fence cuttings, and rustling as methods of attacking the current owners of the contested land grants—including the U.S. Forest Service lands where grazing permits were issued.

On July 4, 1966, members of the Alianza movement marched uphill from Albuquerque to Santa Fe and presented their grievances to the governor of New Mexico, again garnering little media attention during these times of national unrest. Later, in August 1966, the Alianza claimed the independent city-state called the Pueblo de San Joaquin del Rio de Chama. Using this as their new base of government, the Alianza movement issued documents reclaiming the lands currently under government ownership. The new Alianza movement's government even went to the extent of issuing deeds to the new owners as well as eviction notices for current occupants. The Alianza movement now was gaining in membership, attracting the urban poor in New Mexico as well as youth activists and owners of small rural Hispanic farms and rancheros. At its height, the movement had some 20,000 adherents in New Mexico.

Trouble began, however, with the occupation of the Carson National Forest in October 1966. These problems came with Alianza's claim of Free State, the Pueblo de San Joaquin del Rio de Chama on federal lands, which led to the occupation of the Kit Carson National Forest. In October 1966, Alianza leaders arrested federal rangers in the national forest and put them on trial. Federal officers quickly intervened, charging five Alianza leaders with misuse of government property and assault on the forest rangers. The following April, Tijerina took his case to the New Mexico governor without any success while District Attorney Alfonso Sanchez pushed for greater disclosure of the Alianza membership, labeling them as a Communist organization. Instead of complying with this order, Tijerina disbanded the Alianza and resigned as president in May 1967 in order to protect the organization's membership.

In June, the Alianza reemerged as the Confederation of Free City States while meeting in Coyote, New Mexico. Soon fires were started and fences destroyed in the national forest lands the group claimed as their own. Sanchez reacted by arbitrarily banning public assemblies and arresting suspected members of Alianza publicly, calling Tijerina a Communist because of his effort to take over the questioned land grants by force. This public altercation led to Sanchez being targeted by the group for a "citizen's arrest"—a legal procedure in New Mexico. This effort resulted in the June 5, 1967, raid on the Rio Arriba courthouse in a search for District Attorney Sanchez. Not finding him at this office, the 20-man vigilante posse took out their frustration on others, resulting in a state patrolman and the jailer being shot and wounded, and a deputy sheriff and a reporter taken as hostages. This raid led to a massive manhunt with 500 National Guard troops activated, along with two tanks, the state police, New Mexico Mounted Patrol, the Apache police, and the FBI in pursuit of the courthouse raiders. The Alianza camp at Canjilon was quickly surrounded and the occupants, men, women, and children, were held by this armed force until Tijerina's arrest. While out on bail, Tijerina attempted to use his notoriety to further rant against the establishment, disparaging Jews and embracing the Black Power movement. He was even the codirector of the Chicano detachment of the Poor People's Campaign, but these attempts at national recognition led to a rapid decline in his Hispanic followers, leading to his resignation of the Alianza leadership.

Tijerina was acquitted of the charges of kidnapping and assault to commit murder in the Tierra Amarilla Court House raid but was later convicted and sentenced on federal charges of destruction and of assaulting officers. He was housed at the federal prison hospital in Springfield, Missouri, from July 1969 until July 1971. Despite Tijerina's high-profile case, Alianza failed to gain attention beyond northern New Mexico, and the land grant controversy went silent until 2004. Until then the Tierra Amarilla land grant of 1832 remained unresolved. The efforts of Hispanic radicals eventually evolved into effective organizations. Currently, the National Council of La Raza (NCLR) is the largest Hispanic nonprofit organization with LULAC second. The NCLR is an outgrowth of the civil rights organization of the 1960s—the National Organization for Mexican American Services (NOMAS), but unlike NOMAS and La Raza Unida, the NCLR encompasses all those of Hispanic origin, not merely those of Mexican descent. It receives funding from major philanthropic groups such as the Ford Foundation, Citigroup, and Wal-Mart, and has regional offices in all the major cities including Atlanta, Chicago, Los Angeles, New York, Phoenix, Sacramento, San Antonio, and San Juan, Puerto Rico.[5]

THE PRO-DEMOCRACY MASSACRE IN MEXICO CITY

Turmoil existed in Mexico during the turbulent 1960s, resulting in the 1968 Tlatelolco Square student massacre in Mexico City. The massacre of hundreds (some contend thousands) of unarmed protestors, mostly students, at a pro-democracy demonstration on October 2, 1968, occurred on the eve of the Olympics in Mexico City and remains one of the worst atrocities of the long-ruling Institutional Revolutionary Party (PRI) regime. This incident happened at the same time of the deadly race riots in major U.S. cities and predated the deadly school shootings at Kent State and Jackson State universities by police and the National Guard. The major difference here is that while the riots in the United States eventually subsided, the PRI dirty war continued and even intensified under President Echeverria's administration from 1970 to 1976. Echeverria, then interior secretary under President Gustavo Díaz Ordaz, was in charge of police and internal security at the time and is the person linked with giving the orders for the killing. Serious efforts to uncover the particulars of the PRI's dirty war were not possible until 2000 and the end of PRI's 71 years of uninterrupted rule when President Vicente Fox's administration appointed a special commission to investigate these incidents. The results to date indicate an active use of the military in the violent suppression of leftist dissidents, including university students. Moreover, the United States is also implicated through the Pentagon, which sent military radios, weapons, ammunition, and riot-control-training support to Mexico before and during the crisis as well as the CIA, which provided reports on developments within the university community from July to October 1968. In the Tlatelolco Square massacre, 360 sharpshooters fired from surrounding buildings into the protesters, resulting in over 300 deaths. These casualties are not attributed to armed students shooting fellow protestors, which was the PRI account at the time. Echeverria was charged with genocide in connection with the massacre in June 2006 only to have the charges dismissed due to the expiration of the statute of limitations. More about this turbulent era in Mexico's history will emerge as the record continues to be examined.[6] On October 2, 2008, thousands of protesters marched across Mexico City demanding justice for the 1968 student massacre by government troops chanting "Dos de Octubre! No se olivide!" On this 40th anniversary of the massacre, Amnesty International joined in the call to President Calderon, challenging his administration to establish an independent inquiry into this dark chapter of Mexican history.

Treaty of Guadalupe Hidalgo and the New Mexico Land Grant Controversy

The land grant commission, initiated in April 1922, provided its final report in June 2004. In the U.S. General Accounting Office (GAO) report, it is noted that the history of this controversy extends back to 1850 and encompassed the greater New Mexico Territory, which was considerably larger than the present state of New Mexico.

The Court of Private Land Claims Legislation (1891 Act)

On March 3, 1891, Congress enacted the 1891 Act, the second principal statute implementing the property protection provision of the Treaty of Guadalupe Hidalgo with respect to land grants in New Mexico. The 1891 Act superseded the 1854 Act that had been in effect for 37 years. The 1891 Act created the Court of Private Land Claims (CPLC) to address land grant claims in the Territories of New Mexico, Arizona, and Utah, and the states of Nevada, Colorado, and Wyoming.

LAND GRANT ISSUES IN NEW MEXICO TODAY

Today, 300 years after Spain made its first land grant in New Mexico and more than 150 years after the Treaty of Guadalupe Hidalgo was signed, concerns and bitterness over the United States' implementations of the treaty still linger. As an example of this perceived disparity, scholars and land grant heirs often point to the treatment given the Tierra Amarilla land grant, and they also allege that the surveyor general of New Mexico failed to comply with U.S. Constitutional requirements of due process of law during his investigation of this grant. As a result of these alleged shortcomings, heirs contend, Congress in 1881 incorrectly patented almost 600,000 acres to an individual instead of to the Tierra Amarilla community. Issues associated with the Tierra Amarilla community's perceived loss of land to private individuals still create a sense of bitterness and an atmosphere of general distrust about the federal government, as reflected in a 1967 confrontation between land grant heirs, their advocates, and state and federal authorities at a courthouse in the town of Tierra Amarilla, New Mexico.[7]

Overview

A number of land grant heirs, legal scholars, and other experts have charged that activities under the two federal statutory New Mexico community land grant confirmation procedures did not fulfill the United States' legal obligations under the treaty's property-protection provisions. Of the 154 community grants in New Mexico, 105 grants—over 68 percent—were confirmed at least in part and the remaining 49 grants—about 32 percent—were wholly rejected. With respect to the confirmed grants, heirs and others have voiced concern about whether the full amount of acreage that they believe should have been awarded was in fact awarded, as well as whether the acreage awarded was confirmed and patented to the rightful owners. With respect to the rejected grants, the heirs' principal concern is that no acreage was awarded at all:

Notwithstanding the compliance of the two New Mexico confirmation procedures with these statutory and constitutional requirements, we found that the processes were inefficient and created hardships for many grantees. . . . For policy or other reasons, therefore, Congress may wish to consider whether further action may be warranted to address remaining concerns.[8]

Industrialization and Internationalization of the Borderlands—Maquiladoras, WTO, and NAFTA

The Quota Law of 1921 and the Immigration Act of 1924 served to further restrict the type of immigration allowed into the United States. These racial provisions were not corrected until passage of the Immigration and Nationality Act (Walter-McCarran Act) in 1952. Yet, it was not until the civil rights laws of the 1960s that the quota and racial-profiling process were changed dramatically. The new rules now provided legal avenues for entry into the United States to family members of American citizens and permanent resident aliens regardless of ethnic origin. The major problem was that these laws did not positively impact upon Mexican immigrants given that the Bracero Program was still in effect until 1964, thus creating an illegal avenue for Mexicans, notably seasonal workers. At this time the Mexican migrant laborers were organizing under the leadership of Cesar Chavez and his United Farm Workers Union.

Hence, the changes brought about since 1965 have seen an increase of immigrants from third world nations, including the Caribbean Basin, South and Southeast Asia (following the Vietnam conflict), and Mexico. Indeed, Mexico now became a corridor for entry into the United States for illegals coming from Central and South America. Mexico now had to contend with human contraband entering their country at its southern border and exiting at its northern border. There was also increased opposition to nonwhites entering the United States under these new immigration rules. The vocal backlash was best articulated by Pat Buchanan, the perennial conservative third-party candidate for U.S. president. In an article in the *Conservative Chronicle,* Buchanan called for the suspension of current immigration practices due to the fear that whites in the United States would soon become a minority. Here he compared the United States with problematic multinational states in the 1990s like Czechoslovakia, Yugoslavia, and Brazil.[9]

Maquiladoras—The Industrialization of the Borderland

Environmental issues have long been associated with minority groups, including migrant workers. Tougher environmental laws in the United States in the mid-1960s led to the proliferation of the maquiladoras, or twin manufacturing plan, where U.S. and other international firms would establish and operate plants in Mexico along the U.S. border in the borderland. The origins of Mexican industrialization extend back to the early years of World War II when Mexico began the process of preparing workers for industrial jobs with the creation of the Camara Nacional de la Industria de Transformacion in 1942. In 1944, the Mexican Congress passed legislation opening the door to foreign participation with the provision that Mexicans hold a controlling stock in any mixed corporation. This action led to the establishment of the maquiladora system which emerged along the U.S./Mexican frontier border, also known as *the borderland.* At the end of World War II, some 300,000 Mexican workers were employed by major U.S. industrial firms. The maquiladoras, in turn, led to a mass migration of mainly females from rural interior Mexico to the frontier borderland. Both these migrants and immigrants (documented and undocumented) contributed to the unique borderland culture, a mix of U.S. Anglo majority and Mexican American subculture.

The original intent of the maquiladora system was to have the component parts of manufactured goods produced in the Mexican plants while the final assembly of the product occurred in U.S. factories. Both plant systems were located close to the international border in order to keep transportation cost low. But the United States never relocated its manufacturing plants from the industrialized Midwest to the borderland region. Instead, the U.S. firms merely erected warehouses to store the product elements manufactured across the border in Mexico and transported these items to their interior assembly plants using U.S. trucking and rail systems. General Electric (GE) opened its first maquiladora in 1971 and soon expanded to eight plants within a decade. GE employed over 8,000 workers to produce circuit breakers, motors, pumps, and coils in its borderland Mexican plants. Soon General Motors followed suit, opening 12 maquiladora plants in Mexico while closing 11 factories in the United States, laying off nearly 30,000 workers. On the eve of the North American Fair Trade Agreement (NAFTA), General Motors was the largest private employer in Mexico with

50 plants and 50,000 workers accounting for a 10th of Mexicans employed by some 2,000 maquiladoras.[10]

With this transformation of the U.S./Mexico border, known as the borderland, came rapid growth. Juarez, the shared capital (with El Paso) of the borderland, had a population of 250,000 in 1960 compared to well over a million today.[11] The same phenomenal growth has affected every *maquilas* zone from Tijuana to Matamoros. In addition to the industrial pollutants came uncontrolled human waste and garbage that contributed to water and air contamination. Protected from U.S. environmental standards, the U.S. corporations operating in Mexico could pollute at will. By the time of NAFTA in January 1994, the Rio Grande was the most contaminated river in North America (Canada, Mexico, United States) evident with high rates of childhood cancers, gallbladder problems, hepatitis, liver cancer, and even anencephalic births on both sides of the international border in the borderland. Moreover, Mexico's industrial accident and illness rate is among the highest in the world, with a rate of 23 per 100,000 workers.[12] Yet, under Mexican law maquiladoras cannot be sued for work-related injuries or illnesses. The only recourse is a legally capped disability payment from the Mexican government. Under this arrangement, U.S. and other foreign companies have little incentive to clean up the work environment of their maquiladoras.

The Mexican jobs along the U.S. border did not eliminate the influx of undocumented workers because the maquiladoras employed women, most of whom left the rural countryside to migrate to the border frontier of Mexico. This disrupted the traditional rural Mexican family and community system where women provided mostly unpaid labor. Soon young unemployed or underemployed men followed the migrating women to the borderland where many crossed into the United States illegally for work on farms, ranches, and in construction. Even then the legal Mexican immigration figures rose from under 500,000 during the period from 1961 to 1970 to over 1,600,000 in the 1991 to 1996 period. Illegal immigration figures are estimated to be even higher.[13]

NAFTA—Mexico's Transformation to Capitalism

In our 2004 book, *NAFTA & Neocolonialism,* Manzanarez articulated the political changes that set the stage for Mexico's entry into the North American Free Trade Agreement. He noted that a struggle within the PRI ruling elite emerged between the politicos and the technocrats with the latter emerging victorious in the last decades of the 20th century. Indeed, the last three presidents, Miguel de la Madrid, Carlos Salinas, and Ernesto Zedillo all held graduate degrees from prestigious U.S. Ivy League schools. Schooled in free market capitalism, Madrid, Salinas, and Zedillo changed the historic politico's revolutionary mandate of government intervention in the social and economic spheres of Mexican life. U.S. influence in promoting these candidates, even in the face of voting irregularities, was evident in President Reagan's highly public congratulation to Carlos Salinas de Gortari in the highly disputed elections of 1988:

Allegations of fraud were widely documented. For instance, ballot boxes stolen or taken by force by PRI sympathizers were found in garbage dumps, along side riverbeds, etc. If the electoral process was tainted during the campaigning period and during election day, the counting of ballots produced an amazing mishap. The night of the counting the whole computer system broke down allegedly to give the PRI-dominated electoral council time to cook up the results. That is, to rearrange the results in order to assure the PRI's candidate victory.[14]

These actions guaranteed Mexico's support for NAFTA while setting the stage for the PRI's political demise. PRI began to lose mayoral races including in Mexico City in 1997, and governorships beginning in 1989, and eventually the presidency itself in 2000. The genesis of NAFTA in Mexico took a different route than what occurred in Canada and the United States:

On the economic side the 1990s showed a mixed picture. The reestablishment of international confidence was based on the pro free market measures undertaken in the 1980s and its rapid, uninterrupted continuation by the Salinas de Gortari administration. Talks about a tripartite free trade agreement began in earnest in the early 1990s. By the fall of 1993, the U.S. Congress had approved the passage of NAFTA. As contrasted with the U.S. where there was debate about the merits of such an agreement both in the public opinion arena and in Congress [as well as among presidential candidates in 1992]—in Mexico such debate did not take place, with the exception of selected groups in the economic and political spheres. In general, then, dissenting views were stifled.[15]

Passage of NAFTA had an immediate negative impact in Mexico when, on the same day that the accord went into effect, January 1, 1994, the Ejercito Zapatista de Liberacion Nacional (Zapatista Army of National Liberation) the EZLN, declared war on Mexico. The EZLN was comprised of Maya Indians living in one of the poorest states in Mexico. Chiapas is located on its southern border with Guatemala, and Guatemalans make up to a third of the state's population. The Zapatistas took their name from the famous revolutionary leader, Emiliano Zapata, who led the Army of the South while Pancho Villa led the Army of the North during the Mexican Revolution. The Zapatistas were concerned that NAFTA would undermine the revolutionary efforts for land distribution and support for the ejidos, the community-owned land tracts doled out to campesinos. Indeed, a major concern was the element of NAFTA that obviated article 27, section 7 of the Mexican Constitution, which guaranteed land reparations especially to indigenous Indian groups. Indian and Mestizo groups knew that they could not compete with U.S.-subsidized agribusiness especially if the Mexican government ended support for small collective farms that have long been the backbone of Mexican agriculture.

The actual war was short-lived, effectively ending less than two weeks later on January 12, 1994. This ceasefire was arranged by Bishop Samuel Ruíz of the Catholic diocese in San Cristobal de las Casa, resulting in the Zapatistas holding on to some of the lands they occupied in the short war. However, even these holdings were lost when the Mexican army invaded the region 13 months later in February 1995. The Mexican army failed to capture the movement's leaders who made public media appearances with face masks. Most notable of these leaders is Subcomandante Marcos. International outrage forced the Mexican government to negotiate with the EZLN. The EZLN became an international symbol for the antiglobalization movement, which fought the internationalization of world markets. Both the World Trade Organization (WTO) and NAFTA became the targets of this opposition. In 1996, the Intercontinental Encounter for Humanity and against Neo-liberalism was held in Chiapas—home to the EZLN. Indeed, pro-Zapatista support groups soon emerged in the United States, Argentina, Austria, Britain, France, Italy, Spain, and Switzerland.

Federal recognition for the EZLN came in 1996 with the signing of the San Andres Accords that reinstated the autonomy and special rights of the indigenous populations. The Zapatistas took the initiative and created 32 autonomous municipalities in Chiapas state despite some federal objections. By 2003 these autonomous units (ejidos) had created their own local governments (juntas) where they implement communal programs. The juntas are in turn organized into larger units—Juntas of Good Government. Together these juntas represent a shadow EZLN government operating alongside the Mexican government (which alone holds the legal authority to tax Mexican residents). Two years from the date of their revolution, the EZLN began "The Other Campaign," extending their influence to all 31 Mexican states, claiming now to represent all workers of the city and the countryside, including laborers, farmers, students, and teachers. In January 2007, Subcomandante Marcos and the EZLN expanded its mandate to include all indigenous peoples of the Americas through its "Intercontinental Indigenous Encounter." A year later, on January 1, 2008, the EZLN held the "Third Encuentro of the Zapatistas People with the People of the World."

According to Manzanarez, as the trade agreement went into effect in January 1994, reactions began immediately. Calling themselves the Frente Zapatista de Liberacion National, or The Zapatista National Liberation Front (EZLN), on the first day of the year and in southern Mexico, a group of hooded rebels, mostly Indians, attacked military posts and took several towns in the southern state of Chiapas, a noted region of the country with large neglected rural and Indian populations. The native Indian tribes (pueblos), felt that by supporting NAFTA the PRI was abandoning the land reforms earned during the Mexican Revolution. In the past campesinos expressed their support for the PRI by herding cattle into cities and towns to parade and show support for PRI political candidates whether he or she was running for local or national office. This practice earned the Indian peasants the term *acarreados*—the herded ones.

Notwithstanding the official revolutionary rhetoric, which promoted the advancement of the rural sector and its population, only on sporadic occasions did the PRI-led political system actually take seriously its own platform. The only president of Mexico (in a very strong presidential system) who attempted to improve the campesino and Indian condition was Lazaro Cardenas. While the dispensation of benefits continued in the form of bank loans and the distributions of fertilizers, and other farm subsidies, some of these efforts were haphazardly done and often only around election times. It certainly appeared that government aid to campesinos was contingent more on the promise of political support for a candidate than on confirmed needs. Another practice was for local authorities to hoard tons of fertilizer and then give it or sell it cheaply to whomever they wanted when soliciting the support of the campesinos. This system of corruption and distribution of government aid permeated the whole political arena in rural Mexico. Small wonder the rural sector, particularly the ejido element, had been severely criticized as inefficient. Much of the aid, it must be added, came late and rarely served to expand agricultural production, only to save whatever was planted that year. In other words, the campesinos received just enough aid to salvage some of their crops and assure them a meager subsistence based on corn and beans. Clearly, this political process created a self-fulfilling prophecy of marginalizing the rural campesino.

The emergence of the EZLN put Indians' plight, most of whom are campesinos, in the forefront of public discussion. Now the ruling elites could no longer hide the horrible conditions in which large segments of Mexico live. The Indians' uprising was a strong reminder that Mexico's perception of itself was at least partially flawed. Ironically, 1994, was the year Mexico was to embark on its quest to join the World Trade Organization and join the other industrialized countries of the world. Instead, it was the year of armed uprisings, political crimes, and economic crisis. Another reminder of political instability in Mexico was when PRI presidential candidate Luis Donaldo Colosio was gunned down in the northern border city of Tijuana [borderland], a well-known center of operations for one of the strongest drug cartels in Mexico. Another assassination followed in September. This time it was Jose Ruíz Massieu, a former governor of the southern state of Guerrero and recently named head of PRI. Both of these high-profile assassinations followed on the heels of the shooting that took Cardinal Posadas Ocampo's life in 1993. None of these assassinations have been fully investigated and are attributed to drug trafficking and political corruption. It appears that one of the biggest capitalist endeavors in Mexico is supplying illicit drugs to its northern neighbors.[16]

CHAPTER 6

Social and Human Justice Issues

IMMIGRATION ISSUES SINCE NAFTA: LAWS AND TRENDS

A review of U.S. immigration laws from the mid-1960s to the present day indicates the changing collective mood of society following the civil rights era up to the reactions of the September 11, 2001, terrorist attacks on New York City and Washington, DC. These social trends resulted in certain adaptations being made to the immigration laws. As stated earlier, the most significant modern changes in U.S. immigration laws occurred with passage of the Immigration and Nationality Act of 1952 (McCarran-Walter Act), when race-based quotas were replaced with nationality-based quotas. The INA created the Immigration and Nationalization Service, the federal agency mandated to enforce the law. The lexicon of the INA defined an "alien" as anyone lacking citizenship or status as a national of the United States. The different categories of aliens included "resident" and "nonresident," "immigrant" and "nonimmigrant," and "documented" and "undocumented." The latter category represents "illegal" immigrants.

It is also important to realize that the U.S. Congress has original jurisdiction and complete authority over immigration issues. While the U.S. president can suggest changes in the immigration laws, his/her authority is limited solely to refugee policy. By the same token, the U.S. judiciary is limited to acting on the constitutionality of aliens' rights. States have limited legislative authority and can only participate in immigration matters as invited partners with federal authorities. The combined effect of the turbulent protests of the 1960s during the civil rights and Vietnam era and the ending of the Bracero Program opened the gates to a flood of illegal immigration into the United States, resulting in the Immigration and Reform Control Act (IRCA) of 1986 during the Reagan administration. The IRCA both toughened legal sanctions for employers hiring illegal aliens and provided amnesty for those already in the country. This act also restrained illegal aliens from participating in federal welfare programs while the Immigration Marriage Fraud Amendments attempted to curtail the practice of phony marriages for the purpose of obtaining U.S. citizenship. The Immigration Act of 1990 revised the standards set forth in 1952, which abolished the exclusions against Asians and gave preference based upon educational and skills levels, by equalizing the allocation of visas across nations, thereby opening up immigration worldwide.

Six years later, as a reaction to the Oklahoma City bombing (a domestic terrorist act), the Illegal Immigration Reform and Immigrant Responsibility Act of 1996 (IIRIRA) reflected the era of stricter immigration policies. The IIRIRA addressed five major areas: (Title I) improvements to border control, facilitation of legal entry, and interior enforcement; (Title II) enhanced enforcement and penalties against alien smuggling and document fraud; (Title III) inspection, apprehension, detention, adjudication, and removal of inadmissible and deportable aliens; (Title IV) enforcement of restrictions against employment; and (Title V) restrictions on benefits for aliens. The term "entry" was changed to "admission," broadening the requirement for all aliens, regardless of point of arrival (designated port or not), to submit to an inspection by U.S. Customs. The same year Congress passed and President Clinton signed the Antiterrorism and Effective Death Penalty Act (AEDPA). The AEDPA reflected the emotions of the time regarding the Oklahoma City bombing while attempting to strengthen the recently reinstated federal death penalty. While the federal jurisdiction is limited to federal lands, including federally recognized Indian reservations, the AEDPA greatly limited the use of habeas corpus reviews in death sentences, regardless of jurisdiction of origin. The AEDPA also restricted the power of federal judges to grant relief to either state or federal capital-punishment adjudications. Many feel that the AEDPA gives too much power to the U.S. Supreme Court in death sentence cases, especially when the question of political influence was raised following the court's involvement in the 2000 presidential elections.[1]

Following the terrorist attacks of 9/11, the United States created the Department of Homeland Security on March 1, 2003, replacing the INS and placing these responsibilities under three agencies: (1) U.S. Customs and Border Enforcement (CBE), (2) U.S. Citizenship and Immigration Services (USCIS), and (3) U.S. Immigration and Customs Enforcement (ICE). The U.S. Border Patrol now falls under the CBE while ICE takes over the INS function of deportation. The U.S. Border Patrol now has some 11,000 agents with more than 9,500 stationed at its southern border, patrolling the U.S. region of the Borderland with plans of expanding this force by 48 percent

again, placing most of the new force in its nine southwest border field offices. Nearly 99 percent of all people currently arrested entering the United
States illegally are citizens of Mexico. The USCIS deals with asylum, naturalization, and permanent residence functions. Specifically, Section 103,
under other officers of the department, provisions were made for the under secretary for border and transportation security with three subordi-
nates: (1) director, Office for Domestic Preparedness, (2) assistant secretary
of the Bureau of Border Security, and (3) director, Bureau of Citizenship
and Immigration Services. Section 402 spelled out the responsibilities of
the under secretary for border and transportation:

- Preventing the entry of terrorists and instruments of terrorism into the U.S
- Securing the borders, territorial waters, ports, terminals, waterways, and air,
  land, and sea transportation systems of the U.S.
- Immigration enforcement
- Controlling visas and conditions for entry of aliens
- Administering the customs laws of the U.S.
- Agricultural import and entry inspection activities[2]

The Politicalization of Mexican Immigration to the United States

Clearly, the terrorist attacks on the United States on September 11, 2001,
were the defining acts that obstructed the progress on the immigration
front following the North American Free Trade Agreement (NAFTA) of
1994. Ironically, progress was being made in February 2001 with the recommendations of the U.S.-Mexico Migration Panel. This momentum was due
mainly to the initiatives of the Carnegie Endowment for International Peace
and the International Migration Police Program in conjunction with the
Faculty of International Relations of the Instituto Technologico Autonomo
de Mexico (ITAM). This panel addressed the incongruence between the exchange of goods and services and labor since the introduction of NAFTA,
stating:

In a process accelerated by NAFTA, the United States and Mexico have intention-
ally sought to deepen levels of economic integration and interdependence. However, conflict is generated by the fact that on the one hand, the free flow of capital,
goods, and services has been institutionalized and expanded, and on the other
hand, the flow of labor has been the subject of massive enforcement efforts and
legal restrictions. If the United States and Mexico wish to reduce significantly the
strain on their extraordinary positive progress on integration, they must appre-
ciate that it will be increasingly difficult to be partners on economic issues and
antagonists on migration issues.

With the rate of integration increasing apace, there is a clear convergence in
the labor markets of both countries, as an even more robust demand for low and

medium skilled workers in the Unites States has relied increasingly on Mexican immigrants, both legal and illegal. . . . Both countries are in the grasp of important demographic transitions that modify the calculus both about the likely size of future emigration flows from Mexico and about their desirability in the United States. On the U.S. side, the baby boom generation will pass into retirement over the next fifteen years, and immigrants and their children will be needed to help pay the taxes that fund their retirement. On the Mexican side, after a period of intense population growth, analysts expect that the nation's declining fertility rate will continue to decrease. This means that the annual growth rate of the population segment most likely to emigrate, those between 15 and 44 years of age, will continue to decrease, and that the number of Mexicans entering the labor force for the first time will actually be declining. If the Mexican economy experiences sustained growth, and if wise social investments in education and social protections are made, migration pressure are expected to recede gradually over the next 15 to 20 years.[3]

This bilateral plan provided the basis for a "grand bargain" whereby migration from Mexico to the United States would be mutually beneficial to both countries as well as being safe, legal, orderly, and predictable. Toward this end the grand bargain would be based on four elements:

- "Improving the Treatment of Mexican Migrants": The basis for transforming the U.S.-Mexico migration relationship is to make legality the prevailing norm. To achieve this, the United States should, over time, make legal status available to unauthorized Mexicans who are established and working, and channel future flows of migrants through legal streams. Moving on one front and not the other will simply perpetuate the unacceptable status quo.

- "Making Legal Status more widely available": Although almost two thirds of the Mexican immigrant population in the United States are legal permanent residents or U.S. citizens, an estimated half of the undocumented immigrants living in the United States are Mexican-born. In recent years, Congress has taken positive steps to regularize the legal status of certain long-established immigrants, including many Mexicans. In contrast to these targeted measures, in 1986, President Ronald Reagan signed into law a comprehensive legalization program that enabled previously undocumented immigrants to enjoy a more stable workforce, families to remain united, individuals to secure social protections, and, over time, immigrants to fully incorporate into and participate in their communities. The panel recommends that the Bush Administration work with Congress to fashion measures that institute legalizing mechanisms for hard-working, taxpaying, and well-established undocumented immigrants . . .

- "Making Legal Work Visas more widely available": For many intended migrants from Mexico, there is simply no available means to obtain a legal visa to enter and work in the United States. Initially, many migrants want to work in the United States for brief periods, usually a matter of months (a process referred to as "circularity"). Over time, some want to establish residence in the United States permanently. Annually, an estimated 150,000 Mexican migrants enter the United States without authorization and remain for longer than a year. . . . As a starting point, the panel believes that programs that bring in immigrant workers on temporary work visas in response to measurable labor market needs should strive to meet the following criteria: equitable labor rights that can be meaningfully enforced (including visa portability, when appropriate), access to social and health protections, and reasonable mechanisms for securing permanent residence for migrants who qualify for it and choose to do so..

- "Special and Equal Treatment for NAFTA partners": The panel believes that unequal treatment of the NAFTA partners is inconsistent with the spirit of the trilateral agreement and recommends equality of treatment with Canada as one of the central themes of the U.S.-Mexico relationship on legal immigration. . . . Furthermore, the panel believes that the special economic relationship institutionalized by NAFTA, based in large part on interdependence and geographic contiguity, warrants a broader and more special immigration relationship. One option that deserves serious consideration is removing both Canada and Mexico from the normal immigration formula (the per country limits that restrict permanent family and employment based immigrant visas per year for any one country to 25,620) as an expression of formally recognizing the special relationship of Mexico and Canada.[4]

The U.S.-Mexico Migration Panel also stated that both countries needed to cooperate in order to curb illegal border activities, including human and drug smuggling. This can only be done, they warned, with joint strategies and coordinated operations. On the other hand, the panel also warned that serious efforts needed to be made toward making the border a safer area for those who do attempt to enter the U.S. illegally. They suggested warning signs be posted near dangerous regions of the border and that both countries coordinate joint training and rescue operations. Most emphatically, the panel wanted the United States to freeze the construction of additional fences along the border. In June 2001, the Mexico-U.S. Advocates Network met in Mexico City adding to these recommendations. The U.S. Advocates had four additions:

- Legalize Mexico-U.S. migration;
- Strengthen labor rights and social protections by including health care benefits and effective labor law enforcement;
- Develop new strategies for immigration law enforcement including accountability and human rights protection; And
- Develop new economic strategies that include the borderlands including financial and infrastructure support from governments and international financial institution.

The Mexican Advocates had three new recommendations:

- Better control deaths in the borderland region;
- Revisit the guest workers program while at the same time providing amnesty for undocumented workers currently in the United States; And
- Develop better immigration and law enforcement strategies in Mexico.

A few months later, in the aftermath of the United States' reaction to the 9/11 terrorist attacks, the work of these bilateral committees became one of the first casualties of America's xenophobia as the backlash of these attacks included hostility directed toward the United States' southern border.

The best demographic data on Hispanic immigrants, notably those of Mexican descent, comes from the Pew Hispanic Center. Hispanic demographics today extend far beyond the borderland region. Nonetheless, a review of the borderland post–September 11, 2001, indicates a region of increasing violence and poverty. In 2006, it was estimated that nearly 12 million people resided on the U.S. side of the U.S./Mexico border with about one-quarter living below the U.S. poverty level often in *colonias*.[5] Colonias abound on both sides of the U.S./Mexico border, providing the most common transitional communities in the borderland. These are unincorporated, semirural hovels consisting of substandard housing, questionable water and sewer infrastructures, and often without public services or police protection. Approximately 300,000 Hispanics live in 1,300 colonias in Texas and New Mexico alone. More exist across the border in Mexico.

Pew estimates of unauthorized migrants in the United States in 2005 shows the top 10 magnet states to be as follows:

- California with 2,500,000 to 2,750,000;
- Texas with 1,400,000 to 1,600,000;
- Florida with 800,000 to 950,000;
- New York with 550,000 to 650,000;
- Arizona with 400,000 to 450,000;
- Illinois with 375,000 to 425,000;
- Georgia with 350,000 to 450,000;
- New Jersey with 350,000 to 425,000;
- North Carolina with 300,000 to 400,000;
- Virginia with 250,000 to 300,000.[6]

The other borderland state, New Mexico, had between 50,000 to 75,000 illegal immigrants, a substantial number given the state's low population density. The other three borderland states, California, Texas, and Arizona, fall within the top 10 also relevant to their population density. Florida, New York, and New Jersey most likely have substantial Hispanic illegals that are not of Mexican descent (Cubans, South and Central Americans . . .). Even with these numbers, the United States issued over 900,000 nonimmigrant visas for Mexicans in 2005, including 732,566 laser visas for those borderland residents who reside in Mexico but who cross the international border daily to work at jobs in the United States.[7]

Immigrants of Mexican descent account for nearly 30 percent of all foreign born in the United States. According to the Pew Hispanic Center, annual birth to Hispanic women in general exceeded one million for the first time in 2006. They estimate that one-in-four children under age five in the United States is of Hispanic origin. Hispanics now comprise 15.5 percent of the U.S. population with 62 percent of this growth attributed to births. Of the unauthorized aliens of Hispanic descent, about 70 percent are from Mexico. Key demographic factors relevant to Hispanic females compiled in 2007 are:

- Hispanic women are younger with a median age of 41 compared to 47 for non-Hispanic women.
- Hispanic women have a fertility rate that is one-third higher than that of non-Hispanic women.
- Over half (52%) of Hispanic women are immigrants and have a fertility rate that is 30 percent higher than their native-born Hispanic counterparts.
- Over 40 percent of Hispanic women who gave birth in 2005–2006 were unmarried compared to 34 percent for non-Hispanic women. Even then the rate was higher for native-born Hispanics (50%) compared to immigrants (35%).
- Hispanic women are less educated than non-Hispanic women with 35 percent having less than a high school education compared to only 10 percent for non-Hispanic women.
- Hispanic women work primarily in blue-collar jobs such as building and landscape services, food preparation, and services and manufacturing.
- Twenty percent of Hispanic women live in poverty compared to 11 percent for non-Hispanic women.

Another family factor is that 88 percent of the children of Hispanics born in the United States speak English well in comparison to only 23 percent for their immigrant parents.[8]

Nearly half of all unauthorized migrants in the United States entered legally through a port of entry such as a border crossing, dock, or airport. Of the estimated 12 million unauthorized migrants (2006 figure) up to six million entered the country legally. Most (four to five-and-a-half million) entered with nonimmigrant visas as tourist or business visitors while another 250,000 to 500,000 entered using Border Crossing Cards. Even then, this represents only a fraction of the estimated 180 million people who enter the United States yearly under these conditions.[9] And Mexicans make up only a fraction of those who enter legally but overstay their visa conditions. Mexican illegal immigrants mainly come to the United States for work or to be with a family member already residing in the country. Interestingly, the Pew Hispanic Center suggests that the vast majority of the over six million undocumented Mexican migrants were gainfully employed in their native land prior to making the trek northward. This fact challenges the assumption that Mexican workers come to the United States due to a lack of employment opportunities. A relevant factor, however, is the economic picture in Mexico, including wages, job quality and security, and occupational mobility. Even then the occupations available for Mexican immigrants include those jobs low in wages and educational requirements. Yet, often these wages and conditions are far superior to the working conditions they had in Mexico. Moreover, the jobs that attract Mexican workers are those with low status in the United States, a condition that does not have that much of an impact on the Mexican worker. The Pew Hispanic Center estimates $300 per/week to be the median wage earned by Mexican migrants in the United States in 2006. The best paying jobs are in construction but the downturn in the U.S. economy has seen reverses in the Hispanic job market during 2008. The unemployment rate for Hispanics in the United States was 6.5 percent in the first quarter of 2008 in comparison to 4.7 percent for non-Hispanics. Hispanic workers lost a quarter million due to the construction slump ignited by the housing crisis in the United States. Competition for work once thought as low status by non-Hispanics has also resulted in the loss of some 130,000 jobs for Hispanic women recently. In the past, these factors have served to slow the flow of immigrants from Mexico. Indeed, the latest figures for 2008 indicate that the illegal immigration population slowed during the period of 2005 to 2008 to about 500,000 per year in comparison to the 800,000 per year for the period 2000 to 2004. Even then the illegal immigration population has grown by more than 40 percent since 2000 with the most recent estimate (March 2008) being 11.9 million, comprising 4 percent of the total U.S. population. Of this, those of Mexican descent account for seven million illegal aliens. The recent economic downturn in the United States has also impacted illegal immigrant families with income falling at a greater rate than that for U.S. citizens.[10]

Farmworkers, among the lowest paid immigrants, continue to be exploited according to the Southern Poverty Law Center, which has initiated a lawsuit against Del Monte Fresh Produce, Inc. In this case, Del Monte claimed that they were not responsible for migrant farmworkers cheated out of legal wages since they were a third party that used subcontractors to provide these workers. The case currently before the United States District Court for the Northern District of Georgia (2008) is to show that Del Monte Fresh Produce Southeast is, in fact, jointly responsible for the hiring and paying of seasonal migrant workers. In the suit it was noted that the plaintiffs are migrant and seasonal agricultural laborers who worked on Del Monte Fresh Produce Southeast's Helena, Georgia, farms at various times during the 2003, 2004, 2005, and 2006 harvest season. These workers were recruited to work on Del Monte Fresh Produce Southeast's farms by a third-party farm labor contractor, Rojas Harvesting. Given that Rojas Harvesting was a subcontractor, Del Monte Fresh Produce Southeast, according to the plaintiffs, (1) failed to pay the promised wage rate for all hours worked on its Helena farms and (2) violated federal laws governing the wages and working conditions of migrant and seasonal agricultural workers while Del Monte contended that the agricultural workers were employed solely by the third-party labor contractors who recruited and directly hired them. But the court found that Rojas Harvesting was Del Monte Fresh Produce Southeast's primary labor contractor and supplied the majority of workers used in Del Monte Fresh Produce Southeast's Helena operations while Del Monte Fresh Produce Southwest provided and serviced all forklifts, tractors, and other field and warehouse machinery used in the Helena operations as well as the sacks for fieldworkers. Essentially, Del Monte provided most of the tools, material, and services critical to the plaintiffs' work. It was also brought out that Rojas Harvesting's main labor recruiter was an agent of Del Monte Fresh Produce Southeast with no specialized training or experience in agriculture. In its decision the court found that the relevant factors in this case weighed in favor of joint employment, and that the plaintiffs were at least as economically dependent on Del Monte Fresh Produce Southeast as they were on their third-party farm labor contractors.[11]

The farmworkers, the majority of Mexican descent, won the first round in this case with the help of the Southern Poverty Law Center, but the case now goes back to court to prove how much the 500 migrant farmworkers were cheated through this Del Monte third-party "filed bosses" scam.

The United States public, in general, continues to have divided views about migrant workers. The Pew Hispanic Center reviewed the state of American public opinion on immigration in 2006 with the following findings:

- The public appeared almost evenly divided on whether immigration is good for the country or not.
- Americans were split over levels of legal immigration. Significant minorities of roughly a third or more favor the opposite approaches of keeping legal immigration at its present levels or decreasing it. A smaller share favors increasing legal immigration.
- A significant majority of Americans saw illegal immigration as a very serious problem and most others see it at least as a serious problem.
- A majority of Americans believed that illegal immigrants are taking jobs Americans do not want.
- A majority of Americans appeared to favor measures that would allow illegal immigrants currently in the United States to remain in the country either as permanent residents and eventually citizens or as temporary workers who will have to go home eventually. When those options were presented, only a minority favored deporting all illegal migrants or otherwise forcing them to go home.
- Americans generally expressed greater confidence in Democrats on immigration issues than Republicans.
- A majority of Americans disapproved of the way that President Bush was handling immigration issues.[12]

During the 2008 U.S. presidential elections the Mexican migrant issue heated up especially in the Southwest, most notably in Arizona, the home state of the Republican candidate—John McCain.

Vigilantes and the Manifestation of Hate for Mexican Migrants

Negative stereotyping of Mexican illegal immigrants is fostered by both the political establishment and certain elements of the media. At the Mexico/U.S. Border Conference held in Puerto Penasco, Mexico, in September 2007, then Homeland Security Secretary Michael Chertoff defended the construction of the border fence along the U.S. side of the international border for environmental reasons: "Illegal migrants really degrade the environment. I've seen pictures of human waste, garbage, discarded bottles and other human artifacts in pristine areas. And believe me, that is the worst thing you can do to the environment."[13] This argument defies logic especially given the remote areas where aliens are now being forced to cross into the United States. Moreover, the Bureau of Land Management (BLM), often referred to as the "Bureau of Livestock and Mining" due to its questionable deals with local ranchers and mining companies, allowed this region to be abused by overgrazing, unrestricted mining, and environmental destruction by all-terrain motorcycles and four-wheelers. The border area has long been trashed, poisoned by slag heaps and heavy metals, and shot up by American citizens who find the cacti inviting targets. These abuses have been rampant since the mid-1800s and it is foolhardy to start blaming Mexican migrants for this problem or to even feign concern for this long-neglected desert region. Indeed, the San Pedro River region of southern Arizona, a popular entry route due to the availability of water, was not protected by the BLM until November 1988 when Congress passed the Arizona-Idaho Conservation Act creating the San Pedro Riparian National Conservation Area. To blame illegal Mexican aliens for abuse of their former land, especially given the harsh conditions the U.S. Border Patrol has created for them in running the border gauntlet, is preposterous.[14] Yet, statements such as this by the government only help fuel the anti-immigration furor along the U.S./Mexico border.

Clearly, white supremacists, including neo-Nazi and militia groups and border-state extremists, are at the center of the anti-immigration hate mongering. These groups include the Minutemen Project, Ranch Rescue, the Minuteman Civil Defense Corps (MCDC), and Skinheads as well as members of the Aryan Nation and other antigovernment militias throughout the Southwest. The Minuteman Civil Defense Corps cited a national citizen neighborhood watch mission statement: "It is the mission of the Minuteman Civil Defense Corps to see the borders and coastal boundaries of the United States secured against the unlawful and unauthorized entry of all individuals, contraband, and foreign military. We will employ all means of civil protest, demonstration, and political lobbying to accomplish this goal."[15] Labeled as a vigilante group by both President Bush and President Fox in 2005, the group's activities have resulted in a slowdown in border crossings, especially in Arizona, which has the highest entry segment of the borderland. Other contributing factors, however, include increased border patrolling on the Mexican side of the border as well as the increasing use of electronic and satellite surveillance, not to mention the increase in border-patrol personnel and the deployment of the National Guard along the U.S. side of the international border.

Aiding and abetting the Minuteman vigilante mission are ultraconservative religious groups and others supporting the white supremacy mantra. The operational compound for the Minuteman Project is located at the Miracle Valley Bible College in southern Arizona. Another ally is the publisher of the *Tombstone Tumbleweed*—a Cochise County periodical. National support for the anti-immigration movement comes primarily from Lou Dobbs, a former CNN anchorman who harped nightly on this issue in his *Broken Borders* segment. The Southern Poverty Law Center (SPLC) challenged Lou Dobbs on his skewed presentation of the illegal Mexican migrant issue.

The SPLC's *Intelligence Report* has long criticized Dobbs for his one-sided and often inaccurate reporting on immigrants. The controversy flared up anew after Dobbs, while appearing on a May 6, 2007, segment of the CBS show *60 Minutes,* defended a report linking immigrants to a sharp rise in the number of leprosy cases. The next day on his show, he said that he stood "100 percent behind it," and he angrily attacked SPLC Intelligence project director Mark Potok, who had appeared on *60 Minutes* as a Dobbs critic.

The SPLC, in an open letter, then urged CNN to retract the leprosy claim—specifically, that there had been 7,000 new cases of the dreaded, but easily treatable, disease in the United States over a recent three-year period. The truth is that there had been just 398 new cases during the period, an easily verifiable fact. "This is not just a matter of journalistic integrity," said SPLC president Richard Cohen. "It's a dangerous situation in which a powerful media figure is using his national platform to vilify an entire group of people. Dobbs' constant, one-sided reporting, laced with distortions, exaggerations and fabrications, poisons the national debate on immigration. And worse, it inflames racial and ethnic passions, encouraging hate and violence toward all Latinos in this country."[16]

The SPLC has documented that the number of hate groups operating in the United States climbed to 844 in 2006—a 40 percent rise since 2000. In just the past two years, 144 new nativist extremist groups also have been formed to harass and intimidate immigrants. And, according to the FBI, hate crimes against Latinos rose 23 percent between 2003 and 2005. Dobbs and some others in the media and politics are regularly using discredited and inaccurate information about immigrants—material that often originates with far-right ideologues and other organizations dominated by white supremacists and nativists.[17]

Another national organization, one authorized by the U.S. Congress, has joined Lou Dobbs in his national campaign against illegal immigrants—notably Hispanics. The American Legion, chartered by the U.S. Congress in 1919 as a patriotic, mutual-help organization for veterans serving during the time of a declared war, regardless if they served in a foreign campaign (a requirement for membership in the Veterans of Foreign Wars—VFW) is the largest veterans organization in the United States with nearly three million members in some 14,000 posts worldwide. This is not the first time that the American Legion has been involved in ultra-right controversy. In 1933, it supported the American Liberty League and its leaders, the captains of U.S. industry (DuPont, Goodyear, Bethlehem Steel, and J.P. Morgan banks) in a clandestine plan to use the veteran's organization to overthrow the Roosevelt administration and doom his New Deal.[18] Other business leaders apparently behind the American Liberty League were Henry Ford, John D. Rockefeller, and John and Allen Dulles. The plan was to muster 500,000 American Legion World War I veterans and march on Washington, DC, under the pretense of protecting the president from plotters. President Roosevelt would then be forced to resign and the American Liberty League would install a "secretary of general welfare" and a fascist regime fashioned upon that in Italy at the time. The plot was unraveled by Marine Corps General Smedley Butler, leading to a congressional investigation—the McCormack-Dickstein Committee. No arrests were made due to the social and political status of those involved.[19]

Apparently, the American Legion has joined Lou Dobbs in denigrating illegal immigrants, focusing on Mexican and other Hispanic peoples in publishing and disseminating a 34-page booklet: *Policy on Illegal Immigration: A Strategy to Address Illegal Immigration in the United States*. The SPLC, in its review of this manuscript, offered the following analysis:

Now, America's largest veterans' organization has launched another campaign—a hard-line attack on undocumented immigrants that's at odds with the legion's mainstream image. As part of this effort, the legion, which purports to speak for 2.7 million members, recently issued a booklet that regurgitates discredited and often completely false information about how "illegals" are bringing crime, disease, and terrorism to this country, even as they wreck the economy for natives. The legion's 34-page booklet, *A Strategy to Address Illegal Immigration in the United States*, asserts that "poverty, political instability, disease and war" are "on our back doorstep" because of porous borders and the failure of the government to stringently enforce immigration laws. But in making its case, the legion repeatedly cites dubious sources, ignores well-known facts and makes baseless claims—such as the false assertion that the undocumented infected more than 7,000 people in America with leprosy during a recent three-year period.

Richard Wright, a Dartmouth College geography professor who specializes in immigration stated: "These are hackneyed stereotypes that have no place in a policy document." That's not all. On April 28, 2008, when it re-leased its booklet—which was actually a repackaged version of a May 2007 legion "white paper"—the group announced that its campaign would in-clude letters to the editor, news releases from posts around the country, and six 60-second radio spots. These spots revisit some of the nastiest claims in the report, portraying undocumented immigrants as sex offenders, gang members, terrorists, and murderers. Remarkably, they are delivered by Rich-ard Fatherly, Kansas City chapter media adviser for the Minuteman Civil Defense Corps—a group whose members President Bush once denounced as "vigilantes."[20]

Fencing the Border and Creating "Death Corridors"

Crossing from Mexico into the United States has always been a journey with risks—the risk of being caught, the risk of being shot, and the risk of dying in the desert or in the hands of the handlers (coyotes). One of the most widely publicized deadly crossing events occurred in May 2003 in Victoria, Texas, as the human cargo headed for Houston. Stuffed into a locked tractor trailer without air conditioning or even adequate ventilation were over 70 Hispanics hoping to enter the United States illegally. Forty-eight were from Mexico, 15 from Honduras, 8 from El Salvador, 1 from Nicaragua, and 1 from the Dominican Republic. When the U.S. driver, Tyrone Williams, opened the container to check on his cargo, the suffering humanity gasped for air as they spilled out of the overheated trailer. Sev-enteen of the illegals were dead at the scene and two more died that night in the hospital. All victims were males including a five-year-old boy. All the females survived. Sixteen of the dead were from Mexico, and one each from Honduras, El Salvador, and the Dominican Republic. The driver fled the scene leaving the survivors to fend for themselves. The resulting binational investigation exposed a smuggling ring that stemmed from Matamoros in the Mexican state of Tamaulipas to southeast Texas. Victor Rodriguez was arrested in Mexico while his wife, Ema, and Karla Chavez were arrested in the United States as the immigrant trafficker leaders. Tyrone Williams was initially charged with a capital offense but was convicted of a lesser charge.

The details of this tragedy are well documented in Jorge Ramos's book, *Dying to Cross: The Worst Immigrant Tragedy in American History.* The book details the human element with interviews of those involved. However, Ramos also provides a critique of why a tragedy such as this occurred in the first place.

Coyotes had long since become a necessity for anyone who wanted to cross the border illegally into the United States. Because of the ever-increasing surveillance along the border—especially after the terrorist at-tacks that took place on September 11, 2001—it became very difficult for people to enter the United States on their own. That is the reason why immigrants were—and are—so willing to pay coyotes thousands of dollars per person. In the past, people could and often did enter the United States near the border towns, but now they were finding themselves forced to travel through white-hot deserts, rugged mountains, and a rapidly rushing river. Once inside the United States, they would often have to travel in sealed truck trailers, railway cars that locked from the outside, and via other exceedingly unsound transportation methods just to get away from the border. That was why so many immigrants were dying.[21]

Even before the terrorist attacks of September 11, 2001, efforts were being made to shore up border security at the major entry points within the borderland, thus forcing illegal aliens into more treacherous desert regions known as *death corridors*. As a consequence of these actions, the U.S. government makes running the border gauntlet all the more deadly. The increased militarization of the borderland region was conceived in 1993 during the Clinton administration and went in effect in 1994. This new strategy known as the Southwest Border Strategy was designed to shore up the most porous sections of the border, those adjacent to San Diego, California; Tucson, Arizona; and El Paso, Texas; and coincided with the economic crisis in Mexico over the devaluation of the peso. The economic crisis in Mexico resulted in a rapid increase in attempted border crossings into the United States in 1994 and 1995. In response, the United States initiated increased border-patrol personnel and the building of barriers in these high-traffic regions. Operation Hold the Line was initiated at the Ciudad Juarez, Mexico/El Paso, Texas, entryway, while Operation Gatekeeper addressed the main California entry from Ciudad Tijuana, Mexico, into the Imperial Beach/San Diego region, and Operation Safeguard reinforced the Nogales, Mexico/Douglas entryway to Tucson, Arizona. Operation Hold the Line was eventually expanded into southern New Mexico, forcing undocumented workers to traverse the remote, harsh desert that extended west from Sun City, New Mexico, to the east of Douglas, Arizona. In California the death corridor meant traversing the desert mountainous terrain in eastern California that extends into the Yuma region of western Arizona. With this border-security operation came the first fencing initiatives. Arizona U.S. congressman Duncan Hunter was able to get military surplus metal landing mats for use as border fencing, which was seen as being superior to the chain-link fencing constructed along the El Paso corridor. This, along with stadium lighting, ground sensors, and infrared cameras, made border security at the U.S./Mexico border resemble that of the borders that once separated Eastern Europe from its western neighbors. The April 19, 1995, domestic terrorist bombing of the federal building in Oklahoma City, Oklahoma, only served to reinforce these efforts. Ironically, these same sentiments and initiatives did not apply to the U.S./Canadian border, although under the recently enacted North American Free Trade Accord (NAFTA) all three countries were assumed to be equal economic partners. The irony is that the border-fence initiative began four years after the fall of the former Soviet Union and the dismantling of the Berlin Wall.

These border operations also resulted in an increase in border-patrol officers along the U.S./Mexico border as well as the introduction of military personnel. Again, it was Congressman Duncan Hunter who first presented legislation leading to the militarization of the borderland. In 1988, Hunter proposed using the U.S. military along the U.S./Mexico border as a supplementary force to the border patrol for the purpose of drug interdiction and for building roads and construction barriers to aid in the war on drugs. In 1994, Hunter sponsored legislation for the construction of 14 miles of security fencing along the San Diego border corridor and in 2005 introduced legislation calling for the construction of a reinforced fence along the entire U.S./Mexico border. Hunter ran unsuccessfully for the Republican presidential candidacy in the 2008 elections, having one of the strongest anti-immigration stances among the field of candidates of any political party. He consistently voted against international trade agreements including NAFTA, the World Trade Organization (WTO), and the more recent Central American Free Trade Agreement (CAFTA). Heeding Congressman Hunter's call for use of the military in the borderland, President George H. W. Bush authorized the use of the military in the war on drugs in 1989, citing these activities to be a threat to national security.

The major issue with using the U.S. military, including federalizing the National Guard, is the 1878 Posse Comitatus Act, which specifically prohibits the use of soldiers or marines as a domestic security force other than for a declaration of martial law. Exceptions included the mustering of National Guard units along the U.S./Mexico border during the Punitive Expedition following Poncho Villa's attack on the U.S. military base in southern New Mexico in 1916. Another notable exception was the federalization of the National Guard for the purpose of protecting black students following the U.S. Supreme Court's school desegregation order in the 1950s during the Eisenhower Administration. And the National Guard was employed during the turbulent riots of the 1960s, climaxing with the killing of students at Kent State University in 1970.

President George H. W. Bush's plan carried over into the Clinton administration, and the clandestine use of the military to police the borderland came under public scrutiny in 1997 when a U.S. Marine sniper team killed 18-year-old Esequiel Hernandez on May 20, making him the first American killed by U.S. military forces on native soil since the 1970 Kent State shooting by the National Guard. Mr. Hernandez was a U.S. citizen living with his family in Redford, Texas. He was tending the family goats when he was shot about a mile from his home. The publicity surrounding this event effectively shut down the military border patrols with the exception of navy and coast guard coast patrols and air surveillance provided by the U.S. Air Force.[22] In 2006, President George W. Bush reintroduced a plan for using U.S. military personnel along the southern border by enticing governors to authorize the use of their National Guard personnel for this duty. This is known as Operation Jump Start. Ostensibly, having the governors authorize the use of the National Guard for federal purposes without the president specifically federalizing them skirts the Posse Comitatus prohibition. These troops would be stationed in the borderland in Texas, New Mexico, Arizona, and California and would supposedly be under the authority of the governor of the state where they were deployed even if they were members of another state's National Guard force. While armed, the National Guard troops' duty would be to assist civilian authorities by providing logistics, intelligence, and surveillance relevant to illegal traffic crossing the international border. They would, however, be able to perform certain police duties as authorized by the governor in the state where they are deployed. The question remains as to the legality of transferring illegal aliens from supposed state authority to the federal agents like the border patrol and ICE agents. At any rate, the use of National Guard troops has extended the security coverage into the death corridor regions of the borderland.

The increase in border-patrol activity coupled with deployment of the National Guard as well as the creation of numerous roads and the environmental damage done by construction vehicles has soured some borderland residents. Other land owners have welcomed the intrusion of military, paramilitary, and increased border-patrol personnel. Some even allow the Minuteman Civil Defense Corps to construct fencing on their property and to patrol with guns and dogs. Some residents and entire communities on the U.S. side of the borderland are concerned about the increasingly widening swath that border security is mandating, with the power of federal eminent domain, to confiscate their lands and carve up their backyards. Moreover, it is questionable if these efforts are really curtailing the drug trade itself especially with more border tunnels being discovered. Unfortunately, the majority of the million plus apprehensions along the border per year are not drug dealers or terrorists but merely Mexicans coming to the United States for jobs. With the current worldwide financial crisis, both the number of illegal immigrants and the resources for extending the border fence seem to be in decline. Even then, the estimated migrant deaths at the U.S./Mexico border for the period of October 2006 to August 2007 stand at 340 verifiable deaths with the Tucson sector registering the highest fatality count with 168 deaths followed by the McAllen, Texas, sector (56 deaths) and Laredo, Texas, sector (44 deaths). El Paso had 23 deaths, Yuma 11 deaths, and San Diego 15 deaths.[23]

BORDERLAND PERILS

The "War on Drugs," RICO, and the Death Penalty Issue

Militarization along the U.S./Mexico border began under the first Bush Administration despite the 1879 Posse Comitatus Act forbidding such domestic use of the military. In 1989, President George H.W. Bush established Joint Task Force-6 (JTF-6) at Fort Bliss in El Paso, Texas. JTF-6 was created in order to provide military support to the war on drugs and was later expanded to curtail undocumented aliens from entering the United States. Here the military provided free support (personnel and equipment) to domestic law-enforcement agencies within federally designated "High Intensity Drug Trafficking Areas" within the borderland and beyond. Subsequently, JTF-6 has become the longest joint task force in U.S. history with some 70,000 troops in 30 states with over 3,000 missions from 1990 to 1997. It was the killing of Esequiel Hernandez, by a U.S. Marine Corps squad in 1997, that drew international public attention to this otherwise clandestine operation. Even then this publicity did not curtail JTF-6; it merely forced a modification in its operational standards. Since the terrorist attacks on September 11, 2001, JTF-6's mandate has increased substantially. JTF-6 is responsible for the border-patrol blockade operations initiated in 1993 (Operations Gatekeeper, Hold the Line, and Safeguard) when common urban entry points in the borderland were saturated by law enforcement coupled with the initiation of blockade fences. These actions forced undocumented aliens entering from Mexico to try more remote and dangerous areas to cross the border, resulting in a substantial increase in deaths.

On the Mexican side of the borderland, there has been increased U.S. involvement in the training of Mexican police. This effort was initiated as a post-NAFTA joint effort to fight the war on drugs as well as to curtail undocumented entries into southern Mexico from Central and South America and to reinforce the Mexican frontier with the United States. This joint law-enforcement effort, known as the Mexico-US Plenary Group on Law Enforcement, was created in 1995. The program involves coordination between the U.S. and Mexican attorney general's offices. In order to coordinate these efforts, Mexico's past president, Vicente Fox, initiated the Mexican Federal Agency of Investigation (AFI) as an independent police agency modeled after the U.S. Federal Bureau of Investigation (FBI). Since then thousands of AFI agents have been trained by the U.S. Drug Enforcement Administration and the French National Police. And before 9/11, Mexico trained its own law-enforcement officers for participation in the joint Border Patrol Search, Trauma, and Rescue Teams (BORSTAR). President George W. Bush built on these joint activities, incorporating them into his administration's Homeland Security Presidential Directive to Help Combat Terrorism. Part of this plan was to create a North American secure perimeter around the entire NAFTA zone. To date, only the Mexico/U.S. border has been jointly reinforced. Canada remains skeptical of any militarization efforts along its shared border with the United States.

The Racketeer Influence and Corrupt Organization Act (RICO) and the death penalty are briefly addressed in chapter 1 in relation to the United States' stance on capital punishment and its views on the World Court. RICO and capital punishment play a role in the undocumented immigration discussion as well. RICO, established in 1970 with subsequent modifications to include the death penalty, is a federal law that provides extended penalties for criminal acts deemed to fall within the category of organized crime. RICO applies when any 2 of 35 crimes (17 federal and 8 state statutes) are suspected of occurring within a 10-year period. These offenses include:

- Any violation of state statutes related to gambling, murder, kidnapping, arson, robbery, bribery, extortion, obscene matter, or violations of the Controlled Substances Act;
- Any act of bribery, counterfeiting, theft, embezzlement, fraud, dealing in obscene matter, obstruction of justice, slavery, racketeering, gambling, money laundering, commission of murder-for-hire, among others, of the Federal Criminal Code (Title 18 U.S.C.):
  - Embezzlement of union funds;
  - Bankruptcy or security fraud;
  - Drug trafficking;
  - Money laundering and related offenses; and/or
  - Bringing in, aiding, or assisting aliens in illegally entering the country—if this action is for financial gain.

It is evident that a number of these categories pertain to the illegal migrant issue and are not restricted to drug trafficking per se. The severity of a RICO conviction is the length of imprisonment (20 years per offense) and the fine ($25,000) as well as forfeiture of all ill-gotten gains made by the "racketeering activity." Moreover, civil litigation against a RICO defendant can recover treble damages (triple the amount of actual/compensatory damages). Among those convicted under this law was the Key West, Florida Police Department. In 1984, the Key West Police Department was declared a criminal enterprise under Federal RICO statutes, resulting in the arrest of high-ranking officials within the department, including the deputy police chief, Raymond Cassamayor, for illegal cocaine smuggling. Another drug-related RICO indictment pertains to the Hispanic gang, the Latin Kings, of the Tampa, Florida, area, resulting in the arrest of 39 members for a host of violations related to drug trafficking, murder-for-hire, and so forth.[24]

The death penalty was under Supreme Court review when RICO was introduced, obviating a capital-punishment clause at the time. However, in November 1988, President Reagan signed the Anti-Drug Abuse Act. This act included the Drug Kingpin Act (DKA), allowing the reinstatement of the federal death penalty for certain drug-related offenses. The federal death penalty was later expanded under President Clinton in September 1994 with enactment of the Violent Crime Control and Law Enforcement Act along with the Federal Death Penalty Act (FDPA). Now 50 federal offenses were death qualified. In April 1996, four more federal offenses were added as capital crimes with passage of the Antiterrorism and Effective Death Penalty Act. Since passage of the DKA in 1988, the Department of Justice requires all 93 U.S. attorneys serving in the 94 separate federal judicial districts in the United States to submit to the U.S. attorney general all death-qualified cases for review and approval. This includes cases in which the U.S. district attorney's office may not choose to select the death penalty for the offense, ultimately leaving this choice to the discretion of the Attorney General's Review Committee on Capital Cases and the U.S. attorney general, who has the final say in these capital cases. A U.S. Department of Justice report dated one year prior to the terrorist attacks on the United States in 2001 stated that from January 27, 1995, to July 20, 2000, U.S. district attorneys submitted 682 cases for review with the attorney general ultimately seeking the death penalty for 159 of these defendants. Of the cases under review, 195 defendants were of Hispanic origin.[25] And during the George W. Bush administration, the U.S. Department of Justice began adjudicating federal death-sentence cases in nondeath-penalty states, attempting to force capital punishment into these jurisdictions.

Most legal executions are conducted at the state level with the largest U.S. component of the borderland, Texas, outdistancing all others, especially since the reintroduction of capital punishment in 1976. Currently, 37 states and the federal government have the death sentence as does the U.S. military under the Uniform Code of Military Justice (UCMJ). Since 1976, capital punishment can only be used in homicide cases (*Coker v. Georgia*, 1977) with the exception of federal offenses of treason, espionage, and crimes under military jurisdiction (desertion, etc.). Two recent U.S. Supreme Court decisions outlawed the execution of the mentally retarded (*Atkins v. Virginia*, 2002) and the execution of youth—those under the age of 18 at the time of the commission of the crime (*Roper v. Simmons*, 2005). All death sentences, regardless of jurisdiction, come under direct review by an appellate court. The next step would be to file a federal habeas corpus suit.

According to the U.S. Department of Justice Bureau of Justice Statistics, 42 individuals were executed in 2007, 11 fewer than in 2006. However, the vast majority of these executions (26) occurred in Texas. Texas also accounts for the most executions since the death penalty was reinstated in 1976 with 405 people killed by the state. The next highest count in 2007 was three executions each in Alabama and Oklahoma. All those legally executed were males. At the end of 2006, 3,228 prisoners were under a sentence of death with the highest death population being in yet another borderland state—California with 660. Of the total, 358 are Hispanic inmates making up 11 percent of those with known ethnicity. Federal habeas corpus, a type of collateral death-sentence review utilized in both federal and state jurisdictions, was greatly restricted under the Antiterrorism and Effective Death Penalty Act of 1996. This act allows only one suit for habeas corpus in federal court and for compelling new evidence or gross procedural errors. If the federal courts refuse to issue a writ of habeas corpus under this law, the state's governor can set an execution date. Many civil libertarians argue that these restrictions do not allow for the discovery of new evidence subsequent to the single federal habeas corpus filing, including recanted witness testimony and DNA evidence. Toward this end, defense attorneys are filing suits under the Civil Rights Act of 1871 (42 U.S.C.: 1983), which addresses civil rights protection provisions. The most common method of execution currently in the United States is lethal injection (upheld by the U.S. Supreme Court in its 2008 decision—*Braze v. Rees*), which is used in 35 states and in federal executions conducted at the Federal Correctional Complex in Terre Haute, Indiana. Nebraska still uses electrocution as the sole method of execution.[26]

Texas leads the nation in legal executions with 361 people put to death overall. This is in addition to the state's long history of summary executions at the hands of legal and quasi-legal groups such as the Texas Rangers. In Texas, hanging was the method of legal execution from 1819 until 1923. Prior to 1923 counties were responsible for their own executions. However, when the electric chair was introduced in 1923, it was located at the State Prison in Huntsville where all subsequent legal executions have been performed. Lethal injection replaced electrocution as the method of death in 1977. Death row itself is located at the Polunsky Unit of the Texas Department of Criminal Justice in Livingston, Texas. Condemned inmates are transported to Huntsville for their execution.[27]

Discrimination charges were leveled against Texas in 1954 relevant to the exclusion of jurors of Mexican descent in petit juries. The case before the U.S. Supreme Court (Warren Court) pertained to that of Pete Hernandez, an American citizen of Mexican descent, who was convicted of murder in Jackson County, Texas, in a process that had no one of Mexican descent serving on either the grand or petit juries. The Supreme Court decision, written by Chief Justice Warren, cited the long-held practices in Texas of systematically excluding Hispanics, notably those of Mexican descent, from jury duty:

In numerous decisions, this Court has held that it is a denial of the equal protection of the laws to try a defendant of a particular race or color under an indictment issued by a grand jury, or before a petit jury, from which all persons of his race or color have, solely because of that race or color, been excluded by the State, whether acting through its legislature, its courts, or its executive officers. Although the Court has had little occasion to rule on the question directly, it has been recognized since Strauder v. West Virginia [1880] that the exclusion of a class of persons from jury service on grounds other than race or color may also deprive a defendant who is a member of that class of the constitutional guarantee of equal protection of the laws. The State of Texas would have us hold that there are only two classes—white and Negro—within the contemplation of the Fourteenth Amendment. The decisions of this Court do not support that view

. . .The Fourteenth Amendment is not directed solely against discrimination due to a "two class theory"—that is, based upon differences between "white and Negro. . . . The exclusion of otherwise eligible persons from jury service solely because of their ancestry or national origin is discrimination prohibited by the

Fourteenth Amendment. The Texas statute makes no such discrimination, but the petitioner alleges that those administering the law do.

. . . The petitioner established that 14% of the population of Jackson County were persons with Mexican or Latin American surnames, and that 11% of the males over 21 bore such names. The County Tax Assessor testified that 6 or 7 percent of the freeholders on the tax rolls of the County were persons of Mexican descent. The State of Texas stipulated that "for the last twenty-five years there is no record of any person with a Mexican or Latin American name having served on a jury commission, grand jury or petit jury in Jackson County."

The petitioner met the burden of proof imposed in Norris v. Alabama [1935]. To rebut [this] strong prima facie case . . . the State offered the testimony of five jury commissioners that they had not discriminated against persons of Mexican or Latin American descent in selecting jurors. They stated that their only objective had been to select those whom they thought were best qualified. This testimony is not enough to overcome the petitioner's case. . . .

Circumstances or chance may well dictate that no persons in a certain class will serve on a particular jury or during some particular period. But it taxes our credulity to say that mere chance resulted in there being no member of this class among the six thousand jurors called in the past 25 years. The result bespeaks discrimination, whether or not it was a conscious decision on the part of any individual jury commissioner. The judgment of conviction must be reversed.[28]

Recent controversial death-penalty cases in Texas include that of Ruben Montoya Cantu and that of Angel Maturino Resendiz, the "Railroad Killer." The Ruben Montoya Cantu case reflects many of the prejudices and corrupt practices long associated with criminal justice in Texas. Cantu was the fifth teenage offender, being 17 at the time of the alleged crime, executed by Texas, a sentence now forbidden by the U.S. Supreme Court in its 2005 *Roper v. Simmons* decision. A high school dropout and special education student who lived in the tough San Antonio barrio was executed on August 24, 1993, for the murder of Pedro Gomez on November 8, 1984. A dozen years following his execution, compelling evidence suggests that he was framed by an overzealous prosecutor and dishonest and vengeful police officers. Another Hispanic male, Juan Moreno, survived the robbery/shootings but could not identify the assailants from the pictures provided by the police, including photos of Cantu. However, four months later following a bar dispute over a game of pool, an off-duty police officer, Joe De La Luz, pulled a gun on Cantu. De La Luz apparently did not identify himself as a law-enforcement officer when the altercation began, and Cantu responded by pulling his own handgun and wounding De La Luz. The police then attempted to frame Cantu with the Gomez murder by pressuring Moreno, an undocumented Mexican, to identify Cantu as the robber/shooter in the November case. Based on Moreno's testimony, Cantu was convicted and sentenced to death.

In the aftermath of Cantu's execution, Sam Millsap, the district attorney in the Cantu case, reviewed the material, drawing the conclusion that Cantu was very likely innocent of this crime. Part of this new evidence is Juan Moreno's claim that he felt pressured by the police to identify Cantu as the killer even though he did not look at all like the shooter. And with the death sentence removed for youth committing murder prior to their

18th birth date, David Garza, who was 15 at the time of the robbery/shooting, admitted that he was an accomplice to the robbery/assault and that Ruben Cantu was not his partner in this crime. Even then, the district attorney at the time of these disclosures, Susan Reed, sought not to go after the corrupt police officers involved but rather to bring charges of "murder by perjury" against Juan Moreno—blaming the victim who was seriously injured by the shootings instead of pursing misconduct charges against the police involved in the case. Susan Reed was the judge who rejected Cantu's 1988 appeal and who set his execution date for 1993.[29]

The case of Angel Maturino Resendiz, known as the Railway Killer, illustrates the complexity of the U.S. criminal-justice system relevant to that of our NAFTA and European counterparts. A major departure concerns the death penalty. Canada, Mexico, and the EU have abolished the death sentence and are reluctant to extradite death-qualified suspects to the United States for adjudication. More problematic is the issue of nation-of-origin representation in U.S. judicial proceedings, especially those with the potential for capital punishment. As mentioned earlier, Mexico took the United States to the World Court (International Court of Justice—ICJ), the judicial arm of the United Nations housed at the Peace Palace in The Hague in the Netherlands. In *Mexico v. United States,* the former accused the latter of violating article 36 of the 1963 Vienna Convention on Consular Relations, which both countries endorsed. Mexico's concern is the failure of U.S. jurisdictions to notify convicted Mexican nationals of their right to consular assistance, including 54 sentenced to death for their crimes. These condemned Mexican offenders were convicted in nine states, including three of the four within the borderland—California, Texas, and Arizona. The other states are Arkansas, Florida, Nevada, Ohio, Oklahoma and Oregon.

Angel Maturino Resendiz represents this international dilemma. Resendiz is alleged to have murdered as many as 15 people using weapons of convenience such as rocks and tools at the site of the crimes. His apparent motive was robbery and burglary. Some of these items were later recovered at his home in Mexico. Many of his victims were assaulted while they slept. His major mode of transportation was hopping trains from one location to the next. Few would argue that this crime wave needed to be brought to a close. The difference was in the method of punishment. Mexico has a 40-year maximum sentence, one that would have put Resendiz in his late seventies or eighties when released if convicted in his own country. But in the United States, this was a death sentence in the states where these crimes occurred—Texas, Florida, Georgia, Kentucky, and Illinois. Another problem was that he was back in Mexico when he was indicted for these crimes and Mexico would not extradite him due to the death-penalty issue. Instead, U.S. law enforcement enticed Resendiz back to Texas under the false pretense that he would not be indicted under a federal death warrant even though he was on the FBI's 10 Most Wanted Fugitives list.

Under this pretense, a Texas Ranger convinced members of Resendiz's family to get him to surrender. The ruse worked, and Drew Carter, a Texas Ranger, brought Resendiz across the border at El Paso, Texas, in July 1999. Convicted in Texas of murder, Resendiz was executed by lethal injection on June 27, 2006. He was 46. During the same period, a Texas jury found white millionaire Robert Durst innocent of any charge, including murder, for killing an elderly neighbor whose body was dismembered and thrown into Galveston Bay. Durst, who is also implicated in other murders, said he accidentally shot his neighbor, Morris Black, and then cut up the body whose head was never found. To complicate matters, Durst was impersonating a female and using a stolen identification of Dorothy Ciner at the time to avoid a New York investigation into the 1982 disappearance of his first wife, Kathleen. Between his indictment and trial Durst jumped bail and was apprehended six weeks later in Pennsylvania when he was caught shoplifting a five-dollar sandwich. So much for Texas justice.[30]

The Resendiz case highlights the issues brought before the International Court of Justice (World Court) by Mexico (*Mexico v. United States*) in January 2003. To reiterate this concern, Mexico aired its frustration relevant to consular input in U.S. courts, in both state and federal jurisdictions, regarding Mexican nationals, notably those charged with capital offenses. Here, Mexico claimed that the United States breached its treaty obligations under article 36 of the 1963 Vienna Convention on Consular Relations. More than a year later, the World Court (ICJ) ruled in favor of Mexico. Among the problems cited was the U.S. court's reluctance to include diplomatic input from the offender's consular's office as well as a failure to address adequate legal remedies in these matters. In its presentation before the ICJ, Mexico noted that it had established 45 consulates in the United States specifically for the purpose of advising and assisting Mexican nationals charged with crimes in the United States. The function of the consulates is to provide interpreters or legal counsel, to advise Mexican nationals of their right to abstain from making statements without legal counsel, and to provide guidance relevant to decisions regarding plea bargaining. The consul's role is also to obtain records, documents, and other relevant evidence for the defense. The consul can also provide family members and other witnesses critical to establishing mitigating circumstances especially in the second phase of U.S. capital cases. All of these efforts were thwarted by U.S. jurisdictions at both the state and federal court levels, resulting in the hastened execution of Mexican nationalists without international due process provisions outlined by article 36.

However, while the ICJ ruled in Mexico's favor, it also deferred to U.S. sovereignty, leaving these corrective measures to the United States to remedy under its judicial review process. This is not likely to happen under the conservative and isolationist U.S. Supreme Court. Prospects for better international relations rests with the Obama administration. With his administration comes the likelihood that he will be able to nominate more new Supreme Court justices in addition to Justice Sotomayor. As it stands now, the U.S. Supreme Court denied certiorari in the 10th circuit case of *Torres v. Mullin* in November 2003. In its decision the Supreme Court rejected an opportunity to review the scope of article 35 or the Vienna Convention on Consular Relations, doing so while the United States was arguing its case before the World Court. And this is the second time the ICJ has ruled against the United States relevant to article 36. In 2001, the ICJ ruled in Germany's favor in the Karl and Walter LaGrand case. This case also determined that these were issues regarding "individual rights" but did not necessarily imply a scenario for a charge of "human rights" violations. Also, in 1999, the Inter-American Court of Human Rights, in its Advisory Opinion OC-16/99, concluded that article 36 constitutes an "individual rights" issue but that it extends protection of "human rights" to foreign nationals especially when denial of article 36 protection constitutes a violation of due process such as in the imposition of the death sentence. The Inter-American Court of Human Rights opinion is as follows:

1. That Article 36 of the Vienna Convention on Consular Relations confers rights upon detained foreign nationals, among them the right to information on consular assistance, and that said rights carry with them correlative obligations for the host State. (Unanimous opinion)

2. That Article 36 of the Vienna Convention on Consular Relations *concerns* the protection of the rights of a national of the sending State and is part of the body of international human rights law. (Unanimous opinion)

3. That the expression "without delay" in Article 36(1)(b) of the Vienna Convention on Consular Relations means that the State must comply with its duty to inform the detainee of the rights that article confers upon him, at the time of his arrest or at least before he makes his first statement before authorities. (Unanimous opinion)

4. That the enforceability of the rights that Article 36 of the Vienna Convention on Consular Relations confers upon the individual is not subject to the protests of the sending State. (Unanimous opinion)

5. That articles 2, 6, 14, and 50 of the International Covenant on Civil and Political rights *concern* the protection of human rights *in the American States.* (Unanimous opinion)

6. That the individual's right to information established in Article 36(1)(b) of the Vienna Convention on Consular Relations allows the right to the due process of law recognized in Article 14 of the International Covenant on Civil and Political Rights to have practical effects in concrete cases: Article 14 established minimum guarantees that can be amplified in the light of other international instruments such as the Vienna Convention on Consular Relations, which expand the scope of the protection afforded to the accused. (vote: six to one)

7. That failure to observe a detained foreign national's right to information, recognized in Article 36(1)(b) of the Vienna Convention on Consular Relations, is prejudicial to the due process of law and, in such circumstances,

imposition of the death penalty is a violation of the right not to be deprived of life "arbitrarily," as stipulated in the relevant provisions of the human rights treaties (*v.g.* American Convention on Human Rights, Article 4; International Covenant on Civil and Political Rights, Article 6), with the juridical consequences that a violation of this nature carries, in other words, those pertaining to the State's international responsibility and the duty to make reparation. (vote: six to one, with U.S. dissenting—Judge Jackman)

8. That the international provisions that concern the protection of human rights in the American States, including the right recognized in Article 36(1)(b) of the Vienna Convention on Consular Relations, must be respected by the American States Party to the respective conventions, regardless of whether theirs is a federal or unitary structure (three judges, including Jackman, offered partial dissenting opinions).[31]

Since the 2004 ICJ ruling, the U.S. Supreme Court had another chance to provide the remedy outlined in the *Mexico v. United States* decision in *Medellin v. Texas,* 2008. In this case, President George W. Bush sided with the defendant, Jose E. Medellin, a Mexican national, one of the 51 plaintiffs named in the 2004 ICJ case, who is on death row in Texas. In 2005, President Bush announced that his administration would abide by the World Court's decision ordering states to reconsider the convictions and sentences of Mexican nationals on death row. In *Medellin v. Texas*, the Texas Court of Criminal Appeals refused to allow reconsideration in this case, including consular review and input. In the October 2007 term, the U.S. Supreme Court overturned the Bush directive and ruled in favor of the State of Texas:

MEDELLIN v. TEXAS [Syllabus] Certiorari to the Court of Criminal Appeals of Texas No. 06-984 Argued October 10, 2007—Decided March 25, 2008

In the *Case Concerning Avena and Other Mexican Nationals (Mex. V. U.S.)*, 2004 I.C.J. 12 (*Avena*), the International Court of Justice (ICJ) held that the United States had violated Article 36(1)(b) of the Vienna Convention on Consular Relations (Vienna Convention or Convention) by failing to inform 51 named Mexican nationals, including petitioner Medellin, of their Vienna Convention rights. The ICJ found that those named individuals were entitled to review and reconsideration of their U.S. state-court convictions and sentences regardless of their failure to comply with generally applicable state rules governing challenges to criminal convictions. In *Sanchez-Llamas* v. *Oregon*, 548 U.S. 331—issued after *Avena* but involving individuals who were not named in the *Avena* judgment—this Court held, contrary to the ICJ's determination, that the Convention did not preclude the application of state default rules. The President then issued a memorandum (President's Memorandum or Memorandum) stating that the United States would "discharge its international obligations" under *Avena* "by having State courts give effect to the decision."

Relying on *Avena* and the President's Memorandum, Medellin filed a second Texas state-court habeas application challenging his state capital murder conviction and death sentence on the ground that he had not been informed of his Vienna Convention rights. The Texas Court of Criminal Appeals dismissed Medellin's application as an abuse of writ, concluding that neither *Avena* nor the President's memorandum was binding federal law that could displace the State's limitation on filings successive habeas applications.

Held: Neither *Avena* nor the President's Memorandum constitutes directly enforceable federal law that pre-empts state limitations on the filing of successive habeas petitions. (8–37)[32]

Borderland Violence—Collateral Damage: Bystanders and Maquilador Workers

There is no disputing that the borderland is deeply involved in the drug trade and by virtue of this fact, one of the main battlefields on the United States' international war on drugs. History shows that the antecedents to the current war on drugs had its roots in western efforts to expand the trade balance with isolationistic Asian nations such as China. In this sense, the Opium War of 1839–42 provided the foundation for the current international drug war. The Opium War was the result of China's ban on the importation of the British opium trade (from India) in 1799. Britain ignored the ban, resulting in China confiscating and destroying over 20,000 crates of British East Indian Company opium supply. Using this incident as a pretense for expanding their influence in China, Great Britain declared war on China in 1839. Here, the Treaty of Nanking (1842) ceded Hong Kong to Great Britain on a 150-year lease and also granted British merchants full access to all the major Chinese ports. Hong Kong reverted back to China in June 1997.

The United States became involved in this conflict two years later with the Treaty of Wanghai (1844) when it gained a foothold in China. The 1855 Treaty of Tientsin served to expand these trade rights for both the United States and Great Britain as well as for France and Russia. Part of the result of this gunboat diplomacy was the exportation of a cheap labor force from China to the United States, a needed commodity in the development of the western region obtained from Mexico, including the building of the transcontinental railroad system. But discrimination against these Chinese laborers in the United States soon led to laws prohibiting their further entry into the country as well as their isolation and the criminalization of their culture (Chinatown ghettos; Harrison Narcotic Act of 1914), including the use of opium—the same drug that was used for the pretense of lubricating the wheels of western capitalism in Asia in the first place. The United States' interest in Asia at the beginning of the 20th century was forged through gunboat diplomacy in both China and Japan as well as by obtaining Spanish holdings in the region (Philippines, Guam) following the Spanish-American War. In 1900, the United States joined the other western colonial powers in putting down the Boxer Rebellion, which was China's attempt to purge itself of these foreign influences; hence, the first use of the military (U.S. Marine Corps) in the war on drugs.[33]

In terms of western capitalism, the drug trade represents a raw, if not illicit, example of the supply-and-demand free market system—one that was initially fueled by western cultures, notably Great Britain and the United States. Legislating morality in the United States alone has resulted in the highest incarceration rate of any western society—many serving sentences for drug-related crimes. Moreover, since the 1970s, a substantial law enforcement enterprise has arisen in the United States as well, creating a self-fulfilling prophecy that has ballooned into a multibillion dollar international market. And where other societies have attempted to minimize the effects of drug use through decriminalization and provide social and health alternatives to incarceration—the United States has continued to polarize its society with strict, if not discriminatory, enforcement of drug laws. The irony is that while tens of millions of dollars have been spent in Colombia on the eradication of drug fields, notably cocaine, opium production has flourished under U.S. military occupation in Afghanistan. Currently, Mexico has been the recipient of U.S. antidrug monies in the attempt to thwart this avenue for homegrown and imported agents such as cocaine, heroin, and marijuana into the United States to satisfy the populace's drug appetite. Consequently, the demands associated with the international drug market have resulted in fierce competition. And with this scenario comes violence, much of it focused in the borderland region on both sides of the international boundary. This violence has spilled over into the border communities with increasing collateral damage—civilian deaths.

Headlines in 2008 illustrate the problem: "21 dead in Mexican shootings, gunbattles [sic]"; "Border drug sweep brings in 175 arrests"; "Immigration arrests up in fed program." Even the quiet town bordering Columbus, New Mexico, made famous by Poncho Villa's 1916 raid on the United States, Puerto Palomos, has become a deadly battleground in the recent drug wars, virtually shutting down its tourist industry. On September 17, 2008, the U.S. Justice Department announced that the Gulf Cartel, the major Mexican drug organization, was dealt a substantial blow with the indictment and arrest of 175 people, capping a 15-month investigation by the Drug Enforcement Administration. Moreover, indictments were also issued for three cartel leaders still at large in Mexico. These efforts are coordinated with Mexico law-enforcement agencies in President Felipe Calderon's battle with drug mafias. Both the U.S. and Mexican governments see the Gulf Cartel as the main source of trafficking heroin, cocaine, methamphetamines, and marijuana from Central and South America to quench the United States' drug appetite. What makes the Gulf Cartel so violent and effective is the Zetas, the enforcement segment of the cartel comprised of former Mexican military and police personnel. These arrests did little to quell the violence. Competitors for the Mexican drug trade include the Juarez cartel, the Tijuana cartel, and the Sinaloan Federation cartel, as well as smaller operations in addition to the Gulf Cartel. In October 2008, an Associated Press article portrayed the daily death count in Mexico's drug wars (21 deaths with over 4,000 overall), which included innocent bystanders and those protesting the violence. Most of the deaths were in the borderland region of Ciudad Juarez, Tijuana, Nogales, and Monterrey. Among the dead were 10 soldiers. The Mexican drug war has also invaded the interior, especially those states bordering the Gulf of Mexico and the Pacific Ocean. In late November 2008, five drug enforcement officers were ambushed and killed in Culiacan, Mexico.[34]

The U.S. Immigration and Customs Enforcement lists the following as its accomplishments for fiscal year 2007:

- ICE implemented a comprehensive interior enforcement strategy focused on more efficiently processing apprehended illegal aliens and reducing the numbers of criminal and fugitive aliens in the United States. In FY07, ICE removed a record 276,912 illegal aliens, including voluntary removals from the United States.

- Under the Secure Border Initiative, ICE decreased processing time for aliens in expediting removal cases—from apprehension to removal—to approximately 19 days. This was accomplished by bringing greater efficiency to the immigration removal process through expanded detention capacity, greater use of expedited removal authority and increased use of the Justice Prisoner and Alien Transportation (JPATS) for repatriating illegal aliens to their countries of origin.

- For the first time, ICE's Detention Enforcement and Processing Offenders by Remote Technology (DEPORT) Center made it possible to identify and screen criminal aliens incarcerated in federal prisons nationwide to ensure they are processed for removal from the United States upon completion of their sentences. Launched in fiscal year 2006, the DEPORT Center was screening criminal aliens at all 114 federal prison facilities by the end of FY07, with 11,292 charging documents issued in FY07 to criminal aliens housed in federal prisons.

- ICE's Criminal Alien Program, which screens aliens in prison to ensure that they are removed from the United States upon the completion of their sentences, initiated removal proceedings against 164,296 criminal aliens.

- ICE targeted the infrastructure that supports the business of illegal immigration, including document and immigration benefit fraud, launching six new Document and Benefit Fraud Task Forces in cities nationwide. In FY07, ICE initiated a total of 1,309 document and benefit fraud investigations leading to a record 1,531 arrests and 1,178 convictions.

- In the last two years, ICE quadrupled the number of Fugitive Operations Teams (FOTs): special teams dedicated to identifying, locating and arresting fugitive aliens. These teams have increased from 18 in FY05 to 50 in FY06 and 75 in FY07. As a result, ICE eliminated more than 100,000 fugitive alien cases in FY07 and reduced the backlog of fugitive cases for the first time in history.

- ICE's more aggressive worksite enforcement strategy targeted the "job magnet" that attracts illegal aliens seeking employment in the U.S. In FY07, ICE dramatically increased penalties against employers whose hiring processes violated the law, securing fines and judgments of more than $30 million while making 863 criminal arrests and 4,077 administrative arrests.

- ICE continued efforts to combat drug smuggling organizations, resulting in significant seizures of 241,967 pounds of cocaine, 4,331 pounds of heroin, 2,731 pounds of methamphetamine and 1.3 million pounds of marijuana. Additionally, ICE drug investigations led to 8,920 arrests and 5,539 convictions of individuals associated with narcotic violations.

- ICE leads the "Tunnel Task Force" for investigations of cross-border tunnels used by criminal organizations to smuggle narcotics and other goods into the United States from Mexico. Since 2003, 26 tunnels have been discovered in the San Diego area alone.

- ICE turned its combined legal authorities on the dangerous human traffickers who exploit the vulnerable, implementing a new Trafficking in Persons strategy in FY07 to emphasize investigation and prosecution of traffickers while providing services to assist trafficking victims. In FY07, ICE human trafficking investigations led to 164 arrests and 91 convictions.

- ICE expanded its partnership with state and local law enforcement agencies in a force multiplier approach to fighting criminal activity. In FY07, the ICE ACCESS program was launched as a collaborative effort to identify key crime-fighting needs and to develop solution action plans.

- ICE's team of attorneys provided legal support and training while representing the agency in administrative and federal courts. In FY07, ICE attorneys participated in the completion of 365,851 cases before immigration courts, including 323,845 removal cases.[35]

Ostensibly, a major contributing factor to the increase in drug trafficking through Mexico to the United States is the fact that the United States has poured tens of millions of dollars into Colombia in an effort to curtail lucrative drug enterprise. In essence, Plan Colombia has been so successful that the venue for drug trafficking is now Mexico. So, instead of eliminating the South American drug pipeline, U.S. antidrug efforts have brought it closer to the United States by bringing this problem to America's southern border. This unintended consequence has now resulted in a new front on the war on drugs along with a new battle strategy—Plan Mexico. This transformation of Mexico from a small-time drug production and distribution enterprise to becoming the major trafficking route to the United States began in the 1990s. And the more the United States got involved in attempting to control these activities, the more rapid this illicit enterprise grew, along with the violence associated with the drug trade. The U.S. Drug Enforcement Administration began its formal interventions in the Mexico drug war in 1996 with Operation Reciprocity, which addressed the distribution of cocaine and marijuana to major U.S. cities. A year later, Operation Limelight focused on the Mexican cocaine and marijuana trade routes while

Operation META added methamphetamine into the mix. In the fall of 1999, Operation Impunity specifically targeted the Amado Carrillo-Fuentes Organization in Juarez, Mexico. And in 2000, Operation Tar Pit was initiated to address the black-tar heroin trade. This level of cooperation is linked to the North American Free Trade Agreement (NAFTA) through the Security and Prosperity Agreement of North America component.

But instead of eliminating the drug trafficking through Mexico to the United States, these tactics appear instead to have created a self-fulfilling prophecy, increasing, instead of curtailing, the level of drugs being routed through Mexico. Moreover, this action has promoted increased violence along Mexico's southern border with Guatemala and other entry points for illicit drugs driven north to the United States. The U.S. State Department, in its 2007 Narcotic Control Strategy Report, admits that Mexico is responsible for 90 percent of the cocaine that enters the United States as well as being the largest foreign supplier of marijuana and methamphetamines. On the Mexican side, President Calderon has deployed some 30,000 military personnel in nine states in order to eradicate crops and intercede in drug shipments. There are concerns being voiced over the increased U.S. influence in Mexican military and police operations, especially since September 11, 2001, when the war on drugs merged with the war on terrorism. Indeed, there is a heated debate in Mexico itself over the increased use of the military in civilian affairs. Mexico has long been regarded as an independent American state—one that did not readily do the biddings of the United States. Now this image is being challenged with increased U.S. influence in Mexican affairs, notably the fear of the Colombianization of Mexico. Laura Carlsen, in a July 2007 *Foreign Policy in Focus* article, noted that the increased level of military presence in Mexico in the war on drugs has resulted in an increase in human rights violations as well as increased violent confrontations with drug traffickers, often resulting in death and injury to innocent bystanders. Carlsen notes that as with Plan Colombia, the war on drugs tends to morph into a war on terrorism, resulting in increased U.S. military presence in foreign lands along with its extra-legal measures that often violate UN human rights stipulations. These abuses are only coming to the forefront. A disclosure in November 2008 exposed the U.S. Central Intelligence Agency (CIA) cover up of its operations in Peru that involved the shooting down of a U.S. missionary plane in 2001. Apparently, the CIA repeatedly violated rules of engagement in its drug-interdiction program whereby they encouraged the shooting down of all unknown aircraft by their agents and the Peruvian Air Force without first giving these planes an opportunity to identify themselves or to land. It appears that it is only a matter of time before these new Monroe Doctrine mandates will be incorporated into Plan Mexico.[36]

Clearly, borderland violence has intensified since passage of NAFTA with intercartel wars since 9/11 and increased U.S. monetary, equipment, and logistical aid to Mexican police and military forces. Brazen murders of police and news media personnel have become commonplace through-out Mexico in the past five years. Corruption within law-enforcement agencies on both sides of the border is yet another hallmark of the current borderland wars. Corrupt officials include high sheriffs in Texas, U.S. border-patrol agents, local police officers, as well as high-ranking officials within Mexico's federal drug-enforcement agency—SIEDO. These kill-ings include the hit on Silvia Molina, the police administrative director of Juarez, in June 2008. This killing has larger ramifications in that she was also investigating the hundreds of unsolved rape/murders in the greater Juarez/Chihuahua area. Since 1993, the period corresponding with the advent of the NAFTA accord, hundreds of teens and young women have been murdered or simply disappeared in the borderland region surround-ing Juarez, Mexico. Prime suspects have included the bus drivers who are responsible for bringing these women from their homes to their workplace in the maquiladoras. Many of these girls have migrated from the interior of Mexico to work in these border plants. The youngest victims from the maquiladora work pool are age 13, three years below the minimum legal age for this type of employment in Mexico. Civil rights groups in both Mexico and the United States fault the maquiladora administrators for these abuses since they obviously do not provide adequate protection for their female workers. These young women are often forced to live in shan-tytowns while the maquiladoras subcontract bus drivers without doing adequate background checks. The United States bears some responsibility here given that 40 percent of the maquiladora factories are U.S.-owned. These companies include Amway, TDK, Honeywell, 3M, Kenwood, and Dupont. Mexican business own 50 percent of the borderland factories while the other 10 percent are owned by other foreign companies. The number of murder victims now exceeds 300. Drug and prostitution gangs, women haters, sexual sadists, and even those trafficking in body parts have come under scrutiny for these crimes. Mexican law-enforcement agencies have been slow in addressing this problem, resulting in a United Nations in-quiry. The UN report of the Committee on the Elimination of Discrimi-nation against Women was disseminated in January 2005. This report provides the most comprehensive analysis of this situation.

Pertinent selections on the Report on Mexico produced by the Commit-tee on the Elimination of Discrimination against Women under article 8 of the Optional Protocol to the Convention, and reply from the Government of Mexico articulate the complex sociocultural and economic dynamics of the maquiladora system in Juarez:

During a visit to the city's western district, the delegation was able to witness the extreme poverty of the local families; most of those households are headed by women who live in extreme destitution. Furthermore, the delegation was informed by various sources that in Ciudad Juarez there is a marked difference between social classes, with the existence of a minority of wealthy, powerful families, who own the land on which the marginal maquilas and urban districts are located, making structural change difficult. The overall situation has led to a range of criminal behaviours, including organized crime, drug trafficking, trafficking in women, undocumented migration, money-laundering, pornography, procuring, and the exploitation of prostitution. In addition, the situation created by the establishment of the maquilas and the creation of jobs mainly for women, without the creation of enough alternatives for men, has changed the traditional dynamics of relations between the sexes, which was characterized by gender inequality. This gives rise to a situation of conflict towards the women—especially the youngest—employed in the maquilas. This social change in women's roles has not been accompanied by a change in traditionally patriarchal attitudes and mentalities, and thus the stereotyped view of men's and women's social roles has been perpetuated. Within this context, a culture of impunity has taken root which facilitates and encourages terrible violations of human rights. Violence against women has also taken root, and has developed specific characteristics marked by hatred and misogyny. There have been widespread kidnappings, disappearances, rapes, mutilations and murders, especially over the past decade.[37]

A more recent portrayal of the situation in the borderland capital was presented in the December 8, 2005, issue of *Newsweek*:

The border between El Paso [population: 600,000] and Juarez [population: 1.5 million] is the most menacing spot along America's southern underbelly. On one side is the second-safest city of its size in the United States [after Honolulu], with only 15 murders so far in 2008. On the other is a slaughterhouse ruled by drugs lords where the death toll this year is more that 1,300 and counting. . . . Juarez looks a lot like a failed state, with no government entity capable of imposing order and a profusion of powerful organizations that kill and plunder at will. It's as if the United States faced another lawless Waziristan- except this one happens to be right at the nation's doorstep.[38]

Unfortunately, the beginning of the 21st century appears to be a repeat of U.S./Mexico relations at the beginning of the 20th century. While the actors have changed, the political scenario is familiar. Instead of Porfirio Díaz, Felipe Calderon is now the U.S.-sponsored ally of the dictates of the Monroe Doctrine with the unintended consequences of increased lawlessness and violence in the borderland. Here again, the United States is using foreign soil for its reactive strategies (arrest and imprisonment) in its war on drugs. In this drama of vulgar capitalism, the unrelenting market demand for illicit drugs in the United States, coupled with a long-failed policy of retribution, instead of proactive programs of prevention and rehabilitation, has contributed greatly to the current level of violence throughout Mexico and especially in the borderland. And as usual these militaristic and police actions have done little to quell either the demand for or the level of drug consumption within U.S. society. While the final chapter on the current situation has yet to be written, it appears that President Calderon's willingness to accommodate America's interest in Mexico, including providing military equipment and advisors, is very likely to suffer similar consequences as that of his role model, President Porfirio Díaz. Past efforts at changing Mexico's long-held socialist-type of government to American-style capitalism have failed. Time will only tell if America is finally successful in bringing radical change to Mexico, forging it into a desired client state, so that it better fits the North American political/economic model.

Epilogue

The noted German sociologist Max Weber alluded to the subjective influences that impact on everyday decisions including scholarly endeavors. These "value orientations" are similarly termed "attribution bias" by psychologists. The point is we usually hold a manifested (intended) or latent (unintended) interest in our topic, interests that transcend a pure empirical pursuit of knowledge per se. In the case of this book, my interests were forged while being on the faculty at one of the oldest Hispanic-serving public universities in the United States.

Western New Mexico University (WNMU), along with a sister facility in Las Vegas, New Mexico, were created by the territorial legislature in 1893 with the specific purpose of training teachers, notably Mexican Americans, to teach the large Hispanic population in the state at that time. Both educational facilities began as normal schools, the forerunner of teacher-education colleges and universities today. Western New Mexico University was designed to serve the southern part of the state, that region falling within the borderland, while Highlands State University was created to serve the northern Hispanic population. A look at the current education dilemma in the borderland provides a broader picture for the reader to better understand the WNMU "Hands across the Border" project with the Puerto Palomas community.

The free exchange of public school children in the rural borderland changed significantly following passage of NAFTA. The new agreement further curtailed the availability of free U.S. education for Mexican families residing along the international border. Since NAFTA, the 1996 U.S. Immigration and Nationalization Reform Act has denied Mexican students F-1 visas, which in the past allowed these children and youth to cross the U.S./ Mexico border to attend U.S. public schools. Prior to 1996, hundreds of Mexican children and youth crossed the international border daily during the school year to attend public schools in the United States' portion of the borderland—a region that once belonged to Mexico. This process allowed Mexican youth to obtain a 12th-grade education that was usually lacking in the rural regions of the borderland. Now only those Mexican children who hold dual citizenship are afforded this luxury. These are the children whose families reside in Mexico but were transported to a local U.S. hospital for their birth. These children hold joint U.S./Mexican citizenship while most of their parents do not. Even then, Hispanics now represent 20 percent of the public school population nationwide with higher proportions within the borderland region—California (60%), and Arizona, New Mexico, and Texas (40% for each state). The current No Child Left Behind law provides additional challenges given that for many of these students, English is a second language, further complicating the language and math aggregate test scores for schools and school districts. New Mexico, with the highest proportion of its population being of Mexican descent while also being largely a rural state, played a unique role in the area of multicultural education.

Western New Mexico University is located in Silver City, a mere 90 miles from the border and the main border towns of Columbus, New Mexico; and Puerto Palomas (aka Los Palomas), Mexico. Silver City is situated in the foothills of the Gila National Forest and is known for its mining activity as well as being the boyhood town of Billy the Kid. Puerto Palomas and Columbus are famous for being the site of Pancho Villa's raid on the United States in 1916. While WNMU is still primarily a teachers college, its mandate has been expanded to include a viable business school with offerings including the MBA, a regional police academy, and one of the best collections of Mimbres pottery and artifacts, housed at the university museum. In its function as a teacher-training facility, WNMU is responsible for providing teachers to the surrounding school districts, including the Deming schools, the Silver City schools, and the schools in Lordsburg—the region comprising the mostly rural region of southern New Mexico extending west from Las Cruces to the Arizona border. WNMU's state mandate also includes providing both undergraduate and graduate educational and clinical (social work) programs in the northwestern region of the state, serving the eastern portion of the Navajo Nation as well as the Zuni and Acoma Pueblos in addition to local whites (Anglos).

As part of the borderland region, southern New Mexico schools, notably those in the Deming Consolidated School System (which includes the schools in the border town of Columbus), have long welcomed Mexican students from Los Palomas. At the time of the North American Free Trade Agreement (NAFTA) in January 1994, some 400 Mexican students were picked up at the international border by New Mexico school buses and taken to the schools in the southern region of the state (Columbus elementary and

Sunshine school) where the majority of the students were of Mexican origin. Most of these students, while residing with their parents in Mexico, hold dual citizenship, given that they were born in the Deming hospital—the only major health care facility within this section of the borderland. Even then, the majority of the Mexican students attended the federal school system in Los Palomas.

The Palomas school system in 1990 consisted of three federal schools—a kindergarten, a primary school, and a secondary school. A private-run alternative school was built later through funding from the Ford Foundation and is known as the Ford School. Primary school, within the Mexican system, includes grades one to six, while the secondary school covers grades seven to nine. Most Mexican students end their education with primary school, although new standards call for a secondary education. Secondary education in Los Palomas consists of training in welding, electrical contracting, and building construction for males, and secretarial skills for female students. Students desiring college training need to leave the area with the closest facilities of higher education being located in the cities of Juarez or Chihuahua. There were no computers in the school system when we initiated our Hands across the Border cooperative educational program between WNMU and the Los Palomas federal schools. Most of our attention was focused on the primary school, a sprawling, one-story, pale blue cinderblock structure that was situated on the international border with only a fence separating the school yard from the United States. It was also located within visual distance of both the U.S. and Mexican border-patrol stations. Puerto Palomas, like most of the border towns acquired under the Gadsden Purchase, does not have a river crossing demarking the international border. So, when a basketball inadvertently is thrown over the fence, its return is dependent on the magnanimity of the U.S. Border Patrol.

My involvement with the Palomas schools began in early 1990 while I was serving as the chair of the Department of Education and Psychology (now the School of Education) at WNMU. One of the faculty, Virginia V. Sanchez, who earned her doctorate at the University of Arizona in bilingual/ ESL (English as a Second Language) education, approached me about forging a liaison with the public schools within the immediate border region, notably those in Puerto Palomas. Although an informal one-way exchange of primary-age children already was in existence, no formal interaction occurred between the faculty and administrators in New Mexico and their Mexican counterparts. At this time, dozens of Mexican children crossed the border daily to attend the elementary schools within the Deming school district. Moreover, relations with the Mexican schools, in particular, and the larger professional community, in general, were strained recently with a *20/20* televised expose of the Mexican primary school system. Here, the docudrama compared the physical structure of the Palomas schools with those of the United States, noting that the Mexican parents had to provide toilet paper and pay for propane gas to heat the classrooms during winter. It also described the poor condition of the schools' buildings, some with cracked windows and with only swamp coolers to ward off the summer heat.

Obviously our reception was met with suspicion. After all, New Mexico schools had a policy of trashing their outmoded equipment instead of sending it to the Mexican schools that were in dire need of these supplies. In our Hands across the Border plan we offered to assist with their needs, allowing the Palomas community to set the program's agenda. One of our first objectives was to work with the governor's office and the Commission of Higher Education (CHE) in getting the restriction on exchange of educational material changed. The New Mexico attorney general's office granted this request on January 6, 1991, issuing the following statement:

Re: *Shipment of Used Books and Equipment*

. . . The legal issue here is whether the giving of these books and equipment violates the antidonation clause in Article IX, Section 14 of the New Mexico Constitution. The antidonation clause provides that "[n]either the state, nor any county, school district, or municipality . . . shall directly or indirectly . . . make any donation to or in aid of any person, association or public or private corporation . . ." A "donation" within the meaning of the provision is "a gift, an allocation or appropriation of something of value without consideration." *Village of Deming v. Hosdreg Co.*, 62 N.M. 19, 28, 303 P.2d 920 (1956). The antidonation clause is to be interpreted "with reference to the evils it was intended to correct." *City of Clovis v. Southwestern Pub. Serv. Co.*, 49 N.M. 270, 276, 161, P.2d 878 (1945).

The evil addressed by the antidonation clause was the investment of public funds in private enterprises. *City of Clovis*, 49 N.M. at 272-77. Thus, New Mexico courts have found violations of the clause when the state and local governments have conferred gratuitous benefits, at taxpayer expense, on entities and individuals for their private use. The prohibition against donations has been extended to school textbooks when they were being provided to private religious schools. *Zellers v. Huff*, 55 N.M. 501, 236 P.2d 949 (1951).

Does the anti-donation clause apply to donations to public institutions outside New Mexico? The prohibition is generally invoked when donations to private individuals or institutions are involved. The New Mexico courts have clearly stated that the anti-donation clause does not apply to donations by the state or a subordinate governmental agency to another New Mexico agency . . . . The prohibition of aid to a governmental entity outside New Mexico has not been addressed . . .

If donations to Mexican educational institutions are arguably prohibited by the New Mexico Constitution, then are the shipments being considered by CHE "donations" by the state under New Mexico law? . . . The issue then is whether these shipments of books and equipment involve the allocation of "something of value" by the state.

In response to the specific scenarios, we offered the following comments:

1. Based on your description of the facts, we assume that the review copies of textbooks were given by publishers directly to, and remain the property of, the individual faculty members. Therefore, the donation would be by the individual faculty members and not by the state educational institution.

2. Based on your description of the facts, we assume that both the books and the equipment that would be sent to Mexico are no longer of any use to the state educational institutions and would normally be discarded or destroyed without any compensation to the institutions. Therefore these books or equipment appear to be of no value to the institution.

Finally, you have described this planned shipment of books and equipment as part of a larger exchange program with Mexican educational institutions. Therefore, assuming the facts as you presented them, the shipping of faculty books and valueless books and equipment as part of an exchange program would not, in our view, violate the antidonation clause of the New Mexico Constitution.

[signed] William R. Brancard, Assistant Attorney General

As soon as state approval was granted, dozens of boxes of math and science books were collected and delivered to the Palomas school faculty. Over the years, thousands of books, including children's books in Spanish, were delivered to Mexican schools under the Hands across the Border program.

Another dimension of the Hands across the Border program was providing continuing education for the Mexican teachers. WNMU was the closest facility of higher education in the borderland region adjacent to Palomas. Federal Mexican teachers, those employed in the public school system, are required to take continuing education classes in order to maintain their teacher-certification credentials. Colleges and universities in Juarez were the closest facilities in Mexico for these teachers. WNMU, on the other hand, was only 90 miles away (later an auxiliary WNMU campus was established in Deming—only 40 miles away). Initially we brought the instruction to the teachers conducting classes in Palomas. The core of these courses was special education, English as a second language, and counseling and psychology. Dr. Richard Rodriguez, director of special education at WNMU, taught the special education component while Dr. Virginia V. Sanchez provided instruction in functional English as a second language, and I taught the counseling and psychology courses. Bilingual graduate students, of Mexican American heritage, assisted in this endeavor. These accredited courses were provided gratis by WNMU. The quid pro quo aspect of the program was for the Mexican faculty to allow students in the education department to do their practicum and/or student teaching in the Palomas schools. During the summer sessions, Mexican teachers as far as Ciudad Juarez participated in the program. Mexican teacher aides, assisting in the Deming public schools closest to the border, Columbus elementary and Sunshine elementary, also benefited from this training program.

The Hands across the Border program did much to minimize the barriers long associated with the international border. Puerto Palomas has long been seen as a safe port to cross by foot or vehicle while the town's many restaurants, liquor outlets, dentists, drug stores, and optometrists conducted a thriving business with U.S. customers. All of this changed with the increased militarization of the border from both sides justified in the name of the war on terrorism. Pressure from both the Mexican police and military and the U.S. National Guard and Border Patrol along the Juarez/El Paso corridor has resulted in the drug cartels move into otherwise stable rural entry points like Palomas.

In 2008, Puerto Palomas became the deadliest Mexican town per capita in the borderland with drug battles fought a few feet from the international border and the public primary school. The situation was so bad that in March the town's police chief sought political asylum across the border in Columbus, New Mexico. This was shortly after his entire 10-man police force quit en masse. The war among the drug cartels has now entered the U.S. side of the borderland with border patrol agents now facing increased firepower from AK-47 assault rifles. Local hospitals, in both El Paso and Deming, have to post guards to keep wounded Mexicans from being murdered by Mexican hit men.

The raging gun battles have killed and wounded civilians while gangsters have resorted to robbing tourists, some while they are in the dentist's chair. The fear of violence, including kidnappings, has cast a pall over Palomas that has essentially shut down all the progress made by the Hands across the Border program. Mexican families, including those of the teachers, are fleeing Palomas. Once a model border town, Palomas now has rows of abandoned homes and businesses and a rapid decline in its population from a high of over 12,000 to fewer than 7,000 and counting. Tourists no longer venture across the once-friendly border. In the meantime, increasing numbers of Mexican law-enforcement personnel are being held in protective custody in both Luna and Dona Ana counties in New Mexico, awaiting the outcome of their asylum requests. Most in the borderland, Mexico, and the United States hold out hope that conditions will improve under the Obama administration. Already President Obama has called for greater border surveillance relevant to the flow of assault weapons from the United States to Mexico as well as setting a new standard for holding illegal aliens booked in local jails. Now, under the Obama Administration, deportable immigrants will be identified by matching their fingerprints to federal databases. Here, those with criminal records will be fast-tracked for deportation, ultimately resulting in 10 times the number of criminal aliens caught under the Bush-era program while, at the same time, reducing the level of harassment for noncriminal aliens, documented and otherwise. What happens in the next few years of this long-standing, if tumultuous relationship, between Mexico and the United States, may dramatically shape the histories of both nations for many decades to come.

Chronology of Major Events

1776   U.S. Declaration of Independence from Britain.

1783   Treaty of Paris ends U.S. Revolutionary War.

1802   President Jefferson doubles the size of the United States with the Louisiana Purchase from France. Treaty ratified by U.S. Senate on October 20, 1803.

1810   Mexico begins revolts against Spanish rule.

1812   U.S. initiates the War of 1812 with Britain in attempt to gain territory in Canada.

1817   General Andrew Jackson starts war with Spain over Florida—First Seminole War—resulting in U.S. acquiring Florida in 1819.

1819   The Adams-Onís Treaty ends the Seminole Wars not only ceding Florida to the United States but also establishing the Mexico/United States border at the Sabine River (ratified in 1821).

1820   Mexican Constitution outlaws slavery and enfranchises all adult males regardless of race or social status.

1821   Mexico gains independence from Spain. Republic of Mexico established September 21, 1821.

        Americans seek land grants (*empresarios*) in northern Mexico (Eastern Interior Provinces). Conditions include converting to Catholicism.

        Texas Rangers begin as "rangers" for policing the Austin empresario in Mexico.

1824   Mexico emperor Augustín de Iturbide's reign is short-lived and replaced with a federalist system, which evolves into a centralized government in 1830.

1826   Fredonian Rebellion: The Edward brothers lead rebellion among Anglo empresarios and declare independence from Mexico, calling the new nation Fredonia. The rebellion ends in 1827 with the rebels escaping back to the United States.

1830   U.S. Congress passes Indian Removal Act to allow whites to take Indian lands east of the Mississippi (Indian Territory established in lands acquired under Louisiana Purchase). U.S. Supreme Court challenges law but President Jackson overrides Justice Marshall.

1833   Antonio López de Santa Anna's first term as president of Mexico.

1836   Texas declares independence, stating opposition to Catholicism and Mexico's antislavery stance.

        Santa Anna's forces defeat rebels at the Alamo (San Antonio).

        U.S. forces defeat Santa Anna's forces at San Jacinto.

        Sam Houston becomes president of the Republic of Texas.

1838   Cherokee Nation forcefully removed to Indian Territory (Oklahoma) in drama termed the "Trail of Tears."

1839   Santa Anna's second term as president of Mexico.

1841   Santa Anna's third term as president of Mexico.

1844   Santa Anna again elected president but is replaced by José Joaquin de Herrera.

1845   Texas annexed by the United States as a slave state.

1846   United States declares war on Mexico.

        Santa Anna's fourth term as president of Mexico.

        Sam Houston becomes U.S. senator from the state of Texas.

1848   Treaty of Guadalupe Hidalgo ends Mexican War with United States gaining half of Mexico.

1850   U.S. Compromise of 1850 and Fugitive Slave Act.

1853   Santa Anna returns from exile in Venezuela and assumes presidency of Mexico for fifth time.

        Ostend Manifesto—ill-fated attempt to force Spain to sell Cuba to the United States to be added as a slave state.

        U.S. president Franklin Pierce gets Santa Anna to relinquish more Mexican territory with the Gadsden Purchase.

1855   Santa Anna again exiled; returns in 1874; dies in 1876.

1859   Sam Houston becomes governor of Texas (loses second term; dies in 1863).

1861   Benito Juárez becomes first full-blooded Indian president of Mexico.

        Tripartite Convention in London initiates armed intervention in Mexico with forces from Britain, France, and Spain arriving in Veracruz due to the default of 82 million pesos in loans.

        U.S. Civil War begins, ending in 1865.

1862   Cinco de Mayo: General Díaz defeats Napoleon III's forces at Puebla on May 5, 1862—an important anniversary celebrated to the present.

        Spanish and British forces withdraw leaving only French forces.

        U.S. president Lincoln enacts Emancipation Proclamations on September 22, 1862, and January 1, 1863.

1864   Archduke Maximilian accepts Mexican crown as European dictator.

1866   Napoleon III withdraws French troops from Mexico.

1867   Maximilian defeated and executed (on orders of General Porfirio Díaz).

1872   Benito Juárez dies.

1877   Porfirio Díaz elected president of Mexico and remains either president (six terms overall) or de facto leader until his resignation and exile to Paris in 1911; he dies in 1915).

1878   Posse Comitatus Act (18 U.S.C.: 1385): Act restricts the use of federal troops in the South during Reconstruction era.

1882   Mexico and United States sign treaty allowing reciprocal border crossings.

1888   Mexico and the United States form International Boundary Commission along with extradition provision.

1898   Spanish-American War: United States declares war on Spain over Cuba and Puerto Rico.

1899   Peace treaty signed with Spain with United States acquiring Puerto Rico and Spanish colonial holdings in the Pacific—Philippine Islands, Guam, Mariana, Carolina, and Marshall Islands. Spain relinquishes control over Cuba. United States begins war in Philippines.

1901   Rebellion in the Philippines ends.

1904   President Theodore Roosevelt issues his Roosevelt Corollary establishing the right of the United States to unilaterally intervene in the Caribbean and Central America to protect them from foreign interventions. U.S. Marines become the international police force for this policy.

1911   Mexican Revolution begins. Ciudad Juarez falls: 20,000 U.S. troops muster along the Mexican/U.S. border.

1914   U.S. troops occupy Veracruz just as the First World War begins in Europe.

Civil War begins in Mexico between Generals Carranza and Obregón fighting Generals Villa and Zapata.

1915   Plan de San Diego exposed as an unlikely revolution to regain Mexican territory lost to the United States. It is initiated by a small radical element of Hispanic revolutionaries. Overreaction by the Texas Rangers leads to excessive force and terror among Mexican Americans living in Texas.

Wilson's critique: President Wilson sides with the Carranza forces (Carranzitas) believing they would better protect U.S. oil interests in Mexico.

1916   General Villa attacks U.S. military facilities in Columbus, New Mexico.

Zimmerman communiqué exposes German attempts to involve Mexico in World War I.

1917   U.S. Immigration Act of February 5, 1917 (39 Statutes-at-Large 874). Mexican laborers exempt due to manpower shortage during World War I.

Mexico establishes a new Revolutionary Constitution restricting presidents to one six-year term and also allowing for a free secular primary education. The constitution has a de facto prohibition for the death penalty for civilian offenses.

The new constitution greatly restricts the role of the Catholic Church in public matters.

U.S. begins 11-month Punitive Expedition into Mexico under General John (Black Jack) Pershing without finding General Villa.

U.S. enters World War I with Pershing as commander of U.S. Expeditionary Forces.

1921   U.S. Quota Law of May 19, 1921 (42 Statutes-at-Large 5).

1922   U.S. Immigration Act of May 26, 1924 (43 Statutes-at-Large 153).

Act of May 28, 1924 (43 Statutes-at-Large 240) establishes U.S. Border Patrol.

1924   U.S. Indian Citizenship Act enfranchises all American Indians and Alaska Natives at the federal level as citizens; Idaho, Maine, Mississippi, New Mexico, and Washington continue to exclude enrolled tribal members from voting until prohibited by the passage of the Indian Civil Right Act in 1968.

1929   Act of March 4, 1929 (45 Statutes-at-Large 1551) articulates deportable classes convicted of felonies.

League of United Latin American Citizens (LULAC) emerges as a political front for Hispanics, notably Mexican Americans.

1931   Act of February 18, 1931 (46 Statutes-at-Large 1171) expands deportation for illicit drugs—heroin, opium, or coca leaves.

1935   Texas Rangers brought under the authority of the Texas Department of Public Services instead of acting as the governor's private police force.

1940   Act of June 14, 1940 (54 Statutes-at-Large 230) transfers INS from the Department of Labor to the Department of Justice.

        Alien Registration Act of June 28, 1940 (54 Statutes-at-Large 670) requires fingerprinting of all aliens over age 14.

1941   U.S. enters World War II on side of the Allies. Conflict ends in 1945.

1942   Bracero Agreement established between Mexico and United States allowing Mexican migrants to work as seasonal agriculture laborers. The program ends in 1964.

1948   American G.I. Forum (AGIF) is formed by Hispanic veterans of World War II.

1951   U.S. involved in Korean Conflict as primary UN force. Conflict ends in 1953. More Hispanics join the AGIF.

1954   Operation Wetback begins under the direction of General Joseph "Jumping Joe" Swing in attempt to entice illegal Mexican workers to return to Mexico.

1958   United States takes over France's role in Southeast Asia leading to the Vietnam conflict, which extends until 1975.

1964   United States enacts Civil Rights Act that prohibits discrimination based on race, color, religion, sex, or national origin.

1965   Cesar Chavez begins to organize Mexican and Filipino farmworkers into the United Farms Workers union.

1968   Pro-democracy demonstration massacre of student protestors in Mexico City.

        Indian Civil Rights Act passed in United States.

1969   MECHA (El Movimiento Estudiantil Chicano de Aztlan) begins at the Chicano Youth Liberation Conference held in Denver.

1970   La Raza Unida Party (LRUP) and Bronze/Brown Power movements bring nonwhite Hispanics together as a political force.

        The Racketeer Influence and Corrupt Organization Act (RICO) is established in the United States.

1972   U.S. Supreme Court finds death penalty unconstitutional.

1976   U.S. Supreme Court reinstates death penalty with conditions for its application.

        Canada outlaws the death penalty.

1988   President Reagan signs the Anti-Drug Abuse Act, which includes the Drug Kingpin Act (DKA), allowing the reinstatement of the federal death penalty.

1989   President George H. W. Bush establishes the Joint Task Force-6 (JTF-6) as part of the U.S. war on drugs.

1994   North American Free Trade Agreement (NAFTA) goes into effect on January 1.

On the same day, the Zapatista Army of National Liberation (EZLN) declares war on Mexico in protest to NAFTA's opposition to land reform and the ejido system.

2000   Vicente Fox becomes first Mexican leader to break the Institutional Revolutionary Party's (PRI) monopoly on the presidency. He was a member of the conservative National Action Party (PAN).

2001   Terrorist attacks on United States on September 11 initiate the war on terror, which combined with the existing war on drugs leads to the increased militarization of the U.S./Mexico border.

2006   President George W. Bush initiates Operation Jump Start, allowing border-state governors to deploy the National Guard along their section of the U.S./Mexico border.

Felipe Calderon succeeds Fox as president of Mexico. He also belongs to the conservative PAN party, and like Fox, has welcomed U.S. aid for the war on drugs.

2009   Obama administration begins in the United States. Obama is the first post-Columbian North American leader of black-African descent.

Notes

CHAPTER ONE

1. See, Leinwand, Donna. (May 22, 2002). Report: Foreigners Linked to Terror Tricked INS. *USAToday,* http://www.usatoday.com/news/sept11/2002/05/22/terrorists-ins.htm..

2. Weber, M. (1958). *The Protestant Ethic and the Spirit of Capitalism* (Parsons, T., translator). New York: Charles Scribner's Sons.

3. See, Churchill, W. S. (1955). *History of the English-Speaking People.* New York: Barnes & Noble.

4. See, Leinwand, *USAToday*: 180.

5. Stephanson, A. (1995). *Manifest Destiny: American Expansion and the Empire of Right.* New York: Hill & Wang.

6. Erikson, K. T. (1966). *Wayward Puritans: A Study in the Sociology of Deviance.* New York: John Wiley & Sons: 48.

7. See, Blue Laws. 2001. *The Columbia Encyclopedia.* Columbia University On-line Press.

8. Op cited #4. Cpt. 2: Destinies and Destinations, 1820–1865: 28–65.

9. Wallner, P. A. (2004). *Franklin Pierce: New Hampshire's Favorite Son.* Concord, NH: Plaidswede Publishing.

10. See, Davis, R. J. (1962). The Polygamous Prelude. *American Journal of Legal History,* Vol. 6: 1–27; the 1862 Morrill Act (Public Law 37–108); and *Reynolds v. United States* 98 U.S. 145 (1879).

11. See, Gusfield, J. (1963). *Symbolic Crusade: Status, Politics and the American Temperance Movement.* Chicago, IL: The University Press; Kobler, J. (1973). *The Rise and Fall of Prohibition.* New York: G. P. Putnam's Sons; and Goode, E. (1999). *Drugs in American Society.* Boston, MA: McGraw-Hill.

12. See, *R v. Big M Drug Mart Ltd* (1985) 1 S.C.R. 295.

13. See, Dillon, R. H. (1983). *North American Indian Wars.* Greenwich, CT: Brompton Books; Jennings, F. (1990). *Empire of Fortune: Crowns, Colonies and Tribes in the Seven Year War in America.* New York: W. W. Norton & Company; Peckham, H. H. (1964). *The Colonial Wars, 1689–1762.* Chicago, IL: University of Illinois Press; and French, L. A., & Manzanarez, M. (2004). *NAFTA & NeoColonialism.* Lanham, MD: University Press of America.

14. See, Calloway, C. G. (1995). *The American Revolution in Indian Country.* New York: Cambridge University Press.

15. Silverstone, S. A. (2004). *Divided Union: The Politics of War in the Early American Republic.* Ithaca, NY: Cornell University Press, 1.

16. Kaufman, S. (2004). *The Pig War: The United States, Britain, and the Balance of Power in the Pacific Northwest, 1846–72.* Lanham, MD: Lexington Books.

17. See, Meyer, M. C., Sherman, L. W., and Deeds, S. M. (1999). *The Course of Mexican History.* New York: Oxford University Press; and Wallner, op cited #8.

18. See, Search the 1790 U.S. Federal Census. *Census Search: Information, Facts, Tips and Searches for the Federal and State Census.* (2000). Washington, DC: U.S. Census Bureau Population Division, Population & Housing Program Branch.

19. See, Stephanson, A. (1995). Choices and Chosenness 1600–1820 in *Manifest Destiny: American Expansion and the Empire of Right.* New York: Hill & Wang, 23.

20. See, Lipscomb, A. A. (ed.). (1903). *The Writings of Thomas Jefferson: Monticello Edition,* Vol. 10. Washington, DC: The Thomas Jefferson Memorial Association; and French, L. A. (2003). *Native American Justice.* Chicago, IL: Burnham, 96.

21. See, Silverstone, op cited # 14.

22. See, Hickey, D. R. (1989). *The War of 1812.*Urbana, IL: University of Chicago Press; and Mahon, J. K. (1972). *The War of 1812.* Gainesville: University of Florida Press.

23. See, *Indian Removal Act* (May 28, 1830), *U.S. Statutes at Large,* 4:411–12; *Cherokee Nation v. Georgia,* 30 U.S. (5 Pet.) 1 (1831); *Worcester v. Georgia* 31 U.S. (6 Pet.) 515 (1832); and French, L. A. (1998). Forced Removal: The Trail of Tears, *The Qualla Cherokee-Surviving in Two Worlds.* Lewiston, NY: Edwin Mellin Press: 45–50.

24. See, *Standing Bear v. Crook,* 25 Federal Cases, 695, 697, 700–01 (1879); and *Indian Citizenship Act. U.S. Statutes at Large,* 43:253 (June 2, 1924).

25. See, *Plessy v. Ferguson* 163 U.S. 537 (1896); and *Brown v. Board of Education* 347 U.S. 483 (1954).

26. See, Wilson, W. (1902). *A History of the American People.* New York: Harper & Brothers; and Stephanson, *Manifest Destiny:* Cpt 1. Falling into the World—1914–1990: 112–122.

27. See, French & Manzanarez op cited Cpt 1, #12. Cpt 8: Comparative Education among NAFTA Partners: 195–214.

28. See, *Furman v. Georgia,* 408 U.S. 238, 345 (1972); *Gregg v. Georgia,* 428 U.S. 153, 96 S. Ct. 2902, 49 L. Ed. 2d 859 (1976); *Jurek v. Texas,* 428 U.S. 262, 96 S. Ct. 2950 (1976); and *Proffit v. Florida,* 428 U.S. 242, 252 (1976).

29. See, French and Manzanarez (2004) op cited Cpt 1, #2. Cpt. 6: Comparative Human Rights Issues in North America: 153–155.

30. See, French, L. A. (2005). Mental Retardation and the Death Penalty. *Federal Probation* (June): 11–20.

31. See, French & Manzanarez, *NAFTA & NeoColonialism:* Cpt. 8.

32. *Apologizing to the Victims of Lynching and the Descendants of Those Victims for the Failure of the Senate to Enact Anti-lynching Legislation.* 109th Congress, 1st Session (S. RES. 39) (February 7, 2005).

33. See, *Miller-El v. Dretke*, 545 U.S. 231 (2005).

CHAPTER TWO

1. See, The Alamo. Web site of The Daughters of the Republic of Texas. http://drt-inc.org.

2. See, Calloway. (1995). *The American Revolution in Indian Country.* Cambridge, UK: Cambridge University Press.

3. See, Saul, J. R. (2005). Negative Nationalism, Cpt. 25 in *The Collapse of Globalism: And the Reinvention of the World.* Toronto, Ontario, Canada, 246–257.

4. See, Bancroft, H. H. (1886). *History of Mexico,* Vol. 15. San Francisco, CA: The Bancroft Library, The History Company Publishers.

5. See, De Leon, A. (1993). *Mexican Americans in Texas: A Brief History.* Arlington Heights, IL: Harlan Davidson.

6. See, McKeehan, W. L. (2001). *Adam-Onís Treaty of 1819.* New-Spain-Index, Sons of Dewitt Colony Texas (online site); and Bevans, C. L. (1974). Amity, Settlement, and Limits in *Treaties and Other International Agreements of the United States of America, 1776–1949,* Vol. 2. Washington, DC: U.S. Government Printing Office: 528–536.

7. See, De Leon, 1993. Texas: A Spanish Outpost, 1716–1790s: 5–18.

8. See, Henderson, M. V. (1928). Minor Empresario Contracts for the Colonization of Texas, 1825–1834. *The Southwestern Historical Quarterly,* Vol. 31 (4): 295–324.

9. Henderson, Minor Empresario Contracts.

10. Ibid.

11. Bancroft, *History of Mexico*; and Barker, E. C. (1925). *The Life of Stephen F. Austin.* Nashville, TN: Cokesbury Press.

12. See, Holt, J. (1977). *The Edwards Empresarial Grant and the Fredonia Rebellion.* Masters-of-Arts Thesis, Stephen F. Austin State University; and Barker, E. C. (1928). *Mexico and Texas, 1811–1835.* Dallas, TX: Turner Publishing.

13. See, Barker, op cited #12, The Racial and Political Background: 1–31.

14. See, Merk, F. (1972). *Slavery and the Annexation of Texas.* New York: Knopf; and Meyer, M. C., Sherman, L. W., & Deeds, S. M. (1999), op cited Cpt. 1, #16.

15. Op cited #4, and #14.

16. See, Barker (1928). Colonial Grievances. Op cited #12: 62.

17. Op cited #16: 85.

18. See, Binkley, W. C. (1925). *The Expansionist Movement in Texas, 1836–1850.* Berkeley: University of California Press; and Nance, J. M. (1963). *After San Jacinto: The Texas-Mexican Frontier, 1836–1841.* Austin: University of Texas Press; and Weber, D. J. (1982). *The Mexican Frontier, 1821–1846.* Albuquerque: University of New Mexico Press.

19. See, *Constitution of the Republic of Texas* (March 17, 1836); Braden, G. D. (ed.). (1977). *The Constitution of the State of Texas: An Annotated and Comparative Analysis,* Vols. 1 & 2. Austin, TX: Advisory Commission on Intergovernmental Relations; and Sayles, J. (1884). *The Constitution of the State of Texas,* 2nd ed. St. Louis, MO: Gilbert;

and Richardson, R.N. (1928). Framing the Constitution of the Republic of Texas. *Southwestern Historical Quarterly* Vol. 31 (2): 191–220.

20. See, Merk, op cited #14; and Campbell, R.B. (1989). *An Empire for Slavery: The Peculiar Institution in Texas, 1821–1865*. Baton Rouge: Louisiana University Press.

21. See, Dufour, C.L. (1968). *The Mexican War: A Compact History, 1846–1848*. New York: Hawthorn Books.

22. See, Connor, S.V., & Faulk, O.B. (1971). Origins of the War in *North America Divided: The Mexican War, 1846–1848*. New York: Oxford University Press, 3.

23. See, Potter, D.M. (1976). *The Impending Crisis, 1848–1861*. New York: Harper & Row: 36; and Wilmot Provisio. (2008). *Encyclopedia Britannica Online*, http://www.britannica.com/eh/article.9077114.

24. See, Wallner, P.A. (2004). *Franklin Pierce: New Hampshire's Favorite Son*. Concord, NH: Plaidswede Publishing; and Wallner, P.A. (2005). Franklin Pierce and Bowdoin College Associates Hawthorne and Hale. *Historical New Hampshire*, Vol. 59 (1): 23–43.

25. See plaque on John P. Hale statue located on front lawn of the New Hampshire capital in Concord, New Hampshire.

26. See, *John P. Hale, of New Hampshire, on the Increase of the Army in Mexico*. (Speech) Delivered in the Senate of the United States, January 6, 1848: U.S. Senate Records and "papers of John P. Hale" in the collections of the Tuck Library, Concord, NH.

27. See, *Treaty of Peace, Friendship, Limits, and Settlement between the United States of America and the United Mexican States, Concluded at Guadalupe Hidalgo, February 2, 1848; Ratified by President, March 16, 1848*; Ratifications Exchanged at Queretaro, May 30, 1848; Proclaimed, July 4, 1848; and Schroeder, J.H. (1973). *Mr. Polk's War: American Opposition and Dissent, 1846–1848*. Madison: University of Wisconsin Press.

28. See, Connor, S.V., & Faulk, O.B. (1971). The Far West, Cpt 4, op cited.

29. See, Bancroft, H.H. (18891). *History of Arizona and New Mexico, 1530–1888*. San Francisco, CA: The History Company Publishers; and Connor, S.V., & Faulk, O.B. (1971). New Mexico and Chihuahua, Cpt. 3, op cited.

30. See, Gomez, L.E. (2005). Off-White in an Age of White Supremacy: Mexican Elites and Rights of Indians and Blacks in Nineteenth-Century New Mexico. *Chicano-Latino Law Review*, Vol. 25 (Spring): 9–59.

31. See Rozwenc, E.C. (ed.). (1957). *The Compromise of 1850: Problems in American Civilization*. Boston: D.C. Heath and Company; and Stegmaier, M.J. (1996). *Texas, New Mexico, and the Compromise of 1850: Boundary Disputes & Sectional Crisis*. Kent, OH: Kent State University Press.

32. See Connor, S.V., and Faulk, O.B. (1971). The Decisive Campaign, Cpt. 5: 102–132. op cited.

33. See Wallner, P.A. (2004). *Franklin Pierce: New Hampshire's Favorite Son*, op cited; and Sewell, R.H. (1965). *John P. Hale and the Politics of Abolition*. Cambridge, MA: Harvard University Press.

34. See Richardson, J.D. (1897). Franklin Pierce, March 4, 1853, to March 4, 1857. *A Compilation of the Messages and Papers of the Presidents 1789–1897: Published by Authority of Congress*, Vol. 5. Washington, DC: U.S. Government Printing Office: 292–293.

35. See, Richardson, J.D. (1897). Op cited: pp. 349–350.

36. See, Carr, A.Z. (1963). *The World and William Walker*. New York: Harper & Row; Richardson, J.D. (1897). Franklin Pierce, op cited: 350, 368–74, 414–417; and

May, R. E. (2002). *Manifest Destiny's Underworld: Filibustering in Antebellum America.* Chapel Hill: University of North Carolina Press.

37. See, *Ostend Manifesto* (2005). *The Columbia Electronic Encyclopedia,* 6th ed. New York: Columbia University Press, http://www.inforplease.com; *Cuba* (2006). *Funk & Wagnalls New Encyclopedia.* New York: World Almanac Education Group; and Aix-la-Chapelle (1954). *Full Text of the Ostend Manifesto* (written & compiled by J. A. Sierra). Historyofcuba.com.

38. See, Faulk, O. B. (1967). *Too Far North, Too Far South.* Los Angeles, CA: Westernlore Press; Goetzmann, W. H. (1959). *Army Exploration in the American West, 1803–1863.* New Haven, CT: Yale University Press; Hine, R. V. (1968). *Bartlett's West: Drawing the Mexican Boundary.* New Haven, CT: Yale University Press; *James Gadsden* (2003). *The Columbia Electronic Encyclopedia.* New York: Columbia University Press, http://www.inforplease.com; Richardson, J. D. (1897). Franklin Pierce, op cited: 241; and Grisworld del Castillo, R. (1990). *The Treaty of Guadalupe Hildago: A Legacy of Conflict.* Norman: University of Oklahoma Press.

39. See, *Gadsden Purchase Treaty: December 30, 1853. Articles 1–9.* The Avalon Project at Yale Law School.

40. See, Michener, J. A. (1990). *The Eagle and the Raven.* New York: Tom Doherty Associates; and Richardson, J. D. (1897). Franklin Pierce, op cited: 195–196.

41. See, Ryerson, S. B. (1968). *Unequal Union: Confederation and the Roots of Conflict in the Canadas, 1815–1873.* New York: International Publishers; and McNaught, K. W. K. (1988). *The Penguin History of Canada.* New York: Viking Penguin.

42. See, Indian First (2005). *National Museum of the American Indian* (Summer). Smithsonian Institution: 31–37; Mora-Torres, J. (2001). *Mexican Border: The State, Capitalism, and Society in Nuevo León, 1848–1910.* Austin: University of Texas Press; and Meyer, M. C., et al. (1999). *The Course of Mexican History.* New York: Oxford University Press.

CHAPTER THREE

1. See, Gammel, H.P.M. (1898). *The Laws of Texas, 1822–1897,* Vol. 1. Austin, TX: Gammel Book Company; and Webb, W. P. (1935). *The Texas Rangers: A Century of Frontier Defense.* Boston, MA: Houghton Mifflin Company.

2. See, Weber, D. J. (ed.) (1973). *Foreigners in Their Native Land: Historical Roots of the Mexican Americans.* Albuquerque: University of New Mexico Press, 187–188; and Webb, W. P. (1935).*The Texas Rangers.*

3. See, Webb, W. P. (1935).*The Texas Rangers,* 31.

4. See, Haven, C. T., & Belden, F. A. (1940). *A History of the Colt Revolver.* New York: Morrow; Parsons, J. E. (1950). *The Peacemaker and Its Rivals: An Account of the Single Action Colt.* New York: Morrow; and Wilson, R. L. (1985). *Colt, an American Legend.* New York: Abbeville Press.

5. See, Harris III, C. H., & Sadler, L. R. (2004). *The Texas Rangers and the Mexican Revolution: The Bloodiest Decade, 1910–1920.* Albuquerque: University of New Mexico Press, 15.

6. See, Johnson, B. H. (2003). *Revolution in Texas: How a Forgotten Rebellion and Its Bloody Suppression Turned Mexicans into Americans.* New Haven, CT: Yale University Press, 12.

7. See, Procter, B. H. (1991). *Just One Riot: Episodes of Texas Rangers in the 20th Century.* Austin, TX: Eakin Press.

8. See, Garner, P. (2001). *Porfirio Díaz: Profiles in Power.* Harlow, England: Pearson Education Limited.

9. See, Manzanarez, M. (2004). The Genesis of Neocolonialism in *NAFTA & Neocolonialism: Comparative Criminal, Human & Social Justice* (French, L.A., & Manzanarez, M.). Lanham, MD: University Press of America, 13–41.

10. See, Harris, L. (1995). *Strong Man of the Revolution.* Silver City, NM: High Lonesome Press.

11. See, Cosmas, G.A. (1971). *An Army for Empire: The United States Army in the Spanish American War.* Columbia: University of Missouri Press; Millis, W. (1931). *A Martial Spirit: A Study of Our War with Spain.* New York: Literary Guild; Roosevelt, T. (1899). *The Rough Riders.* New York: Charles Scribner's Sons; Roosevelt, T. (1917). *The Foes of Our Own Household.* New York: George H. Doran Company; Trask, D.F. (1981). *The War with Spain in 1898.* New York: Macmillan; Smythe, D. (1973). *Guerrilla Warrior: The Early Life of John J. Pershing.* New York: Charles Scribner's Sons; Smythe, D. (1986). *Pershing: General of the Armies.* Bloomington: Indiana University Press; Vandiver, F.E. (1977). *Black Jack: The Life and Times of John J. Pershing,* Vols. 1 & 2. College Station: Texas A&M University Press; and Manchester, W. (1978). *American Caesar: Douglas MacArthur 1880–1964.* Boston, MA: Little, Brown and Company.

12. See, Ai Camp, R. (1993). *Politics in Mexico.* New York: Oxford University Press.

13. See, Ai Camp, R. (1993). Op cited; Garner, P. (2001). Op cited; Hall, L.B., & Coerver, D.M. (1988). *Revolution of the Border, the United States and Mexico, 1910–1920.* Albuquerque: University of New Mexico Press; and Knight, A. (1987). *U.S.-Mexican Relations, 1910–1940, An Interpretation.* Monograph Series 28. San Diego, CA: Tinker Foundation.

14. See, Butler, S.D. (1935). *War Is a Racket.* New York: Round Table Press: 51–52; Marks, III, F.W. (1979). *Velvet on Iron: The Diplomacy of Theodore Roosevelt.* Lincoln: University of Nebraska Press; and Mitchell, N. (1999). *The Danger of Dreams: German and American Imperialism in Latin America.* Chapel Hill: University of North Carolina Press.

15. See, Brenner, A. (1971). *The Winds That Swept Mexico.* Meridian CT: The Meridian Gravure Company; Manchester, W. (1978) op cited; Mitchell, N. (1999) op cited; Hall, L.B., & Coerver, D.M. (1988) op cited; & Bishop, J.B. (1920). *Theodore Roosevelt and His Times Shown in His Own Letters,* Vol. 2. New York: Scribner Press.

16. See, Clendenen, C.C. (1961). *The United States and Pancho Villa: A Study in Unconventional Diplomacy.* Ithaca, NY: American Historical Association, Cornell University Press; Pinchon, E. (1933). *Viva Villa! A Recovery of the Real Pancho Villa— Peon . . . Bandit . . . Soldier . . . Patriot.* New York: Harcourt, Brace and Company; Ibanez, V.B. (1920). *Mexico in Revolution,* trans. A. Livingston and J. Padin. New York: E.P. Dutton & Company; and Taylor, V.H. (1965). *Memoirs of Pancho Villa.* Austin: University of Texas Press.

17. See, Johnson, B.H. (2003). *Revolution in Texas: How a Forgotten Rebellion and Its Bloody Suppression Turned Mexicans into Americans.* New Haven, CT: Yale University Press; Harris III, C.H. and Sadler, L.R. (2004). *The Texas Rangers and the Mexican Revolution: The Bloodiest Decade, 1910–1920.* Albuquerque: University of New Mexico Press; and Sandos, J. (1992). *Rebellion in the Borderlands: Anarchism and the Plan of San Diego, 1904–1923.* Norman: University of Oklahoma Press.

18. See, Johnson, B.H. (2003). Op cited: 113.

19. See, Johnson, B.H. (2003). Op cited: 120.

20. See, Johnson, B. H. (2003). Op cited; Harris III, C. H. and Sadler, L. R. (2004). Op cited; Sandos, J. (1992). Op cited; and Coerver, D. M., and Hall, L. B. (1984). Op cited.

21. See, Tompkins, F. (1934). *Chasing Villa: The Last Campaign of the U.S. Cavalry.* Harrisburg, PA: Military Service Publishing Company; and French, L. A. (2004). Comparative Human Rights Issues in North America in *NAFTA & Neocolonialism* (French, L. A., & Manzanarez, M.). Op cited: 153–168; Hurst, J. W. (2000). *The Villista Prisoners of 1916–1917.* Las Cruces, NM: Yucca Tree Press.

22. See, Mclynn, F. (2000). *Villa and Zapata: A History of the Mexican Revolution.* New York: Carroll and Graf Publishing; Knight, A. (1987). *U.S.-Mexican Relations, 1910–1940*; Hall, L. B., & Coerver, D. M. (1988). *Revolution on the Border*; and French, L. A., & Manzanarez, M. (2004). *NAFTA & Neocolonialism.*

CHAPTER FOUR

1. See, Manzanarez, M. (2004). Genesis of Neocolonialism in *NAFTA & Neocolonialization: Comparative Criminal, Human & Social Justice* (French, L. A., & Manzanarez, M.). Lanham, MD: University Press of America, 24.

2. See, Ai Camp, R. (1993). *Politics in Mexico.* New York: Oxford University Press.

3. See Isbister, J. (1996). *The Immigration Debate: Remaking America.* West Hartford, CT: Kumarian Press; French, L. A., & Manzanarez, M. (2004). North American Socio-Economics and Social Justice, Cpt. 4. in *NAFTA & Neocolonialism:* 83–118; *Immigration Act of February 5, 1917 (39 Statutes-at-Large 898); Immigration Act of May 26, 1924 (43 Statutes-at-Large 153)*; Van Nuys, F. (2002). *Americanizing the West: Race, Immigrants, and Citizenship, 1890–1930.* Lawrence: University Press of Kansas; and Goldberg, D. J. (1999). *Discontented in America: The United States in the 1920s.* Baltimore, MD: Johns Hopkins University Press.

4. See, Van Nuys, F. (2002). Op cited; Reisler, M. (1976). *By the Sweat of Their Brow: Mexican Labor in the United States, 1900–1940.* Westport, CT: Greenwood Press; and De Leon, A. (1993). *Mexican Americans in Texas.* Op cited.

5. See, Hoffman, A. (1974). *Unwanted Mexican Americans in the Great Depression: Repatriation Pressures, 1929–1939.* Tucson: The University of Arizona Press; and Stoddard, E. R. (1973). *Mexican Americans.* New York: Random House.

6. See *The Official Bracero Agreement of August 4, 1942 with Modifications Agreed Upon on April 26, 1943* (Public Law 45—August 2, 1942—December 31, 1947).

7. See, Gamboa, E. (1990). *Mexican Labor and World War II: Braceros in the Pacific Northwest, 1942–1947.* Austin: University of Texas Press.

8. See *Mexican Labor Agreement of 1951; 1961; 1963* (Public Law 78); Senate Agriculture Committee Hearing, 1951; House Agriculture Committee Hearing, 1963; Craig, R. B. (1971). *The Bracero Program: Interest Groups and Foreign Policy.* Austin: University of Texas Press; Galarza, E. (1964). *Merchants of Labor: The Mexican Bracero Story.* Charlotte, CA: McNally and Loftin; and McBride, J. (1963). *Vanishing Bracero: Valley Revolution.* San Antonio, TX: Naylor Press.

9. See Stoddard, E. R. (1973). Op cited: pg. 187.

10. See, Garcia, J. R. (1980). *Operation Wetback: The Mass Deportation of Mexican Undocumented Workers in 1954.* Westport, CT: Greenwood Press.

11. See De Leon, A. (1993). *Mexican Americans in Texas.* Op Cited; Garcia, J. R. (1980). *Operation Wetback: The Mass Deportation of Mexican Undocumented Workers in*

1954. Westport, CT: Greenwood Press; and Samora, J. (1971). *Los Mojados: The Wetback Story.* Notre Dame, IN: University of Notre Dame Press.

12.   See, Quinones, J. G. (1990). *Chicano Politics: Reality & Promise 1940–1990.* Albuquerque: University of New Mexico Press, 62–63.

13.   See, Stoddard, E. R. (1973). The Period of Cultural Accommodation (1910–1941) in *Mexican Americans.* New York: Random House, 183–188.

14.   See Stoddard, E. R. (1973). Mexican American Education in *Mexican Americans.* New York: Random House, 123–134.

15.   See, Quinones, J. Q. (1990). *Chicano Politics: Reality & Promise 1940–1990.* Albuquerque, NM: University of New Mexico Press; and *Mendez v. Westminster School District,* 64 F. Supp. 544 (C.D. Cal. 1946), *aff'd* 161 f.20 744 (9th Cir. 1947) (en banc); and *Westminster School District v. Mendez,* 161 F.2d 774 (9th Cir., 1947).

16.   See *Delgado v. Bastrop ISD,* Civ. No.388 (W.D. Tex., June 15, 1948); *Hernandez v. Driscoll CISD, 2 Race Rel. L. Rptr.* 329 (S.D. Tex., 1957); *Hernandez v. Driscoll CISD,* Civil Action (Civ.A.) 1384, U.S. District Court of the Southern District of Texas (S.D. Tex., 1957); Stoddard, E. R. (1973). *Mexican Americans.* Op cited; De Leon, A. (1993). *Mexican Americans in Texas.*; San Migual, Jr., G. (1987). *"Let All of Them Take Heed": Mexican Americans and the Campaign for Educational Equality in Texas, 1910–1981.* Austin: University of Texas Press; and Ettinger, D. S. (1979). The History of School Desegregation in the Ninth Circuit. *Loyola of Los Angeles Law Review,* Vol. 12:481, 484–487.

CHAPTER FIVE

1.   See, Johnson, B. H. (2003). Legacies, Cpt. 7 in *Revolution in Texas: How a Forgotten Rebellion and Its Bloody Suppression Turned Mexicans into Americans.* New Haven, CT: Yale University Press, 180.

2.   See, Wheeler, B. W., & Becker, S. D. (2002). *Discovering the American Past: A Look at the Evidence,* Vol. 2: Since 1865. Boston, MA: Houghton Mifflin Company.

3.   See, Wheeler, B.W., & Becker, S. D. (2002). A Nation of Immigrants: The Fourth Wave in California, Cpt. 11, op cited: 290–307.

4.   See, Quinones, J. G. (1990). *Chicano Politics: Reality & Promise 1940–1990.* Albuquerque: University of New Mexico Press; and Stoddard, E. R. (1973), *Mexican Americans,* op cited.

5.   See, Rosaldo, R., Seligmann, G. L., & Calvert, R. A. (1974). *Chicano: The Beginnings of Bronze Power.* New York: William Morrow & Company; and Stoddard, E. R. (1973). *Mexican Americans,* op cited.

6.   See, Poniatowska, E. (1975). *Massacre in Mexico* (Lane, H.R., translator). New York: Viking.

7.   See, GAO Report number GAO-04-59 (June 4, 2004). *Treaty of Guadalupe Hidalgo: Findings and Possible Options Regarding Long-standing Community Land Grant Claims in New Mexico.* Washington, DC: U.S. Government Printing Office, 37–38.

8.   Ibid., Cpt. 3: 80–82.

9.   See, *Immigration and Nationalization Act* (Public Law 106-554) at www.ins.usdoj.gov.; and Buchanan, P. (1995). Immigration Should Be Suspended to Preserve the Nation in *Immigration Policy.* San Diego, CA: Greenhaven Press: 31–33.

10.   See, Manzanarez, M. (2004). Mexico's Full Circle Journey, Cpt. 1 in *NAFTA & Neocolonialism: Comparative Criminal, Human & Social Justice* (French, L. A. & Manzanarez, M). Lanham, MD: University Press of America: 38–41.

11.   Ibid., Cpt. 1: 38–41.
12.   Ibid., Cpt. 1: 37, 38.
13.   See, Lorey, D. E. (1999). Migration in *The U.S.-Mexican Border in the Twentieth Century: A History of Economic and Social Transformation.* Wilmington, DE: A Scholarly Resource Book, 162–169; and U.S.-Mexico Border (June 2006). *Migration Information Source.* Washington, DC: Migration Policy Institute.
14.   See, Manzanarez. M. (2004). *NAFTA & Neocolonialism: Comparative Criminal, Human & Social Justice* (French, L.A., & Manzanarez, M.). Lanham, MD: University Press of America, 35.
15.   Ibid., Cpt. 1: 36.
16.   Ibid., Cpt. 1: 13–41.

CHAPTER SIX

1.   See, AEDPA, Antiterrorism and Effective Death Penalty Act of 1996 (Public Law 104–132, 110 Stat. 1214).
2.   See, Homeland Security Act of 2002 (Public Law 107–296; Sections 103, 402).
3.   See, Summary of Recommendations. (February 14, 2001). *Mexico-U.S. Migration: A Shared Responsibility.* Carnegie Endowment for International Peace (Global Policy Program): 2, http://www.ceip.org/files/publications.
4.   Ibid., 3–4.
5.   See, Non-Citizen Immigrant Households Experience Sharp Decline in Income. (October 2, 2008); Growth of the Unauthorized Immigrant Population Slows. (October 2, 2008), etc. *Pew Hispanic Center,* pewhispanic.org.
6.   See, Estimates of the Unauthorized Migrant Population for States based on the March 2005 CPS. (April 26, 2006). *Pew Hispanic Center (Fact Sheet),* www.pewhispanic.org.
7.   See, Migration & Population: Modes of Entry for the Unauthorized. (May 22, 2006). *Pew Hispanic Center (Fact Sheet),* www.pewhispanic.org.
8.   See, Felisa Gonzales. (May 14, 2008). Statistical Portrait on Hispanic Women in the U.S., *Pew Hispanic Center (Fact Sheet),* www.pewhispanic.org.
9.   See, Entry for the Unauthorized Migrant Population. (May 22, 2006). *Pew Hispanic Center (Fact Sheet),* www.pewhispanic.org.
10.   See, Rakesh Kochhar. (June 4, 2008). Latino Labor Report, 2008: Construction Reverses Job Growth for Latinos, *Pew Hispanic Center,* www.pewhispanic.org.
11.   See, *Hector Luna, Julian Garcia, Francisco Javier Lorenszo, Santos G. Maldonado, Patricia Woodard and Bartolo Nunez, individuals and on behalf of all other similar situated v. Del Monte Fresh Produce (Southeast), Inc. and Del Monte Fresh Produce N.A., Inc.* (Civil Action No. 1:06-CV-2000-JEC). (March 18, 2008). United States District Court for the Northern District of Georgia Atlanta Division.
12.   See, *The State of American Public Opinion on Immigration in Spring 2006: A Review of Major Surveys. Pew Hispanic Center.* (May 17, 2006): 1615 L Street, NW, Suite 700, Washington, DC, www.pewhispanic.org.
13.   See, Sullivan, E. (October 10, 2007). Politics: Chertoff Defends Border Fence. *Associated Press.*
14.   See, Hanson, R. B. (2001). *The San Pedro River: A Discovery Guide.* Tucson: University of Arizona Press: 14–20.

15. See, Mission Statement, The Minuteman Civil Defense Corps: National Citizens Neighborhood Watch—Securing the American Border. 7558 W. Thunderbird Road, Ste. 1 PMB 622, Peoria, AZ 85381.

16. See, SPLC Challenges Lou Dobbs on Immigration Falsehoods. (2007). *SPLC Report*, Vol. 37 (2; Summer): 1; and Beirich, H., & Potok, M. (2005). Broken Record. *Intelligence Report: Prairie Fire* (Winter): 43–45.

17. Ibid., 1 SPLC Report.

18. See, French, L.A., & Manzanarez, M. (2004). Economic and Social Issues in *NAFTA & Neocolonialism: Comparative Criminal, Human & Social Justice*. Lanham, MD: University Press of America, 100–102.

19. Ibid.

20. See, Scherr, S. (2008). Legionnaires' Disease. *Intelligence Report* (31; Fall): 28–35.

21. See, Ramos, J. (2005). *Dying to Cross: The Worst Immigrant Tragedy in American History*. New York: HarperCollins Publishers: 149.

22. See, Herrick, T. (May 22, 1997). Marine on Anti-drug Duty Shoots, Kills Student. *Houston Chronicle*: 37A.

23. See, Migrant Deaths at the U.S.-Mexico Border. (2007). *Latin American Working Group*, www.lawg.org/countries/mexico/deaths_07htm.

24. See *Racketeer Influenced and Corrupt Organization Act (RICO)*; section 901(a), Organized Crime Control Act of 1970 (Public Law 91–452, 84 Stat. 922, enacted October 15, 1970).

25. See, *Capital Punishment Statistics: Summary Findings*. U2.S. Department of Justice, Office of Justice Programs, Bureau of Justice Statistics, www.ojp.usdoj.gov/bjs/cp.htm.

26. See, *The Federal Death Penalty System: A Statistical Survey (1988–2000)*. (September 12, 2000). Washington, DC: United States Department of Justice.

27. See, Crawford, B. (2008). *Texas Death Row: Executions in the Modern Era*. New York: A Plume Book; as well as the following court cases: *Atkins v. Virginia*, 536 U.S. 304 (2002); *Baze v. Rees*, 128 S. Ct. 1520 (2008); *Coker v. Georgia*, 433 U.S. 584 (1977); *Roper v. Simmons*, 543 U.S. 551 (2005); and the *U.S. Civil Rights Act of 1871* (42 U.S.C : 1983).

28. See, *Hernandez v. Texas* [347 U.S. 475, 74 S. Ct. 667, 98 L.Ed. 866 (1954)].

29. See, Olsen, L. (2005). Did Texas Execute an Innocent Man?: Eyewitness Says He Felt Influenced by Police to ID the Teen as the Killer. *Houston Chronicle*, www.chron.com/cs/CDA/printstory.mpl/chronicle.

30. See, Turner, A. (June 27, 2006). 'Railroad Killer' Loses Bids to Stop Execution: Parole Board and Federal Judge Don't Halt Today's Lethal Injection of a Man Linked to 13 Deaths. *Houston Chronicle*, http://www.HoustonChronicle.com; and Lozano, J.A. (November 11, 2003). Millionaire Innocent of Texas Murder. *Associated Press*, http://story.news.yahoo.com.

31. See, *Inter-American Court of Human Rights: Advisory Opinion OC-16/99 of October 1, 1999 Requested by the United Mexican States*: "The Right to Information on Consular Assistance in the Framework of the Guarantees of the Due Process of Law;" and *Torres v. Mullin* 124 S.Ct. 562 (November 17, 2003).

32. See, *Medellin v. Texas*, 552 U.S. (no. 06-984), 2008.

33. See, Beeching, J. (1977). *The Opium Wars in China, 1834–1860*. London: Harcourt Brace Jovanovich; Collis, M. (1947). *Foreign Mud: Being an Account of the Opium*

Imbroglio at Canton in the 1830s and the Anglo-Chinese War that Followed. New York: Knopf; and Inglis, B. (1976). *The Opium War.* London: Hodder and Stoughton.

34. See, Schmitt, R. B. (September 18, 2008). Border Drug Sweep Brings in 175 Arrests: Cartel Indictments a 'Substantial Blow.' *Los Angeles Times*; Moreno, I. (September 22, 2008). Immigration Arrests Up in Fed Program: States Take Advantage of Training Initiative. *The Associated Press*; and Montemayor, M. (October 24, 2008). 21 dead in Mexican Shootings, Gunbattles [*sic*]: Anti-violence Activist, Toddler among Victims. *Associated Press*; Wilkinson, T. (November 21, 2008). 5 Police Among Latest Victims in Drug War. *Los Angeles Times*; and Brophy, S. (2008). Mexico: Cartels, Corruption and Cocaine: A Profile of the Gulf Cartel. *Global Crime,* Vol. 9 (3; August): 248–261.

35. See, *U.S. Immigration and Custom Enforcement FY07 Accomplishments.* (January 2008). U.S. Immigration and Customs Enforcement publication, www.ice.gov.

36. See, International Narcotics Control Strategy Report. (March 2006; March 2008). *Bureau for International Narcotics and Law Enforcement Affairs*; Hanson, S. (June 28, 2007). Mexico's Drug War. *Council on Foreign Relations*; Carlsen, L. (July 12, 2007). Militarizing Mexico: The New War on Drugs. *Foreign Policy in Focus*; and Miller, G. (November 21, 2008). Report: CIA Covered Up Plane Attack [Missionaries' Aircraft Shot Down in 2001]. *Los Angeles Times.*

37. See, "Report on Mexico Produced by the Committee on the Elimination of Discrimination against Women under Article 8 of the Optional Protocol to the Convention, and Reply from the Government of Mexico." (2005). United Nations, Convention on the Elimination of All Forms of Discrimination against Women: Committee on the Elimination of Discrimination against Women, 32nd session, January 10–28 (CEDAW/C/2005/OP.8/MEXICO).

38. See, Campo-Flores, A., & Campbell, M. (December 8, 2008). "Bloodshed on the Border: Life in Juarez, Where Drug Violence Has Created the Equivalent of a Failed State on Our Doorstep." *Newsweek,* Vol. 152 (23): 50–54.

Bibliography

Adams, E. D. 1918. *British Diplomatic Correspondence Concerning the Republic of Texas, 1836–1846.* Austin: Texas State Historical Association.

Ai Camp, R. 1993. *Politics in Mexico.* New York: Oxford University Press.

Alba, V. 1967. *The Mexicans: The Making of a Nation.* New York: Praeger.

Allsup, C. 1982. *The American G.I. Forum: Origins and Evolution.* Monograph 6. Austin: University of Texas Center for Mexican American Studies.

Alvarez, R. P. 1987. *Familia: Migration and Adaptation in Baja and Altra California, 1800–1975.* Berkeley: University of California Press.

Aquilar Camín, H., & Meyer, L. 1990. *A la sombra de la Revolución Mexican.* Mexico City: Mexico: Cal y Arena.

Arreola, D. D., & Curtis, J. R. 1993. *The Mexican Border Cities.* Tucson: University of Arizona Press.

Atwood, J. D., & Ruiz, R. E. 1969. *Out from Under: Benito Juarez and the Struggle for Mexican Independence.* Garden City, NY: Doubleday & Company.

Bailey, G., & Bailey, R. G. 1986. *A History of the Navajos.* Santa Fe, NM: School of American Indian Research Press.

Bailey, J. 1988. *Governing Mexico: The Statecraft of Crisis Management.* New York: St. Martin's Press.

Bancroft, H. H. 1886. *History of Mexico,* Vol. 15. San Francisco, CA: The Bancroft Library, The History Company Publishers.

Bancroft, H. H. 1889 (Reprinted 1962). *History of Arizona and New Mexico, 1530–1888.* Albuquerque, NM: Horn & Wallace,

Barbour, S. 1995. *Immigration Policy.* San Diego, CA: Greenhaven Press.

Barbour, W. 1994. *Illegal Immigration.* San Diego, CA: Greenhaven Press.

Barker, E. C. 1925. *The Life of Stephen F. Austin.* Nashville, TN: Cokesbury Press.

Barker, E. C. 1928. *Mexico and Texas, 1821–1835.* Dallas, TX: Turner.

Baumgartner, F. R., De Boef, S. L., & Boydstun, A. E. 2008. *The Decline of the Death Penalty and the Discovery of Innocence.* New York: Cambridge University Press.

Bean, F. D., et al. 1997. *At the Crossroads: Mexican and U.S. Immigration Policy.* New York: Rowman and Littlefield.

Beeching, J. 1977. *The Opium Wars in China, 1834–1860.* London: Harcourt Brace Javanovich.

Bernard, J. 1972. *Voices from the Southwest: Antonio Jose Martinez, Elfego Baca, Reies Lopez-Tijerina.* New York: Scholastic Book Services, Firebird Books.

Binkley, W. C. 1925. *The Expansionist Movement in Texas, 1836–1850.* Berkeley: University of California Press.

Bishop, J. B. 1920. *Theodore Roosevelt and His Time Shown in His Own Letters,* Vol. 2. New York: Scribner Press.

Blumenson, M. 1985. *Patton: The Man Behind the Legend, 1885–1945.* New York: William Morrow and Company.

Bonfíl Batalla, G. 1944. *México profundo: una civilización negada.* Mexico City, Mexico: Editorial Grijalbo.

Borah, W. 1951. *New Spain's Century of Depression.* Folcroft, PA: Folcroft Press.

Borjas, G. (editor). 2000. *Issues in Economics of Immigration.* Chicago, IL: University of Chicago Press.

Boyle, P., Halfacree, K., & Robinson, V. 1998. *Exploring Contemporary Migration.* Harlow, Essex, England: Longman.

Brenner, A. 1971. *The Winds That Swept Mexico.* Meridian, CT: The Meriden Gravure Company.

Brown, J. H. 1893. *History of Texas from 1685 to 1892,* 2 Vols. St. Louis, MO: Daniell.

Buchanan, P. 1995. Immigration Should Be Suspended to Preserve the Nation. *Immigration Policy.* San Diego, CA: Greenhaven Press.

Buffington, R. M. 2000. *Criminal and Citizen in Modern Mexico.* Lincoln: University of Nebraska Press.

Bulmer-Thomas, V., Craske, N., & Serrano, M. (editors). 1994. *Mexico and the North American Free Trade Agreement: Who Will Benefit?* New York: St. Martin's Press.

Burma, J. H. 1954. *Spanish-Speaking Groups in the United States.* Durham, NC: Duke University Press.

Butler, S. D. 1935. *War Is a Racket.* New York: Round Table Press.

Cabrera, Y. A. 1971. *Emerging Faces: The Mexican Americans.* Dubuque, IA: William C. Brown.

Calloway, C. G. 1995. *The American Revolution in Indian Country.* New York: Cambridge University Press.

Camp, R. A. 1993. *Politics in Mexico.* New York: Oxford University Press.

Campbell, R. B. 1989. *An Empire for Slavery: The Peculiar Institution in Texas 1821–1865.* Baton Rouge: Louisiana State University Press.

Cardoso, L. A. 1980. *Mexican Emigration to the United States, 1877–1931.* Tucson: University of Arizona Press.

Carr, A. Z. 1963. *The World of William Walker.* New York: Harper & Row.

Chase, S. F., & Dunston, H. L. 1922. *The Standard Dictionary of Facts.* Buffalo, NY: The Frontier Press.

Chavez, L. R. 1998. *Shadowed Lives: Undocumented Immigrants in American Society.* Fort Worth, TX: Harcourt Brace College Publishers.

Christian, A. K. 1922. *Mirabeau Buonaparte Lamar.* Austin, TX: Von Boeckmann-Jones.

Churchill, W. S. 1955. *History of the English-Speaking People*. New York: Barnes & Noble.

Clark, M. W. 1971. *Chief Bowles and the Texas Cherokee*. Norman: University of Oklahoma Press.

Clayton, L., Hoy, J., & Underwood J. 2001. *Vaqueros, Cowboys, and Buckaroos*. Austin: University of Texas Press.

Clendenen, C. C. 1961. *The United States and Pancho Villa: A Study in Unconventional Diplomacy*. Ithaca, NY: American Historical Association, Cornell University Press.

Cline, H. F. 1963. *Mexico: Revolution to Evolution: 1940–1960*. New York: Oxford University Press.

Coerver, D. M., & Hall, L. B. 1984. *Texas and the Mexican Revolution: A Study in State and National Border Policy, 1910–1920*. San Antonio, TX: Trinity University Press.

Coerver, D. M., & Hall, L. B. 2000. *Tangled Destinies: Latin America and the United States*. Albuquerque: University of New Mexico Press.

Coles, H. L. 1966. *The War of 1812*. Chicago, IL: University of Chicago Press.

Collis, M. 1947. *Foreign Mud: Being an Account of the Opium Imbroglio at Canton in the 1830s and the Anglo-Chinese War That Followed*. New York: Knopf.

Connor, S. V., & Faulk, O. B. 1971. *North America Divided: The Mexican War, 1846–1848*. New York: Oxford University Press.

Cosmo, G. A. 1971. *An Army for Empire: The United States Army in the Spanish American War*. Columbia: University of Missouri Press.

Costo, R., & Henry-Costo, J. 1977. *Indian Treaties: Two Centuries of Dishonor*. San Francisco, CA: Indian Historian Press.

Costo, R., & Henry-Costo, J. 1987. *The Missions of California*. San Francisco, CA: Indian Historian Press.

Cothran, D. A. 1994. *Political Stability and Democracy in Mexico: the "Perfect Dictatorship"?* Westport, CT: Praeger.

Craig, R. B. 1971. *The Bracero Program: Interest Groups and Foreign Policy*. Austin: University of Texas Press.

Crawford, B. 2008. *Texas Death Row: Executions in the Modern Era*. New York: A Plume Book.

Cuellar, G. L. 2008. *Voices of Marginality: Exile and Return in Second Isaiah 40–55 and the Mexican Immigrant Experience*. New York: Peter Lang.

Daniel, C. E. 1981. *Bitter Harvest: A History of California Farmworkers, 1870–1941*. Ithaca, NY: Cornell University Press.

D'Antonio, W. V., & Form, W. H. 1965. *Influentials in Two Border Cities: A Study in Community Decision-Making*. Notre Dame, IN: University of Notre Dame Press.

Davis, R. J. 1962. The Polygamous Prelude. *American Journal of Legal History*, Vol. 6: 1–27.

De Leon, A. 1993. *Mexican Americans in Texas: A Brief History*. Arlington Heights, IL: Harlan Davidson.

De Leon, A., & del Castillo, R. G. 2006. *North to Aztlan: A History of Mexican Americans in the United States*. Wheeling, IL: Harlan Davidson.

Delgado, R., & Stefancic, J. (editors). 1998. *Latino Condition: A Critical Reader*. New York: New York University Press.

Delgado, R., & Stefancic, J. 2001. *Critical Race Theory: An Introduction*. New York: New York University Press.

Dillon, R. H. 1983. *North American Indian Wars*. Greenwich, CT: Brompton Books.

Driggs, K. 1988. The Prosecutions Begin. *Dialogue*, Vol. 21: 109–125.

Driscoll, B. 1999. *The Tracks North: Program of World War II*. Austin, TX: CMAS Books.

Dudley, W. 2002. *Illegal Immigration: Opposing Viewpoints*. San Diego, CA: Greenhaven Press.

Dufour, C.L. 1968. *The Mexican War: A Compact History, 1846–1848*. New York: Hawthorn Books.

Eisenhower, J.S.D. 1993. *Intervention: The United States and the Mexican Revolution, 1913–1917*. New York: W. W. Norton & Company.

Elting, J.R. 1991. *Amateurs to Arms! A Military History of the War of 1812*. Chapel Hill, NC: Algonquin.

Erikson, K.T. 1966. *Wayward Puritans: A Study in the Sociology of Deviance*. New York: John Wiley & Sons.

Esty, D.C. 1994. *Greening the GATT: Trade Environment and the Future*. Washington, DC: Institute for International Economics.

Ettinger, D.S. 1979. The History of School Desegregation in the Ninth Circuit. *Loyola of Los Angeles Law Review*, Vol. 12: 481, 484–487.

Everett, D. 1990. *The Texas Cherokees: A People between Two Fires, 1819–1840*. Norman: University of Oklahoma Press.

Faragher, J.M. 2005. *A Great and Noble Scheme: The Tragic Story of the Expulsion of the French Arcadians from Their American Homeland*. New York: W. W. Norton & Company.

Farris, N. 1968. *Crown and Clergy in Colonial Mexico, 1759–1821*. London: University of London Press.

Fatemi, K. (editor). 1990. *The Maquiladora Industry: Economic Solution or Problem?* New York: Praeger.

Faulk, O.B. 1967. *Too Far North, Too Far South*. Los Angeles, CA: Westernlore Press.

Fehrenbach, T.R. 1968. *Lone Star: A History of Texas and the Texans*. New York: Macmillan.

Feldman, N. 2005. *Divided by God: America's Church-State Problem and What We Should Do about It*. New York: Farrar, Straus and Giroux.

Fernández-Kelly, M.P. 1983. *For We Are Sold, I and My People: Women and Industry in Mexico's Frontier*. New York: State University of New York Press.

Foran, J. 1996. Reinventing the Mexican Revolution. *Latin American Perspectives*, Vol. 23(Fall): 115–117.

Ford, J.S. 1963. *Rip Ford's Texas* (Oates, S.B., editor). Austin: University of Texas Press.

Ford, J.S. 2003. *Native American Justice*. Chicago, IL: Burnham (Lexington Books).

Forman, H.C. 1938. *Jamestown and St. Mary's*. Baltimore, MD: The Johns Hopkins Press.

French, L.A. 1994. *The Winds of Injustice. American Indians and the U.S. Government*. New York: Garland.

French, L.A. 1998. *The Qualla Cherokee-Surviving in Two Worlds*. Lewiston, NY: Edwin Mellin Press.

French, L.A. 2003. *Native American Justice*. Chicago, IL: Burnham.

French, L.A., & Manzanzarez, M. 2004. *NAFTA & Neocolonialism: Comparative Criminal, Human & Social Justice*. Lanham, MD: University Press of America.

Fry, R. 2008. *Latino Settlement in the New Century*. Washington, DC: Pew Hispanic Center (info@pewhispanic.org).

Fukumi, S. 2008. *Cocaine Trafficking in Latin America: EU and US Policy Responses.* Hampshire, UK: Ashgate Publishing.

Galarza, E. 1964. *Merchants of Labor: The Mexican Bracero Story.* Charlotte, NC: McNally and Loftin.

Gamboa, E. 1990. *Mexican Labor and World War II: Braceros in the Pacific Northwest, 1942–1947.* Austin: University of Texas Press.

Gambrell, H. P. 1934. *Mirabeau Buonaparte Lamar: Troubadour and Crusader.* Dallas, TX: Southwest Press.

Gamio, M. 1930. *Mexican Immigration to the United States.* Chicago, IL: University of Chicago Press.

Gammel, H.P.M. 1898. *The Laws of Texas, 1822–1897.* Austin, TX: Gammel Book Company.

GAO. 2004. *Treaty of Guadalupe Hidalgo: Findings and Possible Options Regarding Long-standing Community Land Grant Claims in New Mexico.* (GAO Report number GAO-04-59). Washington, DC: U.S. Government Printing Office.

Gara, L. 1991. *The Presidency of Franklin Pierce.* Lawrence: University Press of Kansas.

Garber, P. M. (editor). 1993. *The Mexico-U.S. Free Trade Agreement.* Cambridge, MA: M.I.T. Press.

Garcia, I.M. 1989. *United We Win: The Rise and Fall of La Raza Unida Party.* Tucson: University of Arizona Press.

Garcia, I. M. 2000. *Viva Kennedy: Mexican Americans in Search of Camelot.* College Station: Texas A&M University Press.

Garcia, J.R. 1980. *Operation Wetback: The Mass Deportation of Mexican Undocumented Workers in 1954.* Westport, CT: Greenwood Press.

Garcia, M.T. 1981. *Desert Immigrants: The Mexicans of El Paso, 1880–1920.* New Haven, CT: Yale University Press.

Garcia, M. T. 1989. *Mexican Americans: Leadership, Ideology, & Identity, 1930–1960.* New Haven, CT: Yale University Press.

Garcia-Johnson, R. 2000. *Exporting Environmentalism: US Multinational Chemical Corporations in Brazil and Mexico.* Cambridge, MA: M.I.T. Press.

Gardner, R. 1970. *Grito! Reies Tijerina and the New Mexico Land Grant War of 1967.* New York: Bobbs-Merrill Company.

Garner, P. 2001. *Porfirio Díaz.* Harlow, England: Pearson Educational Limited.

Goetzman, W.H. 1959. *Army Exploration in the American West, 1803–1863.* New Haven, CT: Yale University Press.

Goldberg, D.J. 1999. *Discontented America: The United States in the 1920s.* Baltimore, MD: Johns Hopkins University Press.

Gómez, L.E. 2005. Off-White in an Age of White Supremacy: Mexican Elites and the Rights of Indians and Blacks in Nineteenth-Century New Mexico. *Chicano-Latino Law Review,* Vol. 25(Spring): 9–59.

Gonzalez, C. P. (editor). 1985. *Las elecciones en México: evolución y perspectivas.* Mexico City, Mexico: Siglo Veintiuno.

Gonzalez, J. 2000. *Harvest of Empire: A History of Latinos in America.* New York: Viking.

Gonzalez, M.J. 2002. *The Mexican Revolution, 1910–1940.* Albuquerque: University of New Mexico Press.

Gonzalez, N. L. 1969. *The Spanish-Americans of New Mexico: A Heritage of Pride.* Albuquerque: University of New Mexico Press.

Goode, E. 1999. *Drugs in American Society.* Boston: McGraw-Hill.

Graham, P. 1938. *The Life and Poems of Mirabeau B. Lamar.* Chapel Hill: University of North Carolina Press.

Grayson, G. 1980. *The Politics of Mexican Oil.* Pittsburgh: University of Pittsburgh Press.

Grebler, L., Moore, J.W., & Guzman, R.C. 1970. *The Mexican-American People.* New York: Free Press.

Griswold del Castillo, R. 1990. *The Treaty of Guadalupe Hidalgo: A Legacy of Conflict.* Norman: University of Oklahoma Press.

Gurney, G. 1966. *A Pictorial History of the United States Army in War and Peace, from Colonial Times to Vietnam.* New York: Crown Publishers.

Gusfield, J. 1963. *Symbolic Crusade: Status, Politics and the American Temperance Movement.* Chicago, IL: The University Press.

Gutierrez, J.A. 1998. *The Making of a Chicano Militant.* Madison: University of Wisconsin Press.

Hagan, W.T. 1997. *Theodore Roosevelt & Six Friends of the Indians.* Norman: University of Oklahoma Press.

Haldeen, B. 1970. *Cock of the Walk; Qui-qui-ri-qui: The Legend of Pancho Villa.* Port Washington, NY: Kennikat Press.

Hall, L.B., & Coerver, D.M. 1988. *Revolution on the Border, the United States and Mexico, 1910–1920.* Albuquerque: University of New Mexico Press.

Hansen, R.B. 2001. *The San Pedro River: A Discovery Guide.* Tucson: University of Arizona Press.

Harris, L. 1995. *Strong Man of the Revolution.* Silver City, NM: High Lonesome Press.

Harris, III, C.H., & Sadler, L.R. 1990. *The Border and the Revolution: Clandestine Activities of the Mexican Revolution: 1910–1920.* Silver City, NM: High Lonesome Books.

Harris, III, C.H., & Sadler, L.R. 2004. *The Texas Rangers and the Mexican Revolution: The Bloodiest Decade, 1910–1920.* Albuquerque: University of New Mexico Press.

Haven, C.T., & Belden, F.A. 1940. *A History of the Colt Revolver.* New York: Morrow.

Hayner, N.S. 1966. *New Patterns in Old Mexico: A Study of Town and Metropolis.* New Haven, CT: College & University Press.

Heer, D.M. 1990. *Undocumented Mexicans in the United States.* New York: Cambridge University Press.

Heller, N.S. 1966. *Mexican-American Youth: Forgotten Youth at the Crossroads.* New York: Random House.

Hellman, J. 1983. *Mexico in Crisis,* 2nd ed. New York: Holmes & Meier.

Henderson, H. 1999. *Beyond Globalization: Shaping a Sustainable Global Economy.* West Hartford, CT: Kumarian Press.

Henderson, M.V. 1928. Minor Empresario Contracts for the Colonization of Texas, 1825–1834. *The Southwestern Historical Quarterly,* Vol. 31(4): 295–324.

Henderson, P.V.N. 1981. *Felix Diaz, the Porfirians and the Mexican Revolution.* Lincoln: University of Nebraska Press.

Heston, A.W., & Weiner, N.A. (editors). 1997. NAFTA Revisited: Expectations and Realities (Rich, P., & de los Reyes, G., Special Editors). *The ANNALS of the American Academy of Political and Social Sciences,* Vol. 550 (March).

Hewitt, H.P. 1990. The Mexican Boundary Survey Team: Pedro García Conde in California. *Western Historical Quarterly,* Vol. 21(May): 258–269.

Hickey, D.R. 1989. *The War of 1812: A Forgotten Conflict.* Urbana, IL: University of Chicago Press.

Higham, J. 2002. *Strangers in the Land: Patterns of American Nativism, 1860–1925*. New Brunswick, NJ: Rutgers University Press.

Hine, R.V. 1968. *Bartlett's West: Drawing the Mexican Boundary*. New Haven, CT: Yale University Press.

Hoffman, A. 1974. *Unwanted Mexican Americans in the Great Depression: Repatriation Pressures, 1929–1939*. Tucson: University of Arizona Press.

Holloway, C.C. 1951. *Texas Gun Lore*. San Antonio, TX: Naylor.

Holt, J. 1977. *The Edwards Empresarial Grant and the Fredonia Rebellion*. masters-of-arts thesis. Nacogdoches, TX: Stephen F. Austin State University.

Horseman, R. 1962. *The Causes of the War of 1812*. New York: A.S. Barnes.

Hurst, J.W. 2000. *The Villista Prisoners 1916–1917*. Las Cruces, NM: Yucca Tree Press.

Ibanez, V.B. 1920. *Mexico in Revolution* (Livingston, A., & Padin, J., translators). New York: E.P. Dutton & Company.

Inglis, B. 1976. *The Opium War*. London: Hodder and Stoughton.

Isbister, J. 1996. *The Immigration Debate: Remaking America*. West Hartford, CT: Kumarian Press.

Iturriaga, J.E. 1951. *La estructura social y cultural de Mexico*. Mexico City, Mexico: Fondo de Cultura Economica.

James, H.C. 1974. *Pages from Hopi History*. Tucson: University of Arizona Press.

Jennings, F. 1990. *Empire of Fortune: Crowns, Colonies and Tribes in the Seven Year War in America*. New York: W.W. Norton & Company.

Johnson, B.H. 2003. *Revolution in Texas: How a Forgotten Rebellion and Its Bloody Suppression Turned Mexicans into Americans*. New Haven, CT: Yale University Press.

Jones, A., & Emory, W.H. 1966. *Memoranda and Official Correspondence Relating to the Republic of Texas, Its History and Annexation; including a Brief Autobiography of the Author*. Chicago, IL: Rio Grande Press.

Katz, F. 1981. *The Secret War in Mexico: Europe, the United States and the Mexican Revolution*. Chicago, IL: University of Chicago Press.

Katz, F. 1998. *The Life and Times of Poncho Villa*. Stanford, CA: Stanford University Press.

Kaufman, S. 2004. *The Pig War: The United States, Britain, and the Balance of Power in the Pacific Northwest, 1846–72*. Lanham, MD: Lexington Books.

Kiev, A. 1968. *Curanderismo: Mexican-American Folk Psychiatry*. New York: The Free Press.

Kiy, R., & Wirth, J.D. (editors). 1998. *Environmental Management on North America's Borders*. College Station: Texas A&M University Press.

Kluckholn, C., & Leighton, D. 1946. *The Navajo*. Cambridge, MA: Harvard University Press.

Knight, A. 1986. *The Mexican Revolution*. West Nyack, NY: Cambridge University Press.

Knight, A. 1987. *U.S.-Mexican Relations, 1910–1940, An Interpretation*. Monograph Series 28. San Diego, CA: Tinker Foundation.

Knowlton, C.S. 1967. *Land-Grant Problems among the State's Spanish-Americans*. Albuquerque, NM: Bureau of Business Research.

Kobler, J. 1973. *The Rise and Fall of Prohibition*. New York: G.P. Putnam's Sons.

Koeninger, R.C. 1968. *The Law: Rape, Race, Time and Death in Texas*. Dallas, TX: Proceedings of the Southwest Social Science Association.

Krauze, E. 1997. *Biografía del poder: Caudillos de la Revolucíon Mexicana (1910–1940)*. Mexico City, Mexico: TusQuets Editores.

Krauze, E. 1997. *La presidencia imperial: Ascenso y caída del sistema político Mexicano (1940–1996).* Mexico City: Mexico: TusQuets Editores.

Kritz, M.M., Lin, L.L., & Zlornik, H. (editors). 1992. *International Migration Systems: A Global Approach.* Oxford, England: Clarendon Press.

Leiker, J.N. 2002. *Racial Borders: Black Soldiers along the Rio Grande.* College Station: Texas A&M University Press.

Levin, J. 2002. *The Violence of Hate.* Boston, MA: Allyn and Bacon.

Levy, D., & Székely, G. 1983. *Mexico: Paradoxes of Stability and Change.* Boulder, CO: Westview Press.

Lewis, O. 1959. *Five Families.* New York: New American Library (Mentor Book).

Lieuwen, E. 1968. *Mexican Militarism.* Albuquerque University of New Mexico Press.

Lipscomb, A. A. (editor). 1903. *The Writings of Thomas Jefferson: Monticello Edition,* Vol. 10. Washington, DC: The Thomas Jefferson Memorial Association.

Loomis, N.M. 1958. *Texan-Santa Fe Pioneers.* Norman: University of Oklahoma Press.

Lorey, D.E. 1999. *The U.S.-Mexican Border in the Twentieth Century: A History of Economic and Social Transformation.* Wilmington, DE: Scholarly Resources.

Machado, Jr., M.A. 1972. The United States and the De la Huerta Rebellion. *Southwestern Historical Quarterly,* Vol. 75(3): 303–324.

Madsen, W. 1964. *The Mexican-Americans of South Texas.* New York: Holt, Rinehart & Winston.

Mahon, J.K. 1972. *The War of 1812.* Gainesville: University of Florida Press.

Manchester, W. 1978. *American Caesar: Douglas MacArthur 1880–1964.* Boston, MA: Little, Brown and Company.

Manuel, H.T. 1965. *Spanish-Speaking Children of the Southwest: Their Education and the Public Welfare.* Austin: University of Texas Press.

Marks, III, F.W. 1979. *Velvet on Iron: The Diplomacy of Theodore Roosevelt.* Lincoln: University of Nebraska Press.

Martinez, O.J. 1983. *Fragments of the Mexican Revolution, Personal Accounts from the Border.* Albuquerque: University of New Mexico Press.

Martinez Jr., R. 2002. *Latino Homicide: Immigration, Violence, and Community.* Oxford, England: Routledge/Taylor & Francis Group.

Matthiessen, P. 1969. *Sal si Puedes: Cesar Chavez and the New American Revolution.* New York: Random House.

May, R.E. 2002. *Manifest Destiny's Underworld: Filibustering in Antebellum America.* Chapel Hill: University of North Carolina Press.

Mayer, F.W. 1998. *Interpreting NAFTA: The Science and Art of Political Analysis.* New York: Columbia University Press.

McBride, J. 1963. *Vanishing Bracero: Valley Revolution.* San Antonio, TX: Naylor Press.

McCartney, L. 2008. *The Teapot Dome Scandal: How Big Oil Bought the Harding White House and Tried to Steal the Country.* New York: Random House.

Mclynn, F. 2000. *Villa and Zapata: A History of the Mexican Revolution.* New York: Carroll and Graf Publishing.

McMurtry, J. 1998. *Unequal Freedoms: The Global Market as an Ethical System.* West Hartford, CT: Kumarian Press.

McNaught, K.W.K. 1988. *The Penguin History of Canada.* New York: Viking Penguin.

McWilliams, C. 1939. *Factories in the Field: The Story of Migratory Farm Labor in California.* Boston, MA: Little, Brown.

McWilliams, C. 1990. *North from Mexico: The Spanish-Speaking People of the United States.* New York: Praeger.

Medina, L. 1978. *Evolución electoral en México contemporaneo.* Mexico City, Mexico: Graceta Informativa de la Commisión Federal Electoral.

Meier, M.S., & Ribera, F. 1972, 1993. *Mexican Americans/American Mexicans: From Conquistadors to Chicanos.* New York: Hill and Wang.

Meinig, D.W. 1971. *Southwest: Three Peoples in Geographical Change 1600–1970.* New York: Oxford University Press.

Melody, M.E. 1989. *The Apache.* New York: Chelsea House.

Merk, F. 1972. *Slavery and the Annexation of Texas.* New York: Knopf.

Meyer, H.N. 2002. *The World Court in Action: Judging among the Nations.* Lanham, MD: Rowman & Littlefield.

Meyer, L. 1995. *Liberalismo Autoritario.* Mexico City, Mexico: Editorial Oceano de México.

Meyer, M. 1967. *Mexican Rebel: Pascual Orozco and the Mexican Revolution, 1910–1915.* Lincoln: University of Nebraska Press.

Meyer, M.C., Sherman, L.W., & Deeds, S.M. 1999. *The Course of Mexican History.* New York: Oxford University Press.

Michener, J.A. 1990. *The Eagle and the Raven.* New York: Tom Doherty Associates.

Millis, W. 1931. *A Martial Spirit: A Study of Our War with Spain.* New York: Literary Guild.

Mitchell, N. 1999. *The Danger of Dreams: German and American Imperialism in Latin America.* Chapel Hill: University of North Carolina Press.

Mocho, J. 1997. *Murder and Justice in Frontier New Mexico, 1821–1846.* Albuquerque: University of New Mexico Press.

Moore, J.W. 1970. *Mexican Americans.* Englewood Cliffs, NJ: Prentice-Hall.

Moore, S.L. 2002. *Savage Frontier: Rangers, Riflemen, and the Indian Wars in Texas.* Plano: Republic of Texas Press.

Moquin, W. (editor). 1971. *A Documentary History of the Mexican Americans.* New York: Praeger.

Mora-Torrez, J. 2001. *Mexican Border: The State, Capitalism, and Society in Nuevo León, 1848–1910.* Austin: University of Texas Press.

Morner, N. 1967. *Race Mixture in the History of Latin America.* Boston, MA: Little, Brown.

Munoz, Jr., C. 1989. *Youth, Identity, Power: The Chicano Movement.* New York: Verso.

Nance, J.M. 1963. *After San Jacinto: The Texas-Mexican Frontier, 1836–1841.* Austin: University of Texas Press.

Nance, J.M. 1964. *Attack and Counterattack: The Texas-Mexican Frontier, 1842.* Austin: University of Texas Press.

Navarro, A. 1998. *The Cristal Experiment: A Chicano Struggle for Community Control.* Madison: University of Wisconsin Press.

Navarro, A. 2008. *The Immigration Crisis: Nativism, Armed Vigilantism, and the Rise of a Countervailing Movement.* Lanham, MD: AltaMira Press.

Newfarmer, R. (editor). 1985. *From Gunboat to Diplomacy: New U.S. Policies for Latin America.* Baltimore, MD: Johns Hopkins University Press.

Newman, G., & Freilich, J. 2006. *Crime and Immigration.* Burlington, VT: Ashgate.

Nugent, W. 2008. *Habits of Empire: A History of American Expansion.* New York: Alfred A. Knopf.

O'Brien, T. 2000. *The Century of U.S. Capitalism in Latin America.* Albuquerque: University of New Mexico Press.

Orchowski, M.S. 2008. *Immigration and the American Dream: Battling the Political Hype and Hysteria.* Lanham, MD: Rowman & Littlefield Publishers.

Park, R. E. 1964. *Race and Culture.* New York: Free Press.

Parsons, J. E. 1950. *The Peacemaker and Its Rivals: An Account of the Single Action Colt.* New York: Morrow.

Peckham, H. H. 1964. *The Colonial Wars, 1689–1762.* Chicago: University of Illinois Press.

Pinchon, E. 1933. *Villa Villa!: A Recovery of the Real Pancho Villa—Peon . . . Bandit . . . Soldier . . . Patriot.* New York: Harcourt, Brace and Company.

Pitt, L. 1970. *The Decline of the Californios: A Social History of the Spanish-Speaking Californians, 1846–1890.* Berkeley: University of California Press.

Pletcher, D. M. 1958. *Rails, Mines, and Progress: Seven American Promoters in Mexico, 1867–1911.* Ithaca, NY: Cornell University Press.

Politi, M, & Gioia, F. 2008. *The International Criminal Court and National Jurisdictions.* Hampshire, UK: Ashgate Publishing.

Poniatowska, E. 1975. *Massacre in Mexico* (Lane, H. R., translator.). New York: Viking.

Potter, D. M. 1976. *The Impending Crisis, 1848–1861.* New York: Harper & Row.

Procter, B. H. 1991. *Just One Riot: Episodes of Texas Rangers in the 20th Century.* Austin, TX: Eakin Press.

Purcell, Robert Allen. 1981. *The History of the Texas Militia.* Austin: University of Texas Press.

Quezada, J. G. 1999. *Border Boss: Manual B. Bravo and Zapata County.* College Station: Texas A&M University Press.

Quinones, J. G. 1990. *Chicano Politics: Reality & Promise 1940–1990.* Albuquerque: University of New Mexico Press.

Quintana, F. L. 1991. *Pobladores: Hispanic Americans of the Ute Frontier.* Notre Dame, IN: University of Notre Dame Press.

Quirk, R. E. 1962. *An Affair of Honor: Woodrow Wilson and the Occupation of Veracruz.* New York: W. W. Norton & Company.

Rajaee, F. 2000. *Globalization on Trial: The Human Condition and the Information Civilization.* West Hartford, CT: Kumarian Press.

Ralston, S. J. 2005. *The Collapse of Globalism: And the Reinvention of the World.* Toronto, Ontario, Canada: Viking Canada.

Ramos, J. 2005. *Dying to Cross: The Worst Immigrant Tragedy in American History.* New York: HarperCollins Publishers.

Reisler, M. 1976. *By the Sweat of Their Brow: Mexican Labor in the United States, 1900–1940.* Westport, CT: Greenwood Press.

Reynolds, D. S. 2008. *Waking Giant: America in the Age of Jackson.* New York: HarperCollins Publishers.

Rhodes, C. 1993. *Reciprocity U.S. Trade Policy and the GATT Regime.* Ithaca, NY: Cornell University Press.

Richardson, J. D. 1897. *A Compilation of the Messages and Papers of the Presidents 1789–1897: Published by Authority of Congress,* Vol. 5. Washington, DC: U.S. Government Printing Office.

Richardson, R. N. 1928. Framing the Constitution of the Republic of Texas. *Southwestern Historical Quarterly* Vol. 31(2): pp. 191–220.

Riggs, A. R., & Velk, T. (editors). 1993. *Beyond NAFTA: An Economic, Political and Sociological Perspective.* Vancouver, BC, Canada: The Frazer Institute.

Rodriquez, R. 2002. *Brown: The Last Discovery of America.* New York: Viking.

Roosevelt, T. 1899. *The Rough Riders.* New York: Charles Scribner's Sons.

Roosevelt, T. 1917. *The Foes of Our Own Household.* New York: George H. Doran Company.

Rosaldo, R., Seligmann, G. L., & Calvert, R. A. 1974. *Chicano: The Beginnings of Bronze Power.* New York: William Morrow & Company.

Rosenbaum, R. A. 1989. *The New American Desk Encyclopedia.* New York: Signet/Penguin Group.

Ross, S. R. 1955. *Francisco I. Madero: Apostle of Mexican Democracy.* New York: Columbia University Press.

Rozwenc, E. C., ed. 1957. *The Compromise of 1850: Problems in American Civilization.* Boston, MA: D.C. Heath and Company.

Rubel, A. J. 1966. *Across the Tracks: Mexican-Americans in a Texas City.* Austin: University of Texas Press.

Ruiz, R. E. 1992. *Triumphs and Tragedy: A History of the Mexican People.* New York: W. W. Norton & Company.

Ryerson, S. B. 1968. *Unequal Union: Confederation and the Roots of Conflict in the Canadas, 1815–1873.* New York: International Publishers.

Sadler, L. R. 2004. *The Texas Rangers and the Mexican Revolution: The Bloodiest Decade, 1910–1920.* Albuquerque: University of New Mexico Press.

Samoa, J. 1971. *Los Mojados: The Wetback Story.* Notre Dame, IN: University of Notre Dame Press.

Samoa, J, & Vandel, P. 1993. *A History of the Mexican-American People.* Notre Dame, IN: University of Notre Dame Press.

Sanchez, G. I. 1967. *Forgotten People.* Albuquerque: University of New Mexico Press.

Sandos, J. 1992. *Rebellion in the Borderlands: Anarchism and the Plan of San Diego, 1904–1923.* Norman: University of Oklahoma Press.

San Migual, Jr., G. 1987. *"Let All of Them Take Heed"; Mexican Americans and the Campaign for Educational Equity in Texas, 1910–1981.* Austin: University of Texas Press.

Saul, J. R. 2005. *The Collapse of Globalism: And the Reinvention of the World.* Toronto, Ontario, Canada: Viking.

Scherr, S. 2008. Legionnaires' Disease. *Intelligence Report,* Vol. 31.

Schmidt, S. 1991. *The Deterioration of the Mexican Presidency: The Years of Luis Echeverría.* Tucson: University of Arizona Press.

Schmitz, J. W. 1941. *Texan Statecraft, 1836–1845.* San Antonio, TX: Naylor.

Schmitz, J. W. 1960. *Texas Culture in the Days of the Texas Republic.* San Antonio, TX: Naylor.

Schroeder, J. H. 1973. *Mr. Polk's War: American Opposition and Dissent, 1846–1848.* Madison: University of Wisconsin Press.

Schroeder, S. 1998. *Native Resistance and the Pax Colonial in New Spain.* Lincoln: University of Nebraska Press.

Serven, J. E. 1974. *Conquering the Frontiers.* La Habra, CA: Foundation Press.

Sewell, R. H. 1965. *John P. Hale and the Politics of Abolition.* Cambridge, MA: Harvard University Press.

Sherwood, M. B. 1982. *Pilgrim: A Biography of William Brewster.* Falls Church, VA: Great Oak Press.

Siegel, S. E. 1956. *A Political History of the Texas Republic.* Austin: University of Texas Press.

Siegel, S. E. 1977. *The Poet President of Texas: The Life of Mirabeau B. Lamar, President of the Republic of Texas.* Austin, TX: Jenkins.

Sierra, J. 1969. *The Political Evolution of the Mexican People.* Austin: University of Texas Press.

Silbey, J. H. 2005. *Storm over Texas: Controversy and the Road to Civil War.* New York: Oxford University Press.

Silverstone, S. A. 2004. *Divided Union: The Politics of War in the Early American Republic.* Ithaca, NY: Cornell University Press.

Simmen, E. (Ed.) 1971. *The Chicano: From Caricature to Self-Portrait.* New York: New American Library.

Simpson, E. N. 1937. *The Ejido: Mexico's Way Out.* Chapel Hill: University of North Carolina Press.

Skeldon, R. 1997. *Migration and Development: A Global Perspective.* Harlow, Essex, England: Addison Wesley Longman.

Skidmore, T. E., & Smith, P. H. 2001. *Modern Latin America.* New York: Oxford University Press.

Smith, J. H. 1911. *The Annexation of Texas.* New York: Baker and Taylor.

Smither, H. 1931. *Journals of the Fourth Congress of the Republic of Texas, 1839–1840.* Austin, TX: Von Boeckmann Jones Company.

Smythe, D. 1973. *Guerrilla Warrior: The Early Life of John J. Pershing.* New York: Charles Scribner's Sons.

Smythe, D. 1986. *Pershing: General of the Armies.* Bloomington: Indiana University Press.

Spero, J. E., & Hart, J. 1997. *The Politics of International Economic Relations.* New York: St. Martin's Press.

Stegmaier, M. J. 1996. *Texas, New Mexico, and the Compromise of 1850: Boundary Disputes & Sectional Crisis.* Kent, OH: Kent State University Press.

Steiner, S. 1970. *La Raza: The Mexican Americans.* New York: Harper & Row.

Stephanson, A. 1995. *Manifest Destiny: American Expansion and the Empire of Right.* New York: Hill & Wang.

Stoddard, E. R. 1970. *Ethnic Identity of Urban Mexican-Americans.* Dallas, TX: Proceedings of the Southwest Sociological Association.

Stoddard, E. R. 1987. *Maquila: Assembly Plants in Northern Mexico.* El Paso: Texas Western Press.

Stoddard, W. R. 1973. *Mexican Americans.* New York: Random House.

Sugden, J. 1997. *Tecumseh: A Life.* New York: Holt.

Sweeney, T. W. 2005. 1st to Head a National Government in Modern Times. *National Museum of the American Indian.* Washington, DC: Smithsonian National Museum of the American Indian (Summer):34.

Tannenbam, F. 1964. *Mexico: The Struggle for Peace and Bread.* New York: Knopf.

Taylor, C. 1994. *Minorities in the United States: A Multicultural Perspective,* 2nd ed. Upper Saddle River, NJ: Prentice-Hall.

Taylor, V. H. 1965. *Memoirs of Pancho Villa.* Austin: University of Texas Press.

Thompson, E. V. 1986. *Republic: A Novel of Texas.* New York: Paper Jacks.

Timmons, W. H. 1990. *El Paso: A Borderlands History.* El Paso: University of Texas Press.

Tompkins, F. 1934. *Chasing Villa: The Last Campaign of the U.S. Cavalry.* Harrisburg, PA: Military Service Publication Company.

Trask, D. F. 1981. *The War with Spain in 1898*. New York: Macmillan.

Tuck, J. 1084. *Poncho Villa and John Reed: Two Faces of Romantic Revolution*. Tucson: University of Arizona Press.

Tyler, D. 1972. Anglo-American Penetration of the Southwest: The View from New Mexico. *Southwestern Historical Quarterly*, Vol. 75(3): 325–338.

Vallier, I. 1970. *Catholicism, Social Control, and Modernization in Latin America*. Englewood Cliffs, NJ: Prentice-Hall.

Vanderwood, P. J. 1988. Writing History with Picture Postcards: Revolution in Tijuana. *The Journal of San Diego History*, Vol. 34(Winter): 38–61.

Vanderwood, P. J., & Samponaro, F. N. 1988. *Border Fury, a Picture Postcard Record of Mexico's Revolution and US War Preparedness, 1910–1917*. Albuquerque: University of New Mexico Press.

Vandiver, F. E. 1977. *Black Jack: The Life and Times of John J. Pershing*, Vols. 1 & 2. College Station: Texas A&M University.

Van Nuys, F. 2002. *Americanizing the West: Race, Immigrants, and Citizenship, 1890–1930*. Lawrence: University Press of Kansas.

Vargas, L. 2009. *Latina Teens, Migration, and Popular Culture*. New York: Peter Lang.

Wallner, P. A. 2004. *Franklin Pierce: New Hampshire's Favorite Son*. Concord, NH: Plaidswede Publishing.

Wallner, P. A. 2005. Franklin Pierce and Bowdoin College Associates Hawthorne and Hale. *Historical New Hampshire*, Vol. 59(1): 23–43.

Wasserman, M. 2000. *Everyday Life and Politics in Nineteenth Century Mexico*. Albuquerque: University of New Mexico Press.

Webb, W. P. 1931. *The Great Plains*. Boston, MA: Ginn.

Webb, W. P. 1935. *The Texas Rangers: A Century of Frontier Defense*. Boston, MA: Houghton Mifflin Company.

Weber, D. J. (editor). 1973. *Foreigners in Their Native Land: Historical Roots of the Mexican Americans*. Albuquerque: University of New Mexico Press.

Weber, D. J. 1982. *The Mexican Frontier, 1821–1846*. Albuquerque: University of New Mexico Press.

Weber, M. 1947. *The Theory of Social and Economic Organization* (A. M. Henderson & T. Parsons, translators). Glencoe, IL: The Free Press.

Weber, M. 1958. *The Protestant Ethic and the Spirit of Capitalism* (T. Parsons, translator). New York: Charles Scribner's Sons.

Wells, T. H. 1960. *Commodore Moore and the Texas Navy*. Austin: University of Texas Press.

Wheeler, B. W., & Becker, S. D. 2002. *Discovering the American Past: A Look at the Evidence*, Vol. 2: since 1865. Boston, MA: Houghton Mifflin Company.

Wilkie, J. W. 1970. *The Mexican Revolution: Federal Expenditure and Social Change since 1910*, 2nd ed. Berkeley: University of California Press.

Wilson, P. A. 1992. *Exports and Local Development: Mexico's New Maquiladoras*. Austin: University of Texas Press.

Wilson, R. L. 1985. *Colt, an American Legend*. New York: Abbeville Press.

Wilson, W. 1902. *A History of the American People*. New York: Harper & Brothers.

Wirth, J. D. 2000. *Smelter Smoke in North America: The Politics of Transborder Pollution*. Lawrence: University of Kansas Press.

Womack, J., Jr. 1968. *Zapata and the Mexican Revolution*. New York: Knopf.

Young, I. M. 1990. *Justice and the Politics of Differences*. Princeton, NJ: Princeton University Press.

Index

About the Author

LAURENCE ARMAND FRENCH is a professor emeritus of psychology from Western New Mexico University and a senior research associate at the Justiceworks Institute at the University of New Hampshire in Durham. He is currently a Senior Fulbright Scholar assigned to the University of Sarajevo in Bosnia and Herzegovina for the 2009–2010 academic year. He holds PhDs in sociology from the University of New Hampshire and in psychology from the University of Nebraska. He has more than 260 academic publications, including 14 books. He received the 1999 NIDA research award for his work in assessing substance abuse among minorities in the U.S. Southwest.